BARRY MANILOW

BARRY MANILOW

Patricia Butler

OMNIBUS PRESS
London/New York/Paris/Sydney/Copenhagen/Madrid/Tokyo

Copyright © 2001 Omnibus Press
(A Division of Music Sales Limited)

Cover designed by Philip Gambrill
Picture research by Patricia Butler & Nikki Lloyd

ISBN: 0.7119.8547.2
Order No: OP 48200

Exclusive Distributors:
Music Sales Limited,
8/9 Frith Street,
London W1D 3JB, UK.

Music Sales Corporation,
257 Park Avenue South,
New York, NY 10010, USA.

Macmillan Distribution Services,
53 Park West Drive,
Derrimut, Vic 3030,
Australia.

To the Music Trade only:
Music Sales Limited,
8/9 Frith Street,
London W1D 3JB, UK.

Every effort has been made to trace the copyright holders of the photographs in this book but one or
two were unreachable. We would be grateful if the photographers concerned would contact us.

Typeset by Galleon Typesetting, Ipswich.
Printed in Great Britain by Creative Print & Design (Wales), Ebbw Vale.

A catalogue record for this book is available from the British Library.

www.omnibuspress.com

Contents

For My Father

Author's Note

In late 1999, when my editor at Omnibus Press first brought up the idea of doing a biography of Barry Manilow, I laughed. Then I told him I'd think about it. I then started poking around the internet and was surprised to find just how active Barry Manilow is, and how many loyal fans he has. The last – and first – time I saw Barry Manilow was in 1982, when he was performing in Orem, Utah. I was a student at Brigham Young University at the time, and my boyfriend had flown in from Michigan to help me celebrate my 21st birthday. His surprise gift to me was tickets to Manilow's concert. I have to admit that my main memory of that event is whiteness – white piano, white clothing, white teeth and, yes, a snowy white audience.

Eighteen years later I was amazed that Manilow was still trotting the globe, playing mainly the same songs to mainly the same audience. Nothing had changed much, it seemed, except Manilow's clothes and piano, both now a mature black rather than the optimistic white of the early days. The audience, however, while older and wider, remained largely unchanged, and no less enthusiastic than when I'd attended that first concert. I was intrigued.

Armed with Manilow-related press clippings, internet printouts, and material sent to me by my editor, I flew to San Francisco and drove up the coast to Arcata, a favourite place to relax and put life in perspective. Here, I felt I would be able to spend some time reading and discussing the idea with my friends in order to come to an intelligent, informed decision.

When I told my friends I was thinking of doing a biography of Barry Manilow, they, too, laughed. In fact, it was beginning to seem that the surest way to lighten any moment was to throw out Manilow's name. "Oh, my god! Is he still alive?" was a common response. Thanks to my short course of research I was able to state, with some degree of authority, that yes, Manilow was indeed alive and, in fact, was thriving. There are active fan clubs all over the world devoted to him, I'd discovered, and his concerts, which I now knew were frequent as he seemed to be perpetually on tour, were routinely sold out. Yet still they chuckled, and still I found myself apologising, just a little bit, every time I admitted I was thinking of pursuing the project.

It was, in the end, this very dichotomy that made up my mind for me. What was it, I had to know, that could cause someone who has been as continually successful as Manilow has, and for as long as he has – nearly three decades! – to still be treated with a knee-jerk derision by the critics and the public at large? That, I decided, would be the subtext of my research.

A year later, I can't offer a definitive answer to this question. But the search for the answer brought to light facets to Manilow's story that showed him to be a far more complex and interesting individual than I'd ever imagined. After you've read this book, you won't know exactly why Barry Manilow can't seem to get any respect, though hopefully you'll be able to put his life and work into a more sensible perspective for knowing some of what the man had to go through to achieve all he has. You will also not know what Barry had for breakfast three years ago last Wednesday, nor what his favourite colour is or the brand of toothpaste he uses. But you may just understand why it is that people still hunger to know these things about this seemingly simple and unassuming Brooklyn boy.

Now, over a year and a half since I first discussed the idea of a Barry Manilow biography with my editor, I no longer laugh when I hear Manilow's name mentioned, nor do I apologise for my involvement in this project. I'm pleased to have had the opportunity to learn more about the performer who so dazzled me that night in Orem back in 1982, and even more pleased to be able to give his fans a clearer picture of the real man behind the performer.

Prologue

It was 1993, and singer Kyle Vincent was thrilled to have been asked to spend the summer touring with Barry Manilow as the legendary entertainer's opening act. Vincent, who describes himself as "kind of a solo male sensitive singer songwriter", had been a long-time Manilow fan, and had patterned much of his own work after Manilow's style.

The July 14th performance at Pittsburgh's Star Lake Amphitheater seemed to have gone well. The place was packed with nearly 10,000 loyal and loudly enthusiastic Manilow fans. Kyle was warmly received by the Manilow faithful, who then went on to raise the rafters when their idol appeared. All in all, a very satisfying experience for everyone. Or, rather, almost everyone.

Writing about the show the next day in the Pittsburgh *Post-Gazette*, reviewer Ed Masley paid tribute to Manilow's ability to still enthrall fans after so many years. In fact, the review verged on a rave, until nearly the end.

> *Of course Manilow, like any great performer, is entitled to an occasional lapse of taste. Hence, his ill-fated decision to dress up 'Could It Be Magic' as a dance number in response to some pathetic remake that's all the rage in England. Fortunately, it was the only real misstep of the evening — unless you count the opening act.*

Kyle, it seems, had not escaped notice. Unfortunately, for all the wrong reasons.

1

> *MCA recording artist Kyle Vincent was joined by members of*
> *Manilow's band for an overly long set of lightweight, generic pop rock.*
> *It sounded like the sort of stuff the token long-haired guy on any given*
> *soap opera sings until he falls off a cliff, loses his memory and opens a*
> *drive-through laundry. With any luck, Vincent will have a bad*
> *experience on* Star Search *and go back to working at Chess King.*

Kyle was devastated. It was his first experience with the often viciously personal attacks that could be meted out by the press, and it left the singer hurt and puzzled, doubting his career choice and his place on the Manilow tour.

The following night in Massachusetts, as show time approached, Kyle sat in his dressing room at Boston's Great Woods Performing Arts Center, re-reading the Masley review for the hundredth time. The thought of going back out on stage again seemed impossible; Kyle didn't think he'd be able to do it.

Finally, Manilow came to Kyle's dressing room. "What's the problem?" Barry asked.

"I'm just really bummed," Kyle said. "I work so hard, I do all this crap – I'm doing a little opening slot, three songs! – and this guy has to take half the review to not talk about you, but *me*, and about how awful I am!"

Barry Manilow looked at the young singer for a moment before responding. "You know," he finally said, "you have nerve. You want to see bad reviews? I'll show you bad reviews. Now go out there and kick ass." And he did.

In a career that has now touched on four decades and crossed a millennium, Barry Manilow has taken more abuse from more sources than most people could begin to imagine. And yet, as he told Kyle Vincent, "I still go out there every night."

For the entire span of his career, Barry Manilow has weathered the slings and arrows not of fortune, which has usually smiled upon him, but of the critics and comics and sceptics and overall nay-sayers who seem to find Manilow an irresistible target. What is it that makes an otherwise successful performer the butt end of so many jokes? The target of so much professional and, most of all, personal criticism? And, perhaps most importantly, what is it that makes this person keep going in the face of such often cruel criticism? What drives Barry Manilow to take these continual beatings and still walk tall?

As the song says, "Freedom's just another word for nothing left to lose." If Barry Manilow has earned a certain freedom from the constraints his critics would place upon him, perhaps it's only because he first had to fight so hard to free himself from the constraints of his own past, a past filled with poverty and loss and perpetual disappointment, just as his father's had been. For Barry Manilow comes from a long line of people with nothing left to lose.

PART I

Childhood

"Shall he, grown grey among his peers,
Through the thick curtain of his tears
Catch glimpses of his earlier years.

And hear the sounds he knew of yore,
Old shufflings on the sanded floor,
Old knuckles tapping at the door?"

– Lewis Carroll, *Phantasmagoria*

Chapter One

When you're young and poor, Brooklyn is nothing but a place to escape. And, if he was nothing else of note, Harold Lawrence Pincus was certainly young and poor.

Harold was a Brooklyn boy by birth. Like many of those born in Brooklyn in the early part of the 20th century, Harold's ancestors were among the teeming millions who arrived in New York during what was known as The Great Migration. Some of those who arrived by ship stayed in New York, and some moved on, heading west to face unknown dangers. The most intrepid would make it all the way to the Pacific coast; others would settle in various locations between the two shores, eventually populating the entire country.

Rising from the Hudson River at the southern tip of Manhattan Island, the Statue of Liberty came to symbolise America's welcome to immigrants from all over Europe. Many came from the Emerald Isle where the Great Famine of 1845–49 set in motion a pattern of migration that would establish large Irish communities in every English speaking nation in the world. The famine caused a quarter of Eire's population of four million to seek a better life in the United States and England and, although the food-chain eventually recovered, migration continued apace throughout the 19th century and beyond. From 1850 to 1870, at least another one million people would leave the country behind in favour of other English-speaking nations, notably the United States. Still more came later as Irish men and women sought to escape British rule, to build a new life for themselves in a land whose constitution recognised no hereditary privileges, only the freedom of the individual to prosper according to their talent and diligence.

Among the millions of people from all over the world seeking a better life in America, it has been estimated that from 1820 to 1900 about four million Irish would eventually migrate to the United States. Among these was the family of Harold Pincus' mother, the former Anna Sheehan. Only one generation away from the old country, Anna was a striking "Black Irish" beauty with raven hair, intense, mesmerising eyes, and a strong will.

Like Anna Sheehan, Harry Pincus, Harold's father, was also a first generation American, though it's unclear from which part of Europe his family had come, or when. What is known, however, is that by the age of 18, the Jewish Harry Pincus had met and married Catholic Anna Sheehan who gave birth to their only child, Harold, on November 26, 1920 in Brooklyn.

But just as the tremendous prosperity of the "Roaring Twenties" gave way to the crippling economic reversals of what became known in America as The Great Depression, any happiness and stability young Harold Pincus might have known at home with his parents gave way to insecurity and crushing poverty when Harry Pincus left his family for parts unknown. Harry's departure left Anna and young Harold to fend for themselves in a cramped three-room apartment on South 4th Street in the Williamsburg neighbourhood of Brooklyn, an area which, at the time, suffered the highest population densities and infant mortality rates in all of Greater New York.

The teenaged Harold had inherited not only his father's thin face, beakish nose, and piercing blue eyes, but also his wanderlust, a desperate, constant longing for escape from the circumstances that trapped him. It was this yearning for freedom that led him, along with some neighbourhood friends, to hop a freight train out of town. None of the boys cared where the train was going, as long as it was going *away*. "Anywhere but here" was the order of the day. It was an innocent, hopeful joyride that would mark Harold for life.

As the train travelled farther and farther away from New York, Harold and his friends amused themselves by manoeuvring between the train's cars. The timing couldn't have been worse. While Harold was suspended dangerously between two cars, the train made a turn, catching Harold unprepared and crushing his foot between the massive steel links connecting the cars to each other. The train was stopped and Harold was extricated from the machinery. It looked to all present as though his entire leg would need to be amputated. By now the train was many miles from New York. While the country doctor in the farming community nearest to where the train had come to a stop did his best to piece together Harold's crushed bones and torn flesh, what remained was barely more than a mangled stump, half a human foot at best, with little or no resemblance to what the appendage had once been.

For the rest of his life, in order to stand and walk as normally as possible, Harold Pincus would have to wear one shoe specially weighted in the front to make up for the missing part of his foot. It was a bitter price to pay for his small bid for freedom, and it wouldn't be the last such toll he would pay.

Ever resourceful, Anna Sheehan Pincus had remarried a Mr Keliher, whose first name seems to have been forgotten over time. The difference between Anna's Catholic upbringing and her first husband's Jewishness may well have been one of the factors leading to the end of their marriage. Regardless of any wishes Harry may have expressed on the matter, Anna made sure that Harold, her only child, was raised a Catholic. Taking on another husband who could not only provide for Anna and her son but also reinforce Harold's Irish Catholic heritage must have seemed to Anna a perfect plan. Unfortunately, Mr Keliher didn't stay with Anna any longer than Harry Pincus had and, at the age of 16, Harold found himself looking for work to help support himself and his mother.

Nothing remarkable occurred in Harold's life over the next few years that anyone has noted for posterity. Like many young men in similar circumstances, he dropped out of high school after the 10th grade in order to work and help support himself and his mother. He landed a job as a chauffeur, his mangled foot evidently not a handicap to driving. It was during this quiet interval that Harold Pincus met Edna Manilow.

Edna was also the child of immigrants, Russian Jews who had come to Williamsburg, Brooklyn, by way of Baltimore, Maryland, where Edna was born on May 27, 1923. Her father, Joseph Manilow, was born in Russia, the son of Louis Manilow and the former Anna Meltzer. He was a quiet, unassuming man who seemed no match for his domineering wife, Esther. Five years younger than her husband, Esther Manilow was also Russian by birth, the daughter of Abraham Yanoff and Bertha Valinsky. Though, by an odd coincidence, Esther and Joseph shared a September 9 birthday, an outsider would be hard pressed to see just what else this seemingly odd couple had in common beyond their marriage vows and their two children, Rose, the elder, and Edna.

One thing the Manilows did share was a solid work ethic. For her part, Edna went to work at age 17 as a stenographer for Siegal and Karpel at 130 West 30th Street. In addition, both Esther and Joseph worked outside the home to make ends meet. Joseph worked at the garment factory of Goldstein & Spiegelman in Brooklyn, while Esther made her way each day to the basement of 69 Wooster Street where she toiled for the Moon & Herman Hat Box Company.

Esther's workday didn't end when she left Moon & Herman. Though their small apartment on Broadway was humble, it was also spotless – Esther saw to that. She also cooked the meals and sewed the clothes; her hand stitching was legendary. Life in Williamsburg was a far cry from her privileged upbringing in Russia, which had lasted only until her father's death when she was eight years old. But eight years had been enough to cement Esther's sense of entitlement. And every minute of every day that she toiled in the hatbox factory, every floor she scrubbed in her family's tiny apartment, every meal she cooked, every garment she sewed was but another reminder of the privilege that had been so briefly hers, and so cruelly taken.

It was perhaps this memory of lost glory, either real or perceived, that accounted for the steely bitterness Esther carried about her always, a fierce rigidity which would later lead her grandson to refer to her as "a ballbuster". While she had been powerless in the face of the events that had shaped her own destiny as a child in Russia, as an adult she was determined to control every aspect of her life, which ultimately meant exercising complete authority over her household and every person within it.

Joe Manilow simply steered clear of his wife whenever possible, and otherwise gave in to her every wish and command. He was a sweet man who didn't like contention, and he had never really felt a match for Esther, in any sense of the word. Edna's older sister, Rose, had married early and moved out of the state altogether, mainly to remove herself from Esther's vice-like grip over her life. This left Edna as the main focus of Esther's smothering control, a situation which, for the headstrong Edna, could only be characterised as untenable, at best.

So it must have been with an enormous mixture of relief and trepidation that Edna came home one day, at age 19, and announced that Harold Pincus, an Irish Catholic chauffeur, had asked her to marry him — and she'd said yes.

Chapter Two

It should come as no surprise that Edna's announcement of her engagement to Harold Pincus was met by her mother with uncontrolled fury. Every mother dreams of a better life for her daughter, but the prospect of Edna marrying a Brooklyn-born chauffeur was almost more than Esther could bear. Beyond that, Harold was Irish and, even worse, Catholic.

The enmity between the different ethnic and religious groups living side by side in Brooklyn was very real, and often turned very ugly. For a Jewish girl to marry a Catholic boy was nearly as unthinkable as the Jewish Harry Pincus' marriage to Catholic Anna Sheehan had been. And Harold's Jewish-sounding name was little consolation to Esther. The fact that he was a Pincus meant nothing in the face of his Catholic upbringing.

But Edna couldn't be shaken from her resolve to marry Harold. He hardly had the good looks of a movie star, but, then again, neither did the skinny, buck-toothed Edna. But Harold was a gentle man, with a joyous sense of humour which was incredibly attractive to the fun-loving Edna. The two also shared an all-encompassing love of music. Whether it was records, radio, or musical theatre, Harold loved to surround himself with music. He had a beautiful singing voice and was often called upon at social events to perform a number or two. Edna shared this love of music, and she also loved to sing and entertain. "They lived music", a friend observed of the couple.

Beyond this shared love of fun and music, marriage for Edna offered the perfect escape route from her suffocating life at home with her parents. To a young woman raised in the early part of the 20th century, marriage was seen not as a journey, but a destination. It was the end of the story, the happily-ever-after. Two radiant young people looked deeply, soulfully into each other's eyes and vowed to have and to hold, sealed with a kiss. The music swells, a happy tear is shed, and the film fades to black. Of course the tragedy is that very few of these fairy tales, in reality, end with a "happily ever after".

Still, undaunted, Harold and Edna set their fairy tale in motion with a trip to the Kings County Clerks Office late on Wednesday afternoon, June 3, 1942 where they obtained their marriage licence. Four days later, at 1.00 p.m. on Sunday, June 7, they were married by Rabbi Abraham Levin at the Rabbi's home on South 8th Street, just a block away from the Manilows' apartment on Broadway. The ceremony was witnessed by Alfred Howe and Frank Miller. It's not known whether either Edna's parents or Harold's mother attended the brief ceremony.

For the newlywed Mr and Mrs Harold Pincus, reality set in quickly. As she had hoped, her marriage to Harold had given Edna an escape from the suffocating restrictions of life under her mother's roof, if only briefly. She and Harold had barely had time to set up housekeeping in their own apartment just blocks from both Edna's parents' apartment and Harold's mother's apartment when Harold received a letter that effectively revoked Edna's new-found freedom. "*Greetings from the President of the United States,*" the letter began. Harold had been drafted.

The attack by Japanese war planes on the US Naval installation at Pearl Harbor on the Hawaiian island of Oahu on December 7, 1941 had provoked America's entry into World War II, a conflict that had already been raging in Europe for over two years. At first only the best and strongest young men in the country were called to fight for what many optimistically believed would be a quick victory. But as the war raged on and the best and the strongest America had to offer were killed off by the thousands, the armed forces couldn't afford to be quite so picky about who they called into service.

The United States Army must have been desperate indeed to want to induct Harold Pincus into its ranks. When Harold reported for his physical, he needed only to take off his shoes to be declared unfit to serve. His mangled stump of a foot, the souvenir of his youthful bid for freedom from Brooklyn and all the poverty and despair it represented, could now be Harold's ticket out of the war. That is it could have been, had Harold so chosen.

But at 22, Harold found himself still poor, still Brooklyn-bound, still caring for his ageing mother, and now further burdened by the responsibility of a wife, a wife who came with a nagging, domineering mother who hated him. His deformed foot could be his ticket out of the war, but the world's war could also provide Harold with a brief respite from his own personal struggles at home. It was not an opportunity he planned to let slip by.

Beyond that, there was a certain stigma attached to being a draft-aged male not in uniform. Explains a friend of Harold's, "They said to him, 'you could be out on a medical discharge'. He used to laugh. Just to get a uniform and be one of the boys, he didn't sign to get out."

Harold convinced the officers presiding over the selection process that there were any number of duties he could fulfil in the Army that would be unaffected by his deformed foot. Yes, he would need a special prosthesis to make up for the missing portion of his foot. But after all, he'd been a chauffeur for several years. If he was up to that, surely the Army could find something for him to do? Anything? Incredibly the Army agreed, and Harold finally found his way out of Brooklyn, if only as far as a camp in the deep south where he stood guard over enemy prisoners of war. The prisoners were, for the most part, grateful simply to be out of the line of fire and receiving three square meals a day. Harold, their guard, was just as grateful to be in uniform and out of Brooklyn.

Edna, left behind in Brooklyn after only a few months of married life, had little choice but to move back in with Esther and Joe in the cramped, sixth-floor walk-up on Broadway. Far from being sympathetic over Edna's situation, Esther used the circumstances to ridicule and criticise her daughter even more severely than before Edna had married. Hadn't Esther told her that the Irishman was no good? Hadn't she begged Edna not to throw her life away on such a bum? And now where was she? Nineteen years old, married without a husband to show for it, and living back under her parents' roof.

But that wasn't the full extent of Edna's situation. Not only was she married with no husband to show for it, but, she soon realised, she was also pregnant. Anticipating her mother's reaction to this latest turn of events, Edna wisely kept the news to herself. It was only early in 1943, when nature was on the brink of making the situation obvious to anyone who cared to glance at her waistline, that Edna confided in her parents.

Edna's fear of telling her mother about her pregnancy had been well founded. "You stupid girl!" Esther reportedly screamed at her daughter when she made what should have been her joyful announcement. And, in case her displeasure and disapproval were not fully evident, Esther punctuated her remark by punching her daughter in the face with such force that she broke Edna's nose.

The next few months in the tiny apartment would have been even more miserable than those that preceded them had not Edna taken such an obvious pleasure in the impending birth of her child. As spring gave way to the oppressive summer heat, Edna busied herself preparing for the new arrival. Perhaps motherhood would provide the escape that marriage hadn't. For once Edna would have someone to love her without question and without criticism; one single human being who would be utterly dependent upon her, who wouldn't leave her, and who would love her no matter what. It would be a boy, she told everyone who would listen, a beautiful boy.

She was right. On June 17, 1943, Edna gave birth to a son she named Barry Alan Pincus. At last she had her beautiful baby boy.

Chapter Three

"*Show Dad You're Glad He's Your Dad! Father's Day, June 20th!*"
On the day Barry Pincus was born, the *New York Times* was
filled with ads reminding conscientious wives and children that no
father would feel fully appreciated without a gift of Flan-L-Tex
Washable Slacks (only $3.95 "At All Convenient John David
Stores"). Ads for "Holeproof Socks" and "Luxurious White Broad-
cloth Shirts" were accompanied by drawings of "typical" fathers –
impossibly tall, trim, and tucked in, their hair slicked neatly back,
some with dapper moustaches, most puffing on a pipe. "*Yes, he's
tough, gruff and He-manly,*" reads an ad for Seaforth shaving products.
"*No presents for him! No remembrances! 'He'll do the giving.' But you
know Father. You know it's only because the old softy's afraid he'll be forgotten that he pretends he wants to be forgotten.*"

When it came to being forgotten, Harold Pincus was given little
choice in the matter. As with every other aspect of her home and
family, Esther immediately took over control of the new baby. Edna
was not that far out of childhood herself, having passed out of her
teens only a few weeks before Barry's birth, so it was a relief to let her
mother take primary responsibility for the child's upbringing. Edna
went back to work and became little more than a sweet smelling
entity in her little son's life. Grampa Joe was the very embodiment of
love and kindness to his grandson, but he was completely powerless
in the home, any resolve he may once have possessed crushed
between the boisterous youth of his younger daughter and the iron-
fisted contempt of his wife. It was a house dominated by women, but
specifically one woman – Esther.

The rigours of even domestic military life proved too much for
Harold, and, after only nine months of service, he was honourably

discharged from the Army on June 30, 1943, just two weeks after his son's birth. But even after so brief an absence, by the time Harold returned home from military service, a family unit had been established that very deliberately excluded him.

Harold had finagled his way into the Army in order to escape Brooklyn and his overwhelming responsibilities there, to be "one of the boys". But in a strange twist of fate that echoed the accident on the freight train which had marked him for life, Harold was now being forced to pay a bitter price for his second great bid for freedom.

Though she often tried, Edna had never really been able to stand up to her mother. When Harold returned to Brooklyn, Edna was faced with a choice – try to resume a life with a man she'd barely had a chance to know before he'd left her for the Army, or remain in a relatively comfortable situation living with her parents. The second option had much to offer. Edna enjoyed her job, and was rising through the ranks there. She enjoyed dressing nicely, associating with people outside of Brooklyn, and socialising with her friends whenever she wanted to, secure in the knowledge that Barry was being well cared for by her mother. In fact, since Barry's birth, Esther had focused so much attention on the baby that there was little time left over to harangue Edna, finally giving Edna a measure of the freedom she had previously hoped to achieve by marrying and moving out of her parents' home.

Given that, there was no longer any real advantage to life with Harold that Edna could see. Should she choose Harold over her mother, she knew she would no longer be able to count on Esther's support. Edna would no doubt have to quit her job and stay home to take care of her child.

But perhaps the real deciding factor between life with Harold and life with her parents was Harold's desire for Barry to receive the same traditional Catholic upbringing his own mother, Anna, had made sure Harold had had. But according to Jewish belief, a child born to a Jewish mother is Jewish and, as such, should be raised according to Jewish beliefs and customs. The thought of Barry Pincus – son of Edna Manilow and, more importantly (at least as far as Esther was concerned), grandson of Joseph and Esther Manilow – being raised as a Catholic was simply unthinkable.

For Harold these religious differences were also causing problems, not only personally but professionally as well. It was shortly after he returned from the Army that Harold began using the surname Keliher rather than Pincus. The name Keliher had no real meaning to him, having simply been the name of his mother's second husband. But the most lucrative jobs to be had in Brooklyn at that time were offered by Schaefer Brewery, the majority of whose workers were Irish Catholics. Certainly Harold was an Irish Catholic, too, but his father's name – Pincus – proclaimed him a Jew, if falsely. Despite the United States' and their European allies' victory over Hitler and his campaign to exterminate the Jews of Europe, the US was rife with feelings of anti-Semitism, which ran unchecked – and largely unacknowledged – in the brewing industry. "Everybody was polite," says a former brewery employee, "but nobody wanted to hire you – people just were not comfortable." The best way Harold could see around this dilemma was to simply assume a new surname. It wasn't that he was lying about his heritage – he was half Irish and had certainly been raised a Catholic. So he decided to abandon the Jewish half of his identity completely, along with his family name.

To Esther, Harold had seemed bad enough as an Irishman with a Jewish name. Now he was presenting himself as the complete Irish Catholic nightmare – Harold Keliher. It was more than Esther would stand, and much less than she thought Edna should settle for. The iron opposition Esther posed was more than either Edna or Harold could bear. So, reluctantly, Harold moved back into his mother's one-bedroom flat, took a job at Schaefer Brewery as Harold "Kelly" Keliher, and began a lengthy and ultimately futile struggle to become a father to his son. In her corner, Esther Manilow made sure that any contact between father and son would require a battle, with Barry as the prize.

As Barry grew into a toddler and began walking and talking, it's unclear how much he may have sensed of the conflict that surrounded him. A visitation schedule had been agreed for Harold to spend time with his son. Each Sunday Edna would dress Barry in his best clothes so he could go with his father to see Anna, Harold's mother. But gradually it seemed that whenever Harold would call for his son, the Manilows were always able to come up with some excuse why his visits had to be cancelled: Barry was sick, or Barry was tired, or Barry was simply "away". It was Esther's hope that if she could keep Harold and Barry apart long enough, the child would eventually lose all memory of having had a father at all and Barry would be truly and wholly hers.

As unfair as it might seem to him, Edna begged Harold not to fight her mother's wishes, as it would only result in grief for all concerned. Much like the long-suffering Grampa Joe, Harold was a man who avoided confrontations. But there finally came a point when Harold had been given one excuse too many, and the situation reached a boiling point, ironically a situation that involved Joseph Manilow.

Walking toward the Manilows' nearby apartment for his pre-arranged visit with Barry one Sunday, Harold caught sight of Joe Manilow leading Barry by the hand in the opposite direction. This was simply the end of Harold's patience with the Manilows and their nonsense, and Harold approached Joe to confront him. As soon as he caught sight of Harold, Joe hastily picked Barry up and clutched the child to his chest. "I'm supposed to have him today," Harold said firmly. He was fed up. This was *his* son – not Joe's, not Esther's, but his – his and Edna's. Indeed, it seemed to him that the two people with the least authority over Barry were his actual parents. It was simply wrong, and Harold wanted it to stop – immediately. He reached for Barry, trying to wrest the terrified child out of his grand-father's arms, but Joe resisted. Harold certainly wasn't about to beat up an old man holding a child – his child. He relented, the brief confrontation ended, and Joe took Barry home.

That wasn't to be the end of it. Whether at Esther's insistence or of his own volition, Joe Manilow called the police and filed an assault complaint against Harold, who received a summons and had to appear in court to defend his actions. Time has lost the official results of that hearing, but the personal results were clear: Harold admitted defeat. He was no match for Esther – no one was. From that point on, Harold chose to keep an eye on his son only from a safe distance.

For all the bitterness and ill will Esther Manilow could dish out to the adults around her, when it came to Barry, she radiated total love and absolute approval. It was as though Barry had been sent to redeem all Esther's past hardships and disappointments; all the pain life had dished out to her was washed clean through the pure, undi-luted love she received from Barry and which she herself showered upon him. It was, in fact, a deluge of such all-consuming love that at times it seemed Barry would drown in it.

"Gramma loved me," Barry wrote in his 1987 autobiography,

Sweet Life. "I mean *really* loved me . . . She was very protective. Too protective. I had no friends for the first ten years of life . . . Gramma kept me pretty much to herself during those years."

In reality Barry had *two* grandmothers who loved him, not just one, a fact that has somehow gotten lost over time. Harold's mother, Anna, was also obliged to suffer the consequences of Harold's differences with the Manilows, which drastically reduced the amount of time she was allowed to spend with her only grandchild, whom she adored. The elementary school Barry attended was just around the corner from Anna's apartment and, during the school's recess periods, Anna had taken to standing outside the chain link fence surrounding the schoolyard to watch Barry at play; he was the very image of his father.

Ironically, it was Edna who was most responsible for seeing to it that her estranged husband's mother was able to enjoy more personal time with Barry. After Harold stopped calling for Barry, on a regular basis Edna would dress Barry in his finest clothes and take him to Harold's mother's apartment for dinner or just a visit. "Anna idolised him," says Annie Keliher, Harold's second wife and widow, who began dating Harold in the late Forties, after her own divorce. "[Barry] would go over there and Anna would stand on her head. She would just take him and show him off; he was her little guy."

Just as Barry had inherited his love of music from his parents, Harold's own love of music had come to him from his mother, who had an Irish brogue and a beautiful singing voice. When Barry was seven, Edna had given him an accordion and arranged for him to start taking lessons. "Barry used to come with his accordion," Annie Keliher recalls. "And Anna had a voice! See, it runs in the family. This is how she used to entertain Barry. The two of them, him with his accordion and her singing with him." Harold, who was living with his mother since his estrangement from his wife and son, would make himself scarce during these visits. It wasn't that Harold didn't want to see his son, but his mother's ongoing insistence that Harold and Edna reconcile was too painful an ordeal to endure, especially in front of little Barry.

Though Harold and Edna had physically separated almost immediately after Harold's return from the Army, they remained legally married until 1950, when Barry was seven years old, divorcing only when Harold decided to remarry. At that time it was not possible to file for divorce on the basis of the now popular "irreconcilable differ-ences" or any other such vague notion that essentially meant a couple had simply made an error of choice. For those wishing to divorce, the choice of grounds was "beat, cheat, or retreat" – physical vio-lence, adultery, or desertion. If none of these applied, but both parties wanted to divorce, couples often simply admitted to non-existent grounds, just for the sake of expediency. It was for this reason that Harold and Edna agreed that, although Harold had never cheated on Edna, she would file for divorce on the grounds of adul-tery, which Harold would not contest.

Even the finalisation of their divorce on January 10, 1951, couldn't stop Anna Keliher from urging a reconciliation between her son and Edna. "When Edna would come over, [Harold] would dis-appear," recalls Annie Keliher. "Because his mother would stick her two cents in, she'd try to get them together." It was a determination that Anna Keliher maintained throughout her life and even took to her deathbed. In her later years she suffered from uremic poisoning and was often hospitalised. By the time of her death, Harold and Annie were married, and were raising Annie's son and daughter from her first marriage. "We get the call she's dying," recounts Annie Keliher, recalling her mother-in-law's last hours. "We have to run to the hospital. My husband was on the job at Schaefer Brewery, and they got hold of him and told him that he has to go to the hospital, his mother is dying. But I got there first. I'll never forget it!" Annie laughs ruefully at the memory of her mother-in-law's stubborn per-sistence. "She's laying in that bed, I'll never forget it, and she says, 'Harold and Edna are going to get together. Why don't you leave Harold alone?'" Annie, Harold's wife of several years by that time, was stunned. "You know, I looked at her in that bed, I could've hit her! I'll never forget that! I told my husband, 'Get me outta here! Your mother hates me!'"

Yet, in retrospect, Annie has come to appreciate Anna's feelings. "In her heart, it must've hurt her that [Harold] was neglecting Barry and raising my children." It was a feeling that really hit home when, several years after their marriage, Annie gave birth to her only child with Harold, a boy. "I gave birth to Tim and [Harold] drove every-one nuts," she recalls. "He was a father who stood on his head with joy. 'I have a son!' And I'd think, my god, you already have a son." But that was only technically true. In reality, Tim was the first son

Harold could really call his own, and he revelled in fatherhood in a way he was never allowed to with Barry.

Even without a father in the home, compared to many of the other children in the surrounding Williamsburg tenement buildings, Barry's upbringing was relatively privileged. Not only did he receive unlimited supplies of unconditional love at home, but his mother had a good job at which she earned more money than many of his schoolmates' fathers at a time when women were routinely paid a small fraction of the salary of their male counterparts. Their divorce agreement had set out a schedule of child support in which Harold would pay Edna "the sum of $10.00 per week for the support and maintenance of the infant issue of this marriage, to wit, Barry Pincus, aged 7 years". The agreement further stipulated that "such payments to be made at the residence of the plaintiff, or at other places she may designate in writing". This arrangement may well have been suggested by Edna's parents, because Edna subsequently told Harold that she thought it would be best if he simply kept his money and stayed away from Barry. Harold agreed.

Williamsburg in the Forties and Fifties was a small, tightly knit neighbourhood; everyone knew everyone, and everyone knew everyone else's business, too. Since Harold had adopted the surname "Keliher" for good, he'd taken to answering to the nickname "Kelly". Since Kelly and Edna knew many of the same people in the microcosm that was Williamsburg, it was inevitable that their paths would often cross. This was fine with Kelly, who never really stopped caring for Edna. Just as Edna had seen to it that Barry maintained a relationship with Kelly's mother, Edna used the opportunities when they ran into each other to update Kelly on Barry's progress. During one of these meetings Edna and Kelly discussed Barry's upcoming birthday.

Edna told Kelly that Barry would love to have a tape recorder. Adds Kelly's widow, Annie, "That came from Edna, then [Kelly] went out and got it. I don't know how he expected to give it to him, but it just so happened Barry was walking down the street, so Kelly gave it to him."

The handing over of the tape recorder was an event that Barry would never forget. Indeed, he has said it was the only meeting he recalled having with his father during his entire childhood. In his autobiography, Manilow recalls that there was only one photo of his father left in all their family photo albums, because Esther had taken a pair of scissors and meticulously cut Harold's face from every photo he appeared in alongside Edna or Barry. Even so, it would have been hard for Barry not to recognise his father, as their faces so closely resembled each other's.

As Manilow recalls the incident, there was a rather stilted exchange between father and son, during which Kelly made reference to Esther's dislike of him, and expressed a fear that if she saw him talking to Barry she might call the police. After giving his son the reel-to-reel recorder, Kelly asked for a kiss and a hug, asked after Edna, then advised Barry not to tell anyone about the encounter. "Tell 'em you found the tape recorder or something, okay?"

Up to that time, Barry's image of his father was drawn exclusively from Esther's bitter tirades against him. Writes Manilow, "I stood there with my new tape recorder, bursting with excitement, but feeling funny, too. For as long as I could remember, I had thought of Harold as this monster person who had been mean to Mom and was uncaring and ugly. Now, here was this nice-looking, gentle guy, treating me affectionately, remembering my birthday, and giving me a great gift. That was my father? He wasn't so bad after all."

Unfortunately Barry wasn't much of a liar, and Esther discovered the truth about the tape recorder's origin within minutes of Barry's arrival home with his gift. "When Mom came home and heard about my visitor, she was upset, too," writes Manilow. It had seemed a good idea to Edna when she and Kelly had discussed the plan at the bar. But all it had really done was cause more turmoil in the household. As Edna had been instrumental in orchestrating the encounter, it is natural to assume that Edna passed the results on to Kelly and asked him not to attempt such an exchange again. Kelly would never again try to contact Barry while Esther was alive.

"Kelly, now, I realise how wrong he was," says Annie Keliher of her husband's decision not to make trouble for Edna with her mother. "He was always afraid of upsetting Edna or Barry or something. And truthfully, now I would say to him, you're 100% wrong! Your instincts were wrong. You should've pushed your way in."

But Kelly wasn't the type to push his way into any situation. He was a kind, gentle man who disliked trouble and certainly didn't want to be the cause of it. Ironically, Barry unwittingly echoed his father's sentiments when he summed up this encounter with his father in this way: "I never felt the need to go searching for my father, and so I never did. I got so much love and I felt so secure with my family and my friends that finding my real father never became an issue. Besides, the family would have gotten really upset and I was never one to make waves."

When Barry Alan Pincus was bar mitzvahed in 1956, at age 13, the family agreed that Edna would have her son's name legally changed to Barry Manilow. "There was no Pincus in our family," Barry later wrote, by way of explanation. "Here I was, about to enter manhood with a name that didn't mean anything to anyone." Barry didn't realise that Pincus was his father's birth name; he always assumed his father's real name was Keliher. Just as Harold had gone from being Harold Pincus to Harold "Kelly" Keliher to ease his way into the brewery, his son went from being Barry Pincus to Barry Manilow in order to eradicate an unpleasant memory for his mother and grandmother. It was the last tie binding Barry to his paternal past, and it was neatly severed with little consideration to what fell away.

Barry Manilow never knew his father yet, in a number of ways, he was like his father. And therein lies the tragic twist at the end of a fractured fairy tale.

Chapter Four

Along with a new name and the traditional Jewish entree into manhood, Barry Manilow's thirteenth birthday also brought him a new stepfather when Edna married Willie Murphy.

In retrospect, it's rather puzzling that Esther Manilow so easily accepted Willie Murphy as Edna's husband after having so violently rejected Harold Pincus. The two men had much in common. Both were Irish, both Catholic, both loved music. In fact, Harold and Willie were friends who had known each other for years and who worked together at the Schaefer Brewery. But where Harold was reserved by nature, Willie, a divorced father of two, was a drinker, a street brawler and had a reputation as a womaniser. Edna, it seemed, was prepared to overlook these faults. By all accounts, she was crazy about him.

Harold, too, had finally moved on. Anna Ceglowska Price – Annie – was a Long Island born, divorced mother of two and had for years moved in the same Williamsburg social circles as Harold, Edna and Willie. "We lived in a neighbourhood in Brooklyn – middle class, some of us lower," she remembers. "Our entertainment would be getting dressed on a Saturday night, going to the local bar, which was harmless. You knew everyone, and that's where you went to dance all night; Edna, sing all night. And the more drinks you had, the more you thought you had a voice." That's how Annie met Harold Keliher.

Harold had grown more handsome as he matured. He was a sharp dresser and, despite his deformed foot, a good dancer. He was also funny and affectionate, a combination Annie couldn't resist. "I just fell in love with him," she says. "His sense of humour. He was very, very kind to me." Both had been through painful divorces, though, so they bided their time before actually marrying again. But, for Annie, there was never any doubt in her mind, from the moment she met Harold, that her future would be with him. "He was going to be mine, and that was it." And so he was.

When Edna and Willie Murphy married, Barry was given the choice of moving with his mother and her new husband to the fourth-floor walk-up they'd rented on nearby Keap Street, or remaining with his grandparents. As much as Barry loved his grandparents, wriggling out from under his grandmother's heavy thumb must have seemed an attractive prospect. Living with his grandparents had been safe; living with his mother and Willie would be an adventure. Of course the new apartment had only one bedroom, but that bedroom had a closet with a door that opened onto the outside hallway; in Brooklyn's grander days, when the building had been constructed, it had been, perhaps, the servant's quarters. It would be a tight fit, but there was sufficient space in the tiny room for a bed, a desk, and a chest of drawers. What more did a teenage boy need? Two weeks after Edna and Willie married, Barry moved into the Keap Street apartment. Yet another family unit was formed.

To Barry, Willie seemed a revelation. While Barry adored his grandfather, his only previous male role model, Joe Manilow was little more than a benign presence in the home dominated by Esther Manilow. Willie, on the other hand, was young and vital and introduced Barry to an exciting new world. "He brought home books I had never heard of and read magazines I had only glanced at," Manilow later wrote. "His taste in everything was way above what I'd been exposed to. But most of all it was his music that changed my life."

The first thing Willie did for his stepson was to take him to a Gerry Mulligan concert. "I'll never forget it," Barry told an interviewer years later. "It was the biggest thing in my life." That was only the beginning of Barry's conversion. Willie also brought to the new home a small stereo and a large record collection. Barry's previous experience with music had been limited to his repertoire on the accordion, standards of the day sung by crooners and a smattering of jazz.

This was an era when popular culture in America was approaching a dramatic crossroads, the stifling conservatism of the Eisenhower years cracking under the strain of progressive attitudes in all the arts, not least music. By the mid-Fifties, Elvis Presley, a former Memphis truck driver with no formal musical training whatsoever, was dominating the American music charts, spreading the gospel according to rock'n'roll with songs like 'Heartbreak Hotel' (1956), 'Hound Dog' (1956) and 'All Shook Up' (1957), all three of which topped the *Billboard* charts. While Barry's classmates at Brooklyn's Junior High School 50 were bopping to Elvis, Jerry Lee Lewis and Chuck Berry, or swaying to the sweeter, softer sounds of Doris Day singing 'Que Será, Será', Barry remained unimpressed by the changes on the popular music scene. Instead, he was hooked on the sounds of Frank Sinatra or Count Basie or Gerry Mulligan coming through the tinny speakers of Willie's stereo.

For his fourteenth birthday, Barry received yet another life-changing gift from his new stepfather: a transistor radio. Before long the discovery of the five-hour nightly midnight jazz show hosted by "Symphony Sid" on radio station WEVD had the teenager staying up nights and sleepwalking through his days. His burgeoning musical knowledge was now stretched to include such jazz greats as trumpeter Miles Davis, clarinet and horn player John Coltrane, and smooth-sounding drummer and vibraphone player Cal Tjader. "I wallowed in Sarah Vaughan, Carmen Macrae, Nina Simone, Joe Williams, Mel Torme," says Manilow. "I couldn't get enough." Nevertheless, trying to reproduce these sublime sounds on the Bakelite keys of his clunky accordion proved somewhat less than satisfying.

The years of accordion lessons paid off in an unexpected way, however, when their downstairs neighbour allowed Barry to play her grand piano. Barry's agility on the 45 keys of the accordion translated nicely to the 88 keys of the grand, and a lifetime love was born. Every day after that, Barry would stop by his neighbour's apartment and practise on her piano until finally Willie and Edna – perhaps at the neighbour's request – decided to buy Barry a piano of his own, an $800 Wurlitzer spinet. Manilow credits his mother with paying for the piano, but told *Songwriter Magazine* that it was Willie's dislike of the accordion that really prompted its purchase. "Get rid of it!" Willie reportedly said of the outdated instrument. "Get him a piano!"

By the age of 15, Barry's life revolved completely around music. He now belonged to a small group of friends who shared his enthusiasm, if not quite to the same extent. Larry Rosenthal and Fred Katz were his two closest friends, and the three would spend much of their time together harmonising on the songs Barry heard on *Symphony Sid* and learning to play them on the piano. Maxine Horn, whom Barry would later characterise as his "steady girl", was also part of this circle of junior high school friends.

"I think it was more a platonic relationship, a group of friends," recalls Maxine. "I wouldn't say that I dated him. We just went out as a group. I don't remember going anywhere alone with him on a date." Even the 9th grade prom was a group experience, though Barry would later recall that he excitedly called Fred to tell him that he had kissed Maxine good night after the dance and "her leg went up in back, just like in the movies," a detail Maxine characterises today as "a little bit embarrassing".

Along with Fred's girlfriend, Susan, the five friends spent most of their free time together. "We were just a nice group," says Maxine. "We hung out together, we had lots and lots of fun. Barry would invite us to his place; he would play the piano. We'd hang out there. We all practised dancing."

The group would watch Dick Clark's *American Bandstand* after school and pick up the latest dances by watching the show's über-teens perform the steps on camera between commercials for soda pop and acne medications. When popular and controversial New York disc jockey Alan Freed announced he'd be holding a dance contest in Manhattan, Fred and Susan, and Barry and Maxine made up their minds to compete – and win.

"Every day after school we would practise, mostly at Susan's house, for hours and hours," says Maxine. "We thought we would win. I remember the prize was a jukebox. And we practised for months. I remember that all of our energies [were] concentrated on practising, because we were really determined we would win."

Finally the big day arrived. "We took the subway into Manhattan, to compete," says Horn. But there was a problem that Maxine and Barry, after days of debate, were still having difficulty working out. "Barry and I, we knew for sure we were going to win this jukebox. But of course we both lived in small apartments in Williamsburg, and we were trying to decide how we would share the jukebox. There was only one jukebox, and we lived in different apartments." So sure were the pair of winning that resolving this dilemma before they arrived at the contest seemed of paramount importance. "I remember we decided one of us would have it for six months, and the other one would have it the other six months," says Horn.

Problem solved, Barry and Maxine arrived, with Fred and Susan, at the ballroom where the contest was being held. What seemed a sure thing while the four teens practised in Susan's living room seemed somewhat less certain as they observed the hundreds of young couples who had all turned out to try to win the jukebox. But the foursome had come to compete, and compete they did. Today Maxine can laugh at the inevitable outcome. "The funny part of the story is, after having practised – it seems to me like we practised a year for this – I would say like in 30 seconds someone comes and taps us on the shoulder and eliminates us. And Barry was a great, great dancer. I thought we danced pretty well together, actually. But obviously the judges did not agree with us." Fred and Susan fared no better. "Within seconds we were all eliminated from the contest," says Maxine. "And we were just completely shocked that we had not won!" The dejected teens had to return to Brooklyn empty-handed.

It was a happy interlude for the group, this relatively carefree period between true childhood and the onset of more adult problems. "I just remember [Barry] was always a very up person," says Maxine. "We were always, always laughing. If you ask me what I remember, that's it – always, always laughing, having a good time."

As he entered 10th grade at Brooklyn's Eastern District High School, Barry's laughter was covering up serious problems at home. By Manilow's own account, Willie would meet Edna at her office after work and the two would head immediately for the bar. "By the time they arrived home," Barry wrote, "they were always loaded. And they had begun to argue."

Their arguments ranged from what Barry considered "harmless" – lasting a few hours – to more serious, with Willie storming out of the apartment and staying out all night, which would put Edna through a night of agony. "Edna was crazy about him, and that's sad," says Annie Keliher, who had known both of them before they were married and who often saw Edna and Willie when they frequented neighbourhood bars in Williamsburg. "He tortured her."

It wasn't only their drinking that caused problems. Willie's philandering ways didn't stop after marrying Edna. "I always said to my husband, what do the women see in this guy?" says Annie. "Arrogant,

conceited – the women would just go nuts for him. I had another personal friend, she would've committed *suicide* for this guy! And he was
not good looking. He had something *I* didn't see. It bothered me. But
that was Edna. She fell in love with him, that son of a gun."

It seems likely that Edna felt the best way to keep tabs on "that son
of a gun" was to keep pace with his drinking. More and more frequently Barry would get a phone call from his mother, obviously the
worse for drink, telling him to "pop in a frozen" for his dinner as she
wouldn't be home to cook for him. "I lived on Swanson's frozen
dinners during my high school days," Manilow has said. Today a
teenager in Barry's position could look to any number of support
groups to help him cope with his parents' alcoholism. In the late
Fifties, all a teenager could do was throw another TV dinner in the
oven and pray that the verbal fighting between his parents wouldn't
suddenly escalate into physical violence.

Music provided a form of support for Barry during this time. He
was often the first student to show up for school in the morning and
the last to leave at night, though it wasn't so much academics he was
seeking as a safe harbour.

Herb Bernstein was Barry's gym teacher at Eastern District High
School. Ironically Bernstein would leave EDHS in 1965 and make a
name for himself in the music business as a singer, composer,
arranger and manager. But he worked his way toward his eventual
music career by teaching gym and coaching the high school basket-
ball team, along with whatever other small school assignments came
his way. "I used to be in charge of the auditorium early in the
morning," Bernstein recalls. "The kids who came into school early,
it was cold out, so we'd let them into the auditorium, and I was kind
of the watchdog." Barry was usually among these early arrivers.
"Barry used to come up to me all the time," says Bernstein. "He'd
say, 'Would you mind if I played the piano?' He was such a nice kid.
I said, 'Ah, sure, go ahead' and he'd play. You know, nice, nothing
sensational. I never knew he had any real talent. I never dreamed that
someday this kid would be as gigantic as he became." To be fair,
Barry probably never imagined his high school gym teacher would
become a force in the music world, either.

Often the first to arrive in the morning to take advantage of auditorium piano privileges, Barry was just as likely to be the last to leave
for the same reason. Iris Richman was another EDHS classmate.

"Sometimes he'd play piano after school in the auditorium," she recalls. "I was always in school late, so I used to sometimes walk in there and listen to some of his original stuff, which I liked. He was always writing and trying different things. He was very good."

Though Barry's grades were nothing special, he was active in the life of the school. Still, he didn't make friends easily, preferring to stay in the relative safety of his already established relationships with Fred and Larry. "Other than being a really nice person, he was shy," Iris says. "He played in the orchestra and he worked in the main office, and I did also. There were a bunch of kids that used to work in the main office for their grade advisors and the guidance counsellors. I worked in the principal's and vice principal's office. We did a lot of stuff, and he did also. And we had classes together. He was just a nice person, never caused any trouble."

Another classmate remembers Barry's stint as a hall monitor. "He used to get upset with me when he caught me cutting classes," she says, then adds ruefully, "Maybe I should've listened to him – I never did graduate!" Iris also remembers Barry as being very mature for his age. "He wasn't hip, hep. He wasn't into games or gangs. He was respectful. Teachers seemed to like him. He was an all-around guy that was low-key, didn't get in anybody's way."

While his classmates seem to universally remember Barry in this way – "just a nice person" – Manilow's own memory of himself during this period is considerably less flattering. The words he uses to describe himself as a teenager range from "skinny" to "geeky" to downright "ugly" ("I have pictures that would curl your hair," he's said). Barry would later speculate that everybody probably has a different impression of themselves than those around them remember. "I always thought I was the shy loner," he said, "but when old friends call me they tell me that I wasn't perceived that way at all."

By the time he entered his last year in high school, Barry had tried his hand at physical labour with a short-lived job at Schaefer Brewery where both his father and stepfather were long-time employees. Barry made beer deliveries with a series of drivers until a careless mistake on his part caused an accident that ended his employment. At one point Barry worked with his father.

"Barry went with his father," says Annie Keliher. "Not a job, they'd 'shape the hall'. In other words, they weren't official – my husband was an official worker, this had to go through the union. But when they'd 'shape the hall', [a non-union worker was assigned] a job for the day. I don't know how or what, but Barry was with him. Kelly got the truck and Barry helped him, worked the day with him. But then Kelly used to laugh . . . All he said when he got home the first day is that Barry said, 'Boy, I wouldn't want to do this for the rest of my life!'" Annie insists that the circumstances of Barry's brief sojourn at the Schaefer Brewery aren't really important in the grand scheme of things. "Who the hell knows?" she says wearily when asked whether it was Harold or Willie who brought Barry to Schaefer. "The men all worked at the brewery. Willie, all his brothers, Kelly – they all grew up together, they all went to school together, they were all involved in each other's lives, their marriages, who stood up for who. That was the neighbourhood." Who did what for whom wasn't as important as making sure the family was supported.

Much seemed to happen for Barry during his last year of high school. He was voted "Best Musician" after campaigning for the title by playing Manuel de Falla's 'Ritual Fire Dance' on the piano, making Barry one of the "Senior Celebrities" of the class of 1961. More importantly, Barry also became part of his first professional band.

Jack Wilkins, who was still living in his parents' Brooklyn home at the time, doesn't remember exactly how he met Barry Manilow, only that he joined his band. "He was a piano player and used to actually come to my place on occasion and we used to play a little bit. I asked him if he wanted to be in this band, and he said, 'Sure.'"

Jack's band was called The Jazz Partners, and comprised Jack, Barry, Fred Clark, a bass player, and Billy Fagan, the drummer. "I played vibes in that band, and guitar," says Wilkins. "We just did a lot of local gigs. We played at this place on the lower east side in Manhattan called the Vivere Lounge, I think – something like that – a little joint on the lower east side. And we played and we had a lot of people come by and sit in, very, very good players. And Barry was just the piano player in the band. He was not egocentric about anything. And he and I used to rehearse and work out arrangements."

The musical world that Willie had opened up for Barry when he was 13 was now eagerly expanded. "Barry was a big fan of that Barney Kessel record, called *Music To Listen To Barney Kessel By*," Wilkins recalls. "He loved that record. We did arrangements of 'Mountain Greenery', which was on that record. And then we discovered this Cal Tjader record, *Live At The Blackhawk.* It was the same instrumentation — piano, vibes, bass drums. We got into it. It was pretty amazing."

"I remember one time I was at his house," Wilkins continues, "and I said, 'What do you listen to? What have you been listening to lately?' And he said, 'Well, I got these records, and I just put the headphones on and listened until the wee hours of the morning.' He was a big jazz fan — a huge jazz hound."

During his senior year Barry began dating Susan Deixler, a pretty brunette a year younger than himself, in her junior year at Eastern District High School. Susan seemed the very antithesis of Barry. Where Barry tended to be shy, Susan was outgoing; while Barry tended to limit his friends to a select few, Susan knew and was liked by everyone. Next to Barry's photo in his senior yearbook, the space available for a listing of his extracurricular activities is blank save for his address and future career and college plans (*Advertising, CCNY*). By contrast, Susan's listing next to her senior photo in the 1962 year-book reads like a catalogue of available school activities: "*President of the G.O.* [student government]; *Chorus; Biology Squad; Chemistry Squad; Bowling Club; Swimming Club; Grade Advisor's Monitor; Orientation Committee; City and Boro. Council.*" Her college ambition was to study nursing at Miami University.

"Oh, she was a doll!" remembers Iris Richman. "Susan was a bubbly person . . . Just a sweetheart, an absolute sweetheart. There wasn't anybody that didn't like Susan."

Susan was supportive of Barry's love of music and, as a piano player and singer herself, she was able to participate in his enthusiasm if only to a limited extent. The two grew steadily closer and were considered an item — if a surprising one — by their classmates. "I was a little surprised," says Iris Richman, though her surprise was tinged by concern for what she viewed as the imprudence of their plans for the future. "To get engaged [to be] married right after she graduated was a little premature, because I don't believe anybody should get married at 18 or 19." Iris wasn't the only one who felt this way. Barry would later admit that even his closest friends thought he was rushing into something neither he nor Susan was ready to handle. "But they seemed to really care about each other," Richman continues. "They seemed pretty solid."

So, after 18 turbulent years, Barry's life seemed finally to be taking a traditional turn. He would go to college and get a steady job. "Then," wrote Manilow, "I would marry Susan, get a house on Long Island with a white picket fence, and have kids, just like every-one else." But, despite his best efforts over the years to simply blend in and be what he perceived to be "normal", Barry had never been "like everyone else"; his life had never run a smooth course. Marriage was certainly not going to change that.

PART II

Picket Fences

"I have to live for others and not for myself; that's middle class morality."

– George Bernard Shaw, *Pygmalion*

Chapter Five

Barry's adult life began with a bit of a whimper. He'd enrolled for evening classes at City College of New York majoring in advertising because, as he explained it, "The choices were listed alphabetically and advertising was first under A." He got a menial job at an advertising agency and wasn't sorry when the firm went bankrupt soon after, leaving him unemployed once again.

Hindsight is one of those luxuries that allows us to look back over a lifetime and pinpoint events which, at the time they occur, seem inconsequential enough but, over time, prove to be pivotal. Barry's next job was one of those pivotal moments.

Through a friend of Willie's who worked at CBS Television in Manhattan, Barry landed a job in the CBS mailroom. He had been warned that during his interview for the job he was not to mention that he had any interest in music, or anything else even remotely related to show business. Once Barry started working in the mailroom, however, he quickly realised that everyone there was trying to use this tenuous TV connection to further a career in some facet of the performing arts, either behind the scenes or in the spotlight. Among these fellow aspirants was Marty Panzer.

Oddly enough, Marty's life and Barry's had been running parallel for many years. They were from the same neighbourhood, attended the same schools, knew the same people but, somehow, never actually met each other until they crossed the Brooklyn Bridge and started working together in the mailroom at CBS.

While Barry was shy, reluctant to draw attention to himself, Marty was flamboyant, emotional. He was also, like Barry, very musically talented, though the two had dissimilar but complementary tastes in music. While Barry had been drawn to cool jazz since he attended that first Gerry Mulligan concert with Willie, Marty loved show tunes and the larger-than-life performers who didn't simply sing the songs, but breathed fire into them.

"He was right," Manilow wrote of the things he learned about music from Marty Panzer. "When you combine passion and hot emotion with music, the result is explosive. It was a lesson I would never forget."

When a co-worker called in sick one day, Barry took over his mail delivery route, which included the building where the CBS recording studios were located, across the street from the corporate headquarters where Barry worked. After delivering the mail to the offices upstairs, Barry decided to explore the rest of the building. It was another innocent action that would again change the course of Barry's life.

His inquisitive nature led him to one of the recording studios on the second floor of the building. The studio seemed deserted, so Barry decided to try out the Steinway concert grand piano that dominated the room. "From then on," Barry wrote, "my mail runs included visits to the studios. Playing the piano in the studios became my first love and I'd reluctantly stop playing to deliver my mail."

Though he didn't realise it at the time, this would be Barry's first step away from the safe corporate world he'd always imagined would be his future. Other CBS workers would drop by to hear Barry play and, before long, Barry found himself doing arrangements for some of the other corporate drones who were, beneath it all, stars waiting to be born.

Marty's feel for passionate show-stoppers manifested itself in a talent to put words to the tunes Barry was constantly composing. It was the beginning of a collaboration that would eventually bring enormous success to both of them. But, for a while yet, they were still just two guys from the mailroom, trespassing in a world not yet theirs.

The next step came almost immediately, when Barry made a spur of the moment decision to give up his pursuit of an advertising degree at CCNY and instead enrol at New York College of Music. Advertising had been only a convenient choice, while NYCM offered courses in the things Barry actually cared about, like orchestra arranging.

Still, even though Barry was finally studying music seriously, he couldn't really see it as a career. Those who are raised with very little find it difficult envisioning life outside of the security of a nine-to-five job. So, while Barry took classes in the evening, his day job became even more important to him. It was the job that paid for the classes, and the job that was the only means Barry could see of paying for whatever his future would bring.

After two years in the mailroom, both Marty and Barry had moved into other, more responsible positions at CBS. Marty was in charge of On Air Operations, while Barry became a Log Clerk, keeping track, on four TV monitors, of what was being aired in each of the country's four time zones from 8.00 a.m. until 4.00 p.m., Monday through Friday. Then Barry would attend classes until late evening, when he would meet Susan, who was working as a secretary in the city, and the two would commute home to Brooklyn.

It had been two years since Susan had graduated from high school, and she and Barry had been dating steadily throughout that time. Things seemed to be sailing smoothly toward marriage until the couple decided it was time for their families to meet. While the first meeting went smoothly enough, the second meeting between Edna and Willie Murphy, and Al and Nettie Deixler ended in an argument over money. The Deixler's wanted a big wedding for their daughter while the Murphys made it clear they were unable to afford an elaborate affair. The fighting between the families escalated from there. Names were called, feelings were hurt, and grudges were born. Finally, out of desperation, Barry, 21, and Susan, 20, decided to bypass their families and simply elope.

Barry asked Marty to witness the brief City Hall ceremony, while Susan asked her best friend from high school, Joan De Santis, to act as her maid of honour. It was to be a simple civil ceremony only, but Susan wanted to make it special. "They were giggly and so full of life and hope for the future," Joan's mother, Anne De Santis, later told an interviewer. "They went to Lord & Taylor's on Fifth Avenue together to get dresses and spent just about every penny they had saved. I remember Joan bought a lovely green velvet dress . . . Susan was such a pretty bride. She had beautiful jet-black hair and was so happy."

Barry and Susan were married on their lunch break. The actual wedding ceremony took place in a judge's chambers, and took far less time to make official than the amount of time the judge insisted

Barry and Susan take before the ceremony to rethink their actions. Not unwisely, the judge thought it prudent to subject them both to a stern admonition about the serious responsibilities of marriage, but neither bride nor groom could be dissuaded. So, vows exchanged, all documentation signed and filed, Mr and Mrs Manilow parted company outside City Hall, and each went back to finish their day's work.

If the couple thought they'd be spending their first night of wedded bliss in each others' arms in the apartment they'd surreptitiously rented on Sullivan Street, they were quite mistaken. When Barry and Susan arrived home after work that night and broke the news to Susan's parents, the Deixlers refused to acknowledge a civil ceremony, and wouldn't even consider letting Susan and Barry move in together until the union had been solemnised by a rabbi.

That weekend, Barry and Susan were again married, and again attended by Marty and Joan. This time, though, the ceremony took place under a chupeh in a rabbi's office, while both sets of parents – each still not speaking to the other – looked on without the beatific smiles that normally grace such occasions. Now the Manilows were joined in the eyes of God and man – and the Deixlers. It was official. Again.

A week later Susan's parents held a lavish wedding reception for the newlyweds. It was a disaster. Grudges firmly in place, the Deixlers refused to invite any of Barry's family other than Edna and Willie, who refused to attend. Out of a sense of family loyalty, Barry said he wouldn't go if Edna and Willie weren't there. Edna finally talked him into attending, though she and Willie maintained their boycott of the event. Because Susan's extended family had been cheated out of the big wedding Nettie and Al had so hoped for, at the reception they produced a rabbi and made Barry and Susan go through the wedding ceremony again, for the benefit of all those assembled.

Then, in a stunning display of one-upmanship, Edna and Willie threw a reception of their own for Barry and Susan the following weekend. Perhaps assuming that Nettie and Al Deixler would boycott the affair in retaliation for Edna and Willie's refusal to attend the earlier event, the Murphys simply neglected to invite the Deixlers. But Edna had learned a lesson from the Deixlers and she, too, produced a rabbi at their reception and insisted that Barry and

Susan take their vows a fourth time, this time for the benefit of the groom's extended family.

If a wedding a week for a solid month can't cement a marriage, then perhaps it's a sign that something about the union was seriously, seriously wrong from the very beginning.

Chapter Six

Not long after Barry and Susan were married, Barry was offered a chance to play piano for the revival of a 19th century stage play, *The Drunkard*. Bro Harrod, who worked as a director at CBS, owned a small theatre on 13th Street called, appropriately enough, the 13th Street Theater. Barry's talents as a pianist, songwriter, and arranger were by now widely known among the CBS personnel. When Bro stopped by Barry's office one day to offer him the job playing piano for the production, Barry jumped at the chance. It paid only $15 a performance, but it was a toe in the door, which was priceless.

Barry's schedule was exhausting. His studies at New York College of Music had led to a brief stint at Juilliard, but he'd had to leave the prestigious music school for lack of funds. Still, he was working a full-time job, still playing gigs with The Jazz Partners, and now he'd taken on a nightly accompanist job with the 13th Street Theater as well. And – oh, yes – he also had a wife.

Susan was determined to play the role of supportive wife, to do whatever it might take to help Barry realise his dreams of becoming a successful professional musician. Jack Wilkins, the leader of The Jazz Partners, remembers: "Susan was very nice, a supportive girl, I liked her. But [Barry] was just completely wasted, he was working so hard to make this work, and he was like almost crying at the piano he was so tired."

To cap it all, it was right around this time that Edna Manilow made her first suicide attempt.

Barry was working at the 13th Street Theater when Susan called to tell him she was on her way to pick him up. She offered no explanation, but simply asked that he be in front of the theatre waiting for her when she arrived by cab. On their way to Brooklyn, Susan explained that Edna had taken an overdose of sleeping pills. Edna would later tell her son that the attempt was prompted by a combination of financial and marital problems. However, friends hint that Edna was despondent over her son's marriage. Indeed, she had tried to talk him out of marrying Susan, whom, some observers noted, Edna resented for taking her son away.

Barry Manilow has never publicly discussed the circumstances of Edna's fortuitous rescue from the brink of death. Someone had called the police before it was too late, but who? If her suicide attempt was timed and staged to get Barry's attention without actually killing herself, it proved most effective: Barry was confused, terrified and racked with guilt. The police were not so moved. They told Barry if his mother attempted to take her own life again, they would have no choice but to commit her to a sanatorium. It was another stone added to the load of stress and guilt Barry was already carrying with him on a daily basis.

As he had always done to escape his troubles, Barry buried himself in his work, his music. In addition to his day job at CBS and evening work with *The Drunkard*, Barry had also finagled his way into conducting music for a community church theatrical group's production of *The Pajama Game* by exaggerating his past experience. Combining his wish to work with his guilt over his neglected wife and troubled mother, Barry even managed to find small parts in the production for both Susan, so she could feel involved in Barry's work, and Edna, so Barry could keep an eye on her. Still, it was a juggling act that was proving impossible to sustain. "Edna wanted to perform, more than anything on the planet," recalls Jeanne Lucas. "And any time that he could make that come true for her, even if she got a little part or whatever in one of these little shows, he would do it. Because he really wanted her to be happy."

*

Jeanne Lucas was a vivacious and talented young woman who had arrived in New York from Michigan with $200 in her pocket. She didn't know anyone in New York, but, like so many young performers, was determined to make it in the big city. Soon she discovered the 13th Street Theater and auditioned for a part in *The*

Drunkard, which is how she first met Barry Manilow. "Before I even left the theatre they told me I had the job," Lucas recalls. "Barry got all enthusiastic and he said, 'Oh, you're the next Ethel Merman, you're the next Judy Garland . . . you have to be in the show.' So I got cast in *The Drunkard* and we rehearsed and worked together in that show where I played Crazy Agnes."

Jeanne and Barry became fast friends immediately. They took to calling each other "Harry" and "Ethel". Explains Jeanne, "We just started fooling around one day and calling each other corny names, and Harry and Ethel hit the wall and stuck. They seemed like the corniest names we could think of."

Barry confided in Jeanne his insecurities about his future. Though he loved music, he craved the kind of financial security he'd never known as a child. He acted as Jeanne's accompanist when she would make the rounds auditioning. "He used to say to me constantly, 'Ethel, I can't imagine myself ever leaving CBS. I have to have security. I couldn't do what you're doing. It's just not possible.'" Still, he kept exploring his musical options. "He once in a while would play the piano and would sing and tape record himself singing," Jeanne says, "and Susan and I would listen to it. And it wasn't good. Even he knew. It was just – we used to tease him about it. But he kept working on it and he kept working on it and he kept working on it."

The problem was, Barry was working on just too many things. So many opportunities were coming his way, he felt he couldn't afford to miss out on any of them, nor did he want to. In fact, he kept seeking out new opportunities that would demand even more of his time. His job at CBS started at 8:00 a.m., and he often didn't get home until 2 or 3 in the morning. Susan had a full-time office job as well and had no desire to stay out until all hours of the morning, so the two were apart far more than they were together.

Like Jeanne, Mary Moesel had also been in New York only a short time when she landed a job as stage manager at the 13th Street Theater. She remembers how the cast and crew of *The Drunkard* would often stay after performances to put on a show of their own, for fun. "Saturday night, after the show was over, those of the people who were talented vocally or whatever way, would stay. And Barry was always willing to stay and play the piano for them while they did their favourite things, other than what was being done in *The Drunkard*. You know, they'd sing their favourite songs, or something

44

they'd like to do. And he was always such a good sport about it that, you know, I thought that was great. He never sat there and played something or sang anything, he always just played for the rest of them. I thought that was a nice thing to do." It also kept him from going home to his wife for another few hours.

"You know what I remember about Susan the most?" says Lucas. "Two things: the smell of Jean Nate – she wore that all the time, and the whole place was just permeated by it, it was just wonderful – and a leopard robe that she wore. She was beautiful. Susan was the most lovely person. She was so sweet and so understanding of him. Because he was out more than he was there. But she had a job and stuff, and she couldn't be out all night."

More often than not, Barry would literally be out all night. After he would finally leave the 13th Street Theater each night, sometimes as late as 10 p.m., he and Jeanne would then start checking out the local clubs. "He was very ambitious," she recalls, "and he would go out to clubs or wherever to try to see what was going on. Because, even though at that time he was working at CBS and he was an accompanist, he had big eyes."

At this stage in his career Barry saw himself as a support mechanism for other people's work, not a front man himself. He played all of Jeanne's auditions and had put together a programme of songs for her to sing that they could take to clubs or theatres. "So we would do the show at the 13th Street Theater," says Lucas, "and then at night we would start hitting some of the small clubs that had piano bars. And he would play music that we'd worked on and I would sing. So we became sort of little regulars at these little places after the show." But even Jeanne couldn't help but wonder at Susan's seemingly endless patience with her husband's constant absence. "She was just very, very sweet about it all. And I remember thinking, god, just what an amazing woman she was because we would stay out nights until 2, 3 in the morning going from club to club to hear people sing and all that kind of good stuff."

The next opportunity that came Barry's way would cause a serious reassessment of priorities. By now he had written music for two stage plays in addition to *The Drunkard*, and one of these productions was about to go on the road. The producer offered Barry the job of musical director for the production. Barry felt excited – and trapped. Music was his passion, and the thought of working in the field full-time was unbelievably tempting. But the job would mean he would have to be away from New York for months, which would mean giving up his day job. The job at CBS was an important security blanket for Barry, one he wouldn't give up lightly. And then there was the fact that he was now a married man.

The marriage had been a bad experiment from the start and by now was effectively over. Barry turned for help to the "Advisor" column in *Playboy* magazine.

Jim Petersen, who has been with *Playboy* since 1973 and acted as *Playboy*'s "Advisor" for 22 years, isn't at all surprised that Barry would have felt more comfortable sharing his doubts and fears with the Advisor than with his friends, family, or even his wife. In fact, he says, scores of young men at the time felt exactly the same way.

"Even when I took the column over in 1973," says Petersen, "the first thing that struck me about the people who wrote to the magazine was that they trusted the magazine before they trusted neighbours, parents, priest, doctors. They had no one in their own life to turn to, so they turned to the voice of the magazine because they trusted our voice." *Playboy* was catering to an intelligent, upwardly mobile male readership that typically wanted more out of life than their fathers had settled for. According to Petersen, the collective consciousness of the typical *Playboy* reader was: "*I will not settle for this; I believe life can be better, help me out.*"

"And that's the underlying sentiment of all the letters," Petersen says. "*I have a great relationship, but . . . I do this, it doesn't work — what's wrong? How do I get out of this situation? How do I catch the bus?*" And, he adds, most importantly, "*I think that you are more like me than the people around me are.*"

"I took over the column right at the crest of the sexual revolution — *Joy of Sex* was out, Masters and Johnson had just published, I had a sexual vocabulary no one had had before me — and I took the Advisor column into the bedroom. But prior to 1973, it was a career counselling guide. It was financial, it was collecting stamps, it was how many holes should I have in my belt, it was what wine goes with what fish; should I deal with my boss this way, should I take this chance with my career. When Barry wrote to [*Playboy*], he might as well have been writing to *Money* magazine, or *Boy's Life*."

There was also a certain New York sensibility about *Playboy*, a cultivated cool that had very little to do with naked women and much to do with simply being too imperturbable and in command to ever have to make compromises. "Hefner always compared *Playboy* to the Sear's catalogue," says Jim Petersen. "We were a dream book, and sex was only one of the dreams. For the first ten years of its life *Playboy* was a jazz magazine with naked women in it. We didn't discover rock and roll until about 1963."

This jazz mentality suited Barry just fine. After all, he'd never been interested in the pop scene, preferring ever-cool swing and be-bop music to the seemingly transitory nature of most pop music and culture. For years, *Playboy* felt exactly the same way. "*My daughter and a number of the other kids in the neighborhood have formed a real cult over the Beatles . . .*" wrote a concerned father in a letter to the Advisor that appeared in the March 1965 edition of *Playboy*. "*If they weren't so darned serious about this, it would be pretty funny. But when Susan doesn't go to church with us because they are having their own service in their Beatle church, I start to worry a little. Worst of all, we have to listen to that awful music over and over and over. What should we do?*" The Advisor's answer was reassuring, if not prescient: " '*And this, too, shall pass away,' said a sage about another plague at another time. We suggest you keep cool until the Beatle bugaboo likewise passes away, as it most assuredly will. In the meantime, when Susan plays her records, do your listening with earmuffs. Yeah, yeah, yeah.*" Oops.

"Our tastes and sensibilities were very much with the jazz world and the showbiz world, the Frank Sinatra world, the Miles Davis world," says Petersen. "I mean Hefner was an urban man at a time when most of America had left the city for the suburbs. So he was sharing the city with jazz musicians and showgirls. So [*Playboy* taught the reader] how to be a man, how to be a success, how to break the mould, how to be an iconoclast, how to do it your way. This was the message on every page of the magazine. And Barry Manilow just got swept up in that."

Indeed, Barry's letter to the *Playboy* Advisor, which appeared in the December 1965 issue of the magazine, seemed heartfelt and sincere, even though he neglected to mention he was married:

> *Music has always been a vital part of my life. Due to financial difficulties, however, I had to stop attending music school and accept a job at a leading radio and television network. Through enormous good fortune, I have been promoted very rapidly and at the age of 22 I hold*

a junior executive position with a very generous salary. The only drawback is that this position has absolutely nothing to do with music.

During these past few years, between working and attending college, I have managed to musically direct and conduct three full-scale musicals at various theatre workshops in New York. I now have an offer to take this last musical out of town for a period of six to eight months at a good salary with the promise of a permanent position as a musical director.

My musical wild oats are screaming to be sown, but it means giving up my secure job. Leaves of absence are rare, so it looks like it's either one or the other. Any suggestions?

— B.M., Brooklyn, New York

Playboy's answer was swift and certain:

Follow your real interest and take the musical out of town. At your age, your financial responsibilities are few. If you remain in the secure job, you may regret for the rest of your life that you didn't sow your notes. You can always go back to radio and television: your ability was recognized once; chances are it would be recognized again — if not with your former employer, then elsewhere.

"I look at that as one of our great letters," says Jim Petersen, "because we read him correctly and we said, fly. Take this chance."

But Barry Manilow wasn't yet ready to try his wings, at least professionally. Personally, his marriage was coming to its inevitable end. In fact, by the time Barry's letter appeared in *Playboy*, Barry and Susan had parted, and Susan had filed for an annulment, charging Barry with fraud. They'd been married just 18 months.

Chapter Seven

His admittedly half-hearted attempt at marriage a failure, Barry headed back to Brooklyn. His mother's response to the situation was, "See, I told you so."

After a brief and uncomfortable stay with Edna and Willie, who were now constantly drinking and fighting with each other, Barry found an apartment in the Flatbush section of Brooklyn. It was in no way convenient – an hour to work and an hour home each day by subway – but the price was right and, for the first time in his life, Barry was alone, his own man.

Bro Harrod, owner of the 13th Street Theater and producer of *The Drunkard*, was open to Barry's musical ideas about the production and, eventually, let Barry replace the public domain songs originally included in the play with all original songs Barry had composed himself. Bro also became a mentor of sorts for Barry, who paid close attention to everything Bro did and tried to learn from him as much as possible about theatre production.

The Jazz Partners were now defunct, but Barry started working as pianist for a jazz trio from eight until midnight on the weekends. He also started working with singers who were referred to him by those who'd worked with him in the past, like Jeanne Lucas. "He is the most gifted arranger I have ever known on the planet," says Lucas. "And everybody knew it and people really wanted him to arrange their material."

Things seemed well on track again. Barry was back in Brooklyn, but at least he was on his own. He still had the security of his day job at CBS, while his nights and weekends were filled with the pursuit of his musical interests. It all seemed ideal until the day his mother knocked on his door to announce that he was about to receive new neighbours – them.

Barry was horrified and felt, as he characterised it, "violated and outraged" by his mother's decision to take the apartment above his without even bothering to ask his feelings on the matter. But, like the good son he'd always been, he kept his thoughts to himself, pushing his feelings of rage deep within himself where they would cause no trouble. At least not for anyone but himself.

It would have been impossible not to realise the extent to which Edna and Willie's relationship had deteriorated in the past few years when evidence of their violent discord came through Barry's ceiling nearly every night, loud and clear. Their fights were fuelled by Edna's insecurity, Willie's infidelities, and above all, alcohol. Their drinking problems ignited all their other problems, so that everything they'd once had in common evaporated in the heat of their quarrels.

As much as Barry wanted to keep his distance from his mother's marital problems, it was inevitable that he would once again be pulled into their private hell. It happened after yet another prolonged screaming match between Edna and Willie, punctuated, as usual, by the slamming door as Willie once again stormed out in a fury. It was late, and Barry had just begun to drift off to sleep in the calm following the storm, when he was pulled back to consciousness by the ringing of the phone. It was his mother.

"I think I've done something stupid again."

This was Edna's third suicide attempt, and the second since she and Willie had moved in above Barry. The previous incident had seemed less threatening. Edna's sister, Barry's Aunt Rose, had suspected something was wrong with Edna when she'd spoken to her on the phone, and Rose had called Barry to alert him to a potential problem. Edna had again taken a bottle of sleeping pills, but Barry was able to revive her with a couple of pots of strong, black coffee, continually walking her around the room until she came out of it.

This time, though, it seemed that Edna was running out of luck. Barry slapped her repeatedly, but couldn't rouse her. He knew that to involve the police again would mean that his mother would be sent to a sanatorium, but he had no choice – better a sanatorium than a cemetery. He called the police emergency number, then rode with his mother in the ambulance to the hospital. It was the first time that Barry was not only scared by his mother's actions, but deeply angry.

He called his family to the hospital, but the sight of their worried faces only enraged him more. How could Edna do this to them? And to him? This couldn't happen again. It wouldn't happen again.

He sat down with the doctor and recounted Edna's entire history – the alcoholism, the fights with Willie, and all three suicide attempts. Yes, they would have to send Edna to a sanatorium. And maybe it was about time.

Several weeks later Barry received a letter from his mother, writing from the Brunswick General Hospital. She explained to him that this latest suicide attempt had been brought on by Willie's ten-day absence, during which time, she said, she never slept, yet never missed a day of work. She closed by spinning steel threads of guilt, designed to pierce her son through the heart and bind him to her forever: "*You're the only thing that's keeping me going. I don't believe in much any more, but I believe in you. In fact, you're all I believe in.*" Barry was Edna's reason for living and Edna's life, now, was clearly Barry's responsibility. Forever.

Chapter Eight

The turbulence of Barry's personal life was offset by continued small successes in his professional pursuits. Also, Barry and Jeanne Lucas had continued to grow close both personally and professionally with Barry continuing to accompany Jeanne to various auditions as both her musical and moral support. They were still regulars at after-hours clubs around New York, and had also started looking for jobs in the outlying resort areas as well.

"We started auditioning for these people who booked the Catskills," Jeanne recalls. "What an assortment of people! There was this one guy, I can't remember his name, but he had the worst breath and he would lean down into your face as he played the violin in his office, because he wanted to play his violin and me to sing. And I remember looking at Barry and saying, 'Don't leave me alone with him, please!' It was not a pretty picture." But a job's a job, and at this stage of their careers, neither Jeanne nor Barry felt they were in a position to be too choosy. "So we got booked at some of these awful places in the Catskills," says Jeanne. "I mean, Blech's Bungalow Colony, and just awful places where there'd be Barry playing the piano, somebody on the drums, somebody on the bass – waiters by day, musicians by night. They had a lot of pimples and you'd smell Clearasil on the stage."

The two continued to play club dates around Manhattan, with Jeanne as the headliner, Barry simply her accompanist. But there came a moment when that balance began to shift a bit.

"I got a job at a place called Charlie Bates'," says Jeanne, "and it was 'Jeanne Lucas and Company' – Barry loved that! I had 40 minutes on and 20 off, and my voice was getting really tired. So I said to Barry, 'Could you please sing a song somewhere in my set because

I'm not going to be able to make it four sets a night; that's a lot of singing.'" Barry seemed a bit horrified at the thought of not only taking centre stage, but doing so as a *singer*. His response to Jeanne's request was unequivocal: "*No, no, no, no – I can't sing, I can't sing, I can't sing.*" But Jeanne knew that Barry had been working on his singing ever since the time she and Susan had teased him about it. Besides, she was desperate. "Yes, you can," she told Barry. "Trust me, you can do it. You'll sound wonderful. You'll do it." And, the clincher: "You've got to do it, otherwise I'm just going to get a bad throat and we're not going to have a job." That did the trick. Barry agreed to work on one or two numbers he could perform solo.

When Barry bowed to this concession, Jeanne decided to go for a somewhat easier one. She said to Barry, "Maybe on a song or two you could do 'ooh aah' in the background with me so I don't have to sing so much and you could carry part of the show?" After agreeing to sing a solo, what were a few "oohs" and "aahs" by comparison? Barry agreed to ooh and aah for Jeanne.

Barry's initial efforts weren't quite stellar, but were still effective. "The first night that we did that, he was hunched over the piano, his head down, like he was so embarrassed he wanted to die," Jeanne recalls. "He was playing the piano and singing, and he did an okay job. He'd really been working. And the thing that they really responded to was when we did a song or two and he did his 'ooh aah' – they really liked that."

While the audiences seemed pleased with the new arrangement, the owner of Charlie Bates' Saloon was less enthusiastic. "I didn't hire you to hear *him* sing," he complained to Jeanne. "That's not what I want. I want *you* to sing." But Barry had been very good to Jeanne for a very long time, and she wasn't about to jettison him at this point. She told the club owner, "If you don't want him, then I'm gone." And so they were.

There were plenty of other clubs and resorts happy to take Jeanne and Barry on more favourable terms. Barry was still working on and off with *The Drunkard* in between coaching sessions with up-and-coming singers and his continuing full-time job with CBS, which continued to bring the financial security he felt he needed in order to pursue his real interests. With all the success Barry was having in his musical pursuits, not to mention the encouragement from *Playboy*, it's hard to understand his reluctance to let go of the job at CBS and commit to music full-time. But no matter how many other music-related jobs he took on, he stubbornly clung to the job at CBS. That's why Jeanne's next bit of good news seemed, to Barry, to be more of a problem than a blessing.

A booking agent had spotted Jeanne at one of her numerous gigs around the city and had called to say that she had an out-of-town booking that would be perfect for Jeanne and Barry – as a singing duo. Were they interested? Jeanne was definitely interested. It didn't matter that the "out-of-town" part of the job meant Richmond, Indiana. It still sounded good to Jeanne, and she wanted to say yes.

Barry was less enthusiastic. For one thing, they weren't a duo, they were a singer and her accompanist. Barry might have been willing to throw a number or two into the middle of Jeanne's act to save her voice, and even give some "oohs" and "aahs" for the good of the team, but he had never aspired to be a singing act, and couldn't see Richmond, Indiana, as the gateway to that new career. But the main drawback was far more serious: if he agreed to take this gig with Jeanne, it would mean finally letting go of his job at CBS.

Jeanne did all she could to persuade Barry that nothing dire would happen to him if he were to leave CBS. He was single again, supporting only himself. He'd never had a problem getting a job before, and it was highly unlikely he'd start having a problem getting jobs now. But, most of all, if he wasn't willing to take any risks, what could he ever hope to gain? All powerful arguments. "But to leave a steady job for a gamble in music went against everything I had learned while growing up," Barry wrote in his 1987 autobiography. "Without that almighty Friday paycheck you were a bum."

After much-soul searching – not to mention constant reminders from Jeanne that the agent was waiting for their answer – Barry went to see his boss, Richard Rector, director of broadcasting at WCBS-TV. Barry laid out his entire professional history for Rector, his growing conflict between the musical and non-musical dual lives he'd been leading, and his reluctance to give up the security that his job at CBS afforded him. Rector told Barry essentially what *Playboy* had – go for it. If things didn't work out musically, Rector assured him, Barry would always have a job at CBS. This time Barry was ready to listen.

"I'll always be grateful to Dick Rector," Barry later said. "He was the last kick in the ass I needed. And I felt somewhat secure knowing I could always come back."

Reassured, Barry left his boss's office and immediately called Jeanne to tell her the news. Harry and Ethel were going to Indiana.

Chapter Nine

On the plane ride to Indiana, Jeanne and Barry eagerly prepared for their Richmond debut. "We decided we would do some more duets because I really enjoyed doing those with him," says Jeanne. "The poor people on the plane! There we are, singing away, and figuring out all the harmonies and things."

They arrived in Indiana with two duets prepared – 'Georgie Girl' to open the act, followed by Jeanne's usual programme of solo numbers, then she and Barry would close with 'Something Stupid'. But when the two arrived to check out the venue, it looked very much as though the title of their closing number could very well describe the entire Indiana sojourn.

"We go to the lounge expecting – I don't know what we were expecting," Jeanne recalls. "We were all dressed to the nines and everything, and we walk in and there's this guy playing a piano and this woman sort of playing these big congo drums. And they're singing these songs we'd never heard in our lives, just dumb songs. And these were the people we were replacing!"

Although it seemed unlikely, apparently the current act was going over big with the audience. The pianist and his drum playing partner, who Barry would later remember as having no teeth, had the crowd stomping, clapping, and singing along, shouting out for more numbers and encores of songs already performed. Jeanne and Barry retired to the bar to contemplate their future in Richmond. It didn't look good. The bartender, recognising the duo from their publicity photo on the poster in the bar, seemed to agree. "You sure have a tough act to follow!" he told them.

Apparently too tough. "We got up to sing the next night and we bombed," says Jeanne. Barry had always taken great care in sequencing their performances, but the Richmond audience wasn't interested in what Barry wanted. "They were asking for requests," Jeanne says. "They wanted us to sing things like 'My Bucket's Got A Hole In It', and all that. I didn't know any of those songs! I'd never even heard of them!" It's been said – and sung – that if you can make it in New York, you can make it anywhere. But if the folks who first expressed those sentiments thought New York was a tough city, apparently they'd never tried to make it big in Richmond, Indiana. Jeanne and Barry were unceremoniously shown the door.

"And there we were," says Jeanne. "We had really taken the plunge. I'd given up my apartment, I'd given away my cat." And Barry had finally given up his job at CBS. "This was going to be the big time," says Lucas. "This was going to be the road to success. We didn't know what to do. All we had was enough money for two bus tickets to my mother's."

Jeanne's mother lived in a small suburb of Detroit. She and Jeanne had been estranged for quite some time. In fact, the rift between the two was so serious that Mrs Lucas had told everyone that her daughter was dead. Now here was her daughter appearing on her doorstep out of the blue. "That was a tough explanation to her friends, I'm sure!" Jeanne laughs. "I was dead, so I had to be resurrected."

Not only had Jeanne made a sudden trip back from the dead, but she'd brought a young man with her as well. "[My mother] was a little leery of Barry, I must say," Lucas recalls. However leery she might have been, though, Mrs Lucas agreed that Jeanne and Barry could stay with her until the two figured out their next move.

Since the pair had blown what little money they'd had left on the bus tickets to Michigan, the most important thing seemed to be to find a job. Jeanne and Barry spent their days at the upright piano in Mrs Lucas' living room, working up a new act. Barry and Marty Panzer had previously written a song for Jeanne called 'The Greatest Thing That Ever Came Down The Line'. It was a song which Jeanne had performed to win the title "The Most Promising Act in New York" awarded in a competition sponsored by NBC; that song went into the act, as did more duets for the two of them.

Jeanne and Barry soon landed a job at Paul's Restaurant and Lounge in Detroit. *Direct from New York*, the ad for their act read. It probably would have been a bit distracting had the ad more honestly read, *Direct from New York Via a Disastrous Few Days in Richmond, Indiana.*

In fact, "The Finest Act in Detroit", as they were billed, met with far more success in Michigan than they had in Indiana. Their meticulous preparations had paid off. The lesson Barry had learned from their ill-starred Richmond experience was that audiences might want something new, but not too new. To address that, he and Jeanne had taken familiar songs the audience was sure to know, but had given each their own spin. This way the audience was hearing something new, yet still reassuringly familiar, while Barry and Jeanne weren't falling over with boredom from performing the same old standards in the same old way. "And that's really where we worked out a lot of our duet songs," says Jeanne, of their frequent onstage experimentations. "We would try them out with people. We wrote a lot of material together; I would write lyrics and he would do the music. We had a lot of fun doing these things."

As could usually be said for life, things were going great – right up until they weren't.

"I got tonsilitis and I had to have my tonsils out," says Lucas. It had looked as though the gig at Paul's could have gone on forever, so enthusiastic was the audience reaction to the new act. But without Jeanne, there was really no point in Barry staying in the area. He decided to go back to New York while Jeanne stayed at her mother's house and recovered.

Even though he'd been assured that there would be a place for him at CBS should he decide he wanted to return, Barry has said that he never even considered going back. Even the constant hustling necessary to try to make a living by making music no longer seemed a drawback. "Even though I wasn't finding fame and fortune in the world," Manilow has written, "I was happier than I'd ever been. I was able to devote all of my energy to making music and each day was more rewarding than CBS had ever been."

Via ads in the trade papers and simple word of mouth, Barry let it be known that he was back in New York and eager to work. Soon he was once again busy coaching and accompanying singers and writing arrangements for their acts.

During this time he also kept in constant touch with Jeanne, even though she had a little trouble communicating by phone in the days immediately following her surgery. "He would call me on the phone," laughs Lucas, "and I couldn't talk so I would shake a tambourine – one shake for "yes", two for "no", a maraca for "what are you talking about" – I had this whole percussion system worked out, so that's how we would carry on a conversation."

Several weeks passed before Jeanne, her voice fully recovered after her tonsillectomy, returned to New York where she and Barry continued working on the act they had begun developing in Detroit. The agent who had booked Jeanne and Barry into the Indiana gig was a woman named Gladys Gross, who was still representing Jeanne and, by extension, Barry. "We used to call her Goldie Groove," says Lucas. "She meant well, but she wasn't the best connected around." But she was connected enough to get Jeanne an audition for a part in the road company of *Sweet Charity*, which had ended its Broadway run in July 1967 after 608 performances. Jeanne would be auditioning for the role that comic actress Ruth Buzzi had originated on Broadway or, as Goldie Groove told Jeanne, "The Ruth Buzzi part".

The audition for *Sweet Charity* turned out to be a comedy of errors. "I didn't know who Ruth Buzzi was, and I didn't know anything about *Sweet Charity*," says Jeanne, "and I thought the name of the character was Ruth Buzzipart. So I went in and I said, 'I'm here to audition for Ruth Buzzipart.'" Beyond that, Jeanne didn't belong to the proper actors union – or any union for that matter – nor did she have a résumé or professional headshots; she instead gave them a snapshot of herself she happened to have handy.

The situation turned to farce when Jeanne finally took the stage. As she walked across the bare stage to deliver a selection from *Once Upon A Mattress* for the producers, Jeanne tripped on a nail that had been left sticking up from the floor after the last set change. "While I was singing," says Jeanne, "I kept patting my foot around the floor trying to find the nail – god forbid I should fall over." She continued to sing and feel the stage with her foot until she completed her number and the producers thanked her for coming. So much for *Sweet Charity*.

On her own, Jeanne had found a job singing backup at a resort in the Catskills. "Now they had a switchboard there that was sort of on when they felt like it and off when they didn't feel like having it on," Jeanne recalls. "What I didn't know was that everybody was trying to call me from New York, including Barry, to tell me that *Sweet Charity* wanted to see me back again. They wanted me to do a call-back for the role."

It turns out that those watching Jeanne's odd movements on the stage as she performed her song didn't realise that Jeanne had simply been trying to check her exit path for further obstacles. "They thought I was doing a bit!" she laughs. "And they thought it was the funniest thing they ever saw. I mean they were just rolling with laughter. And I got the job on the spot."

Once again, though, this blessing was delivered with a built-in curse. "Barry was happy," says Jeanne, "but he wasn't thrilled because now I was leaving, and who was he going to work with?" *Sweet Charity* would end its tour in Chicago, several months hence. Jeanne and Barry agreed that they would meet there and Barry would try to find a short-term job while Jeanne finished out the play's run. That way they could continue working on their act between her performances. A booking agent recommended to Barry by a friend found Barry a job working at The Little Corporal Lounge located in the Meadowview Shopping Center in Kankakee, Illinois, about 50 miles south of Chicago. It was no Richmond, Indiana, but it would do.

Besides putting Barry in close enough proximity to Jeanne for the two to continue to perfect their act together, his two-week stint at the Little Corporal Lounge was yet another turning point in Barry's life. Up to this point, he had only performed publicly as part of a larger act. More often than not he'd been the anonymous piano player providing accompaniment to the headliner. In fact, up until his arrival in Kankakee, his act with Jeanne was the closest Barry had come to being centre stage, and even then Jeanne was still the headliner. But at the Little Corporal Lounge, the sign outside the doors said BARRY MANILOW AT THE KEYBOARD. For the first time ever, it was Barry Manilow, and Barry Manilow alone sitting in the spot-light. Sure, it was a foot-operated spotlight he had to turn on and off himself. And sure his dressing room was the seedy motel across the street from the shopping mall where the Little Corporal's manage-ment was putting Barry up during his stay in Kankakee. But when Barry donned his tuxedo and took his place on the bar stool behind the piano each night, he was a star.

"At the end of my first week there," wrote Manilow in his

autobiography, "I would walk into the place feeling dull and plain. But I'd climb up to the piano, click on the spotlight with my foot, and I would become attractive, worldly, witty."

It's a magical place, Kankakee, Illinois. Don't let anyone ever tell you otherwise.[1]

---

[1] After more than 35 years in business, the Little Corporal Lounge in Kankakee, Illinois, closed briefly, reopening in October 1996 under new management. Though the name of the establishment has changed – it's now America's Bistro – the piano at which Barry Manilow first felt himself a star remains, bearing a plaque that says simply BARRY MANILOW.

Chapter Ten

After his two weeks in Kankakee, Barry started working in downtown Chicago at a restaurant called Henrici's, where he continued to explore the advantages of being a solo act, a position in which he felt increasingly at ease. Though he still wasn't completely comfortable with what he felt were his limitations as a singer, the audiences seemed to like him, as did Henrici's management. The downtown Chicago location also made it easier for him and Jeanne to see each other.

"I would do a matinee, then we would work on the songs, then I'd go do the evening show," says Lucas. "Then after I was done with the show we would go to the really cool places in town and we would get up and sing. And it was really great because at that time, there were people there like Len Cariou, and people who became huge Broadway stars. And we were all in there, just kind of getting up, and it was just wonderful."

In the same way Barry tended to fill every waking minute of his life with frantic activity when at home in New York, life in Chicago quickly became just as frenetic. He worked from four o'clock to eight o'clock in the evening at Henrici's, practised with Jeanne, then hit the local clubs until all hours. While Jeanne was sometimes free during the day as well, Barry still had a lot of daylight to fill, so he decided to continue his musical education by taking orchestration classes at Chicago's DePaul University.

They'd made themselves at home in Chicago, and life there had become very comfortable, very quickly. But they'd always known their stay would be temporary and, as soon as *Sweet Charity* ended its run, Jeanne and Barry said their goodbyes and headed for home.

Back in New York, the two landed a job at the upscale Downstairs at the Upstairs, which led a dual life as Upstairs at the Downstairs. Upstairs at the Downstairs was, as the name suggested, the night-club's upper floor, which could seat several hundred. Downstairs at the Upstairs, the club's first floor, was more intimate. While Upstairs could present larger stage revues, Downstairs was reserved for small acts – singers, comedians. Barry and Jeanne had auditioned in front of the club's owner, Irving Haber, Joan Rivers, whose act Jeanne and Barry would end up opening for two seasons, Joan's husband, Edgar Rosenberg, and an agent from the William Morris Agency. Jeanne sang for the group, solo, with Barry accompanying her, then Jeanne and Barry performed a duet or two from the act they'd worked so hard to perfect. The response was yes, and no: Yes to Jeanne, no to Barry. Just as she had told the owner of Charlie Baits' Saloon that hiring her must also mean hiring Barry, Jeanne explained to Irving Haber that the act was strictly a twosome. "Well, here's the deal," Haber told Jeanne. "I pay $125 a week and if you want to share it with him, fine, that's all there's going to be." Jeanne agreed. Joan Rivers had herself an opening act, at a bargain two-for-one rate.

A series of mis-communications and just plain bad luck followed the William Morris agent's subsequent offer to sign Jeanne and Barry as an act. The William Morris offices in New York, Chicago and Los Angeles operated independently of each other. There was talk of a record deal, but then the New York agent died and the deal fell through. Then, with a new William Morris representative, there was talk of a TV show, but a pre-emptive move by the West Coast William Morris office ended that deal, even as the contracts were being negotiated in the New York William Morris office. The final straw came when Jeanne and Barry were offered a two-week stint at the Playboy Club in Chicago. As time went by, and still no contracts for the Playboy job arrived, Jeanne grew frustrated. She finally called the manager of the Playboy Club, whom she knew, and inquired why they hadn't yet received a contract when the job was less than two weeks away. "What are you talking about?" he asked. "The William Morris office here in Chicago is telling us you can only work a split week, you can't work two weeks, and I don't want that. Do you want to come or don't you want to come? If you're going to come you're going to come for two weeks." And that was the end of the William Morris Agency as far as Jeanne was concerned.

Despite these frustrations, the contracts were finally negotiated, and Barry and Jeanne did head back to Chicago to play the two-week gig at the Playboy Club. "The Playboy Club was really funny," Jeanne recalls. "Because whoever is the manager for the evening, the maître d' or whoever he is, gives you points for how well you perform. And it's based on how much the audience claps. And you're looking at these guys, working at the Playboy Club, as waiters who then became managers, giving points for your performance! We couldn't believe it! I guess we did okay because we got asked back again."

During this busy period in their professional lives, Jeanne started seeing an actor named Howard Honig. It was this relationship, more than anything, that would spell the end of Jeanne and Barry as a performing team.

"Barry was very possessive of people," says Jeanne. "You were either possessed by him in his life and loyal, fiercely loyal to him, or you were out. But I didn't realise that until way later. Because we were so close then, it didn't matter, it was all happening that way anyway."

Where previously Jeanne's entire world had revolved around her work, most of which involved Barry in one way or another, suddenly Jeanne had a new interest that was diverting her attention from work, and from Barry. "Every time I was with a guy for any period of time," Jeanne recalls, "Barry would say, 'Ethel, Ethel, is this the one you're going to marry?' And usually I'd say, 'Nah, you kidding?'" But Howard was something special. So this time when Barry asked Jeanne if she'd found the man she wanted to marry, her response was, "Yeah, you know, I think so."

By this time Jeanne and Barry had been together for so long, it was almost as if they themselves were already a married couple. They worked together, played together, travelled together and had, on a couple of occasions, lived together. In fact, early on in their relationship, Jeanne had even found herself falling for Barry.

"This was in the very, very beginning," Jeanne says now, "and I really couldn't understand why he wasn't reciprocating." Jeanne was attractive and intelligent, with a lively personality, a quick laugh, and the same kind of talent and drive to make it in show business that Barry himself possessed. It was only natural for her to assume, with all they shared in common, that any spark she felt between them would be mutual. The fact that this didn't seem to be the case was causing Jeanne much pain and confusion.

"When we were working at Charlie Baits'," says Jeanne, "there was this wonderful woman, she was English, I just loved her to pieces. I think she was the manager there. And I confided in her, because I was just miserable because Barry just wasn't picking up on my vibes I was sending out." At this point Jeanne was not long out of the midwest, where she'd led a reasonably sheltered existence. So the restaurant manager's response to Jeanne at first only puzzled the girl even more. Explains Lucas, "She said, 'Darling, don't you understand? Don't you know?' And I said, 'What? Know what?' And she sat me down and she said, 'He's not for girls.'"

Chapter Eleven

Even after the manager at Charlie Baits' had clued Jeanne in about the reason Barry wasn't returning her romantic feelings toward him, it still took a while for the truth of the situation to make itself manifest to Jeanne.

"Let me tell you something, I was very naive coming from Michigan. It was like you had to hit me over the head with it," Jeanne explains. "I wasn't getting it, because I never thought that. Even when she told me I really found it hard to believe." Homosexuality was hardly the accepted way of life that it is, for the most part, today. In 1964 if someone had talked about an alternative lifestyle, they were probably referring to someone who chose to live in the suburbs rather than the city. For anyone trying to build a career for himself at that time, to be openly gay would most likely mean you were also openly unemployed, and even openly shunned by society, friends, and family. And it was hardly a subject likely to pop up over the dinner table in a nice middle-class home in suburban America.

Later in his career, after he'd become a household name, Barry would do all he could to avoid questions about his personal life, insisting it was simply too boring to talk about. Though rumours about his sexuality have always run rampant, at the height of Manilow's fame, few would dare turn the whispers into a direct question. When one Canadian interviewer did manage to stammer out, "I don't know, I never really thought about it" – a sure sign the interviewer had been thinking about nothing else but this subject since he knew he'd netted the assignment – "but . . . I was wondering if . . . you are gay?" Manilow's reply was emphatic: "Well, I'm not. No, no, I'm not." Then, as though to offer proof positive, he added, "I've been married."

Indeed, Barry had told everyone that he was divorced, but in truth the marriage between Barry and Susan had been voided via annulment. Susan's cousin, Marshall Deixler says that the story within the family was that "the marriage was annulled for not being consummated, and presumably it wasn't consummated because he was homosexual." It's important to note, though, that Deixler prefaces his remarks by admitting that the conclusion is based on little more than speculation within the family. Susan herself denies there's any truth to the story, and declines to offer any alternative explanation for her actions at the time. And, amid all the speculation and guesswork regarding the dissolution of the brief marriage, the one clear certainty is whatever really happened between Barry and Susan, only Barry and Susan know for sure.

Having worked so closely making music with Barry for so long, Jeanne Lucas can understand the bond that once existed between Susan and Barry, a bond that went far beyond the physical. "When they were in high school," she says, "as I understood it from Barry, Susan was always there with him musically, with everything that he did. Now I can tell you, and I'm sure any other person who's had this kind of relationship could say the same, it's very seductive when you're working musically with somebody that closely. A bond forms on some other plane, a real spiritual bond, a real loving bond, and it's as if you really become connected at the soul. And just like I mistook that in the beginning for being in love with him, I'm sure that he and Susan had that kind of bond."

Unfortunately, it was a bond that even four wedding ceremonies couldn't cement. After Barry left her, Susan, bitterly upset, filed for an annulment which would mean, in essence, that the marriage never existed. According to the laws of New York, an annulment is granted if one or both of the parties can prove that the union was invalid from the start. A situation that would constitute a valid reason for an annulment would include one or both of the parties being already married, the two parties being siblings or close relatives, one or both of the parties being underage, one or both of the parties being mentally retarded or mentally ill, or that the marriage was never consummated, or was based on fraud. When filing her complaint, Susan chose the last option.

Barry was served with a summons on September 10, 1965, advising him that a hearing on the matter would be held on

November 12. Like his father before him, when Edna had filed for divorce, Barry chose not to respond to the summons. So, without Barry present, Susan gave testimony on the matter in open court on December 3, 1965, "*sustaining the allegations set forth in the complaint.*" The Interlocutory Judgment goes on to state that the Court, "*having thereupon fully heard and considered the proofs offered and having made a decision in writing, separately stating the findings of fact and conclusions of law, deciding that plaintiff is entitled to judgment against defendant annulling the marriage between the parties hereto pursuant to law because of the fraud of the defendant.*" In the eyes of the law, Barry and Susan had never been married.

Outside the courthouse and across the country, news-stands were carrying the December issue of *Playboy* magazine, containing the letter Barry had written in which he'd expressed his desire to sow his "musical wild oats". *Playboy* had granted him permission to take a chance. Now he was legally free to do so, unencumbered. And certainly no one questioned the process that brought Barry to that point. In fact, most were simply happy to see him available again.

"Barry was very charming, and women went nuts for him – let me just tell you that," says Jeanne Lucas. "He could charm the pants off of any lady. They would just, *oh Barry, Barry, Barry.* All these women." But of all the women vying for Barry's attention, at that time it was Jeanne who had it, more often than not. "I always felt like I was the chosen one," she says, "because I was the one he chose to really be with and work with and live with and whatever. And I had a cache among other women because of Barry, of all things."

From the time the manager at Charlie Baits' had opened her eyes to the reality of the situation, Jeanne began to really observe what was going on with her partner. And, as they continued to spend the majority of their time together, Barry eventually felt comfortable enough to trust Jeanne with this aspect of his life and simply be himself when they were together.

"Wherever we would perform," says Lucas, "when we were in Detroit or wherever, I used to drop him off at these places, where they were just storefronts and you didn't know what was behind there. We went into one gay club, and in that parking lot was every Cadillac and every high-end car you ever wanted to see. And if anybody would walk in, all heads would turn because everybody was scared." At that time, every state but Illinois (which had repealed its sodomy law in 1961) had a law on its books prohibiting homosexual acts between consenting adults. With its "crime against nature" law, carrying a penalty of 15 years in prison, Michigan was – and still is – among these.[2]

"There were a lot of very wealthy and successful people in there," Jeanne continues, "and Barry and I went in there, and the guy who sang a song called 'Hot Nuts' was singing." Doug Clark and his Combo had had an instant success with the silly and mildly raunchy song when they were playing at fraternity parties around their home state of North Carolina. Once the song became a hit, the group changed its name to Doug Clark and the Hot Nuts and had built a career on playing somewhat racy venues around the country, where their style of telling dirty jokes and singling out audience members had proven extremely successful. While John Clark, who has been with the group since 1955, doesn't remember the band playing any gay clubs in Detroit, he acknowledges that lots of bands playing such venues as a secret gay club in Detroit at the time would have been very likely to appropriate their songs.

"The singer came over to the table where Barry and I were," says Jeanne, "and I was wearing some pearls. And there's this verse, I just remember this so well, he sang, '*There's a girl, with a string of pearls, she ain't got hot nuts, cause she's a girl.*' It was unbelievable! But that was one of the clubs."

Once Jeanne understood what Barry was going through, it wasn't difficult for her to accept the fact that the friendship they shared would be just that – a friendship. They already shared so much. Keeping Barry's secret became just another facet of their partnership. "I was very sensitive to his needs," she says, "and wherever we were – whether it was Chicago or wherever – I would help him find that community, and that's what was going on."

Sometimes this became a problem when the "community" in question was a little too close for comfort. "When we were working Upstairs at the Downstairs, we were supposed to be America's Sweethearts there. And there was a gay bar across the street, and in between our sets he would run across to the gay bar. And I would go

---

[2] Currently in the United States only eight states, the District of Columbia and some cities have enacted laws prohibiting discrimination against homosexuals in employment, housing and other areas.

in there and grab him out and say, 'Are you crazy? Don't be doing this now! We're America's Sweethearts! Irving's got us billed as the little love bugs. Do whatever you want, but don't do it right across the street from where we're working!' "

Even as Jeanne became comfortable with her new knowledge about Barry's life, she could sometimes catch glimpses of what seemed to be his own unease with the situation. "I remember one day," she recalls, "he said to me, 'You know, I really am not sure I want to go that route. But when I visit people that are in that world, they know how to live, and they're very sophisticated, and they understand the arts, and they've got money, and they know how to dress. I love that world. I want to live like that.' " Adds Jeanne, "Besides being gay, he loved the trappings."

Though he seemed supportive of her plans, when Jeanne announced that she and Howard Honig were to be married, Barry saw himself losing a valuable and trusted playmate, as well as a musical partner. "If he decided to call me up at 11 o'clock, 12 o'clock at night and say, 'Ethel, come on down to the Improv' – because we used to perform there a lot – I would just *run*," says Jeanne, "wherever he wanted me to come and sing, above and beyond the job, without hesitation." But with Howard in the picture, what little free time Jeanne had was usually spent with him. Barry treated Howard with his usual friendly charm, but the two had little to do with each other. When Jeanne asked Barry to play the music at their wedding, he declined. "What he did do, though," says Jeanne, "was write a song for me and get me a piano for my wedding, which was very lovely."

The owner of the 13th Street Theater, Bro Harrod, gave Jeanne away, and Bro's wife, Diane, acted as maid of honour. Among all their friends and Howard's family, Barry was in attendance, as was his mother.

Later in Barry's career, when he had become an object of interest to fans and the press, Edna used to tell people who inquired about her son's love life, "He just hasn't found the right girl yet." But while Jeanne was a naive young woman from Michigan when she learned the truth about Barry's lifestyle, Edna was Brooklyn born and raised, and undoubtedly knew that her son was not looking for the right girl, or any girl for that matter. Still, a mother can hope. Edna always liked Jeanne. In fact, Edna and Willie had even made a trip to visit when Jeanne and Barry were staying at Jeanne's mother's house in Detroit.

Because Jeanne had been estranged from her own mother for so long by the time she met Barry, Edna Manilow had become a sort of surrogate mother for her. "She was as much a part of my life as he was in many ways," remembers Jeanne fondly. "She was just very involved and cared a lot." At the time she was married, Jeanne was once again estranged from her mother who, as Jeanne puts it, "boycotted my wedding". That left Jeanne with no family in attendance, save for one "rebel" aunt, and Jeanne's surrogate mom, Edna. After the ceremony, in the cab they were sharing on the way to the reception, Edna, seeming quite upset, turned to Jeanne's aunt and said, "There goes my last chance of grandchildren.

PART III

The Divine Mr M

"More Hebrews worked on this act than built the pyramids."

– Bette Midler, *Mud Will be Flung Tonight*

Chapter Twelve

As a decade, the Seventies was, as one observer once put it, "the last good time." The seeds of unrest sown in the Sixties had only just started to take root by the beginning of the next decade. Many old mores had been destroyed, and new paradigms were being created from the fragments. There was a new freedom, a sense of abandon that seemed to bear no ill consequences. Hair was longer, music louder, sex freer. No one could yet foresee the heavy price that would one day be paid for all this freedom, but its time would come.

When Barry left his Flatbush apartment after his mother's last suicide attempt, he did all he could to close the door on Brooklyn forever, or at least as close as he could come with his grandparents, his mother and Willie still living there. When he did have to go back it was, says a friend, "a painful experience for him". While most of us harbour fond memories of childhood homes, Brooklyn held little nostalgia for Barry. Certainly he had been loved there more wholly and unconditionally than he would ever be loved again, but still Brooklyn represented hard times and bad memories.

"He didn't want to go back to Brooklyn – ever," says Pamela Pentony, who would become Barry's neighbour on West 27th Street.

Pamela and her boyfriend, Bob Danz, lived in one of three apartments connected by a backyard "garden", which had been created on top of a parking garage. Pamela was a singer and actress. Her boyfriend, Bob, was also a musician who, between gigs, was studying to be a dentist. Another neighbour was an elderly gentleman named Fred Norring, an Austrian by birth and a mathematician by trade. Norring shared his neighbours' love of music, preferring classical to jazz. In his younger days, he'd sung in the collegiate chorale.

The last neighbour in the triumvirate of apartments was a woman named Jean Ross. Ross was a hard drinking woman who owned an ever-present little poodle she would refer to, in her low, raspy voice, as "poor little shit".

"I wasn't a wide-eyed innocent," says Pentony, "but Jean really was very colourful. She loved music and she used to tell me about going to see Billie Holiday and stuff like that."

When Ross decided to move out of her studio apartment, she promised Pamela and Bob that she wouldn't let anyone move in unless Pamela and Bob approved of them first. Pamela's worry was that Jean's spot might be filled by someone who was, as she puts it, "a jerk who didn't like music". They needn't have worried. The first applicant they interviewed was Barry Manilow.

"He had to sit and talk to Jean, but he also had to sit and talk to me," Pentony recalls. The interview took place just after Barry had done a series of appearances on the local WCBS daytime show *Callback!*, which Jeanne had hosted. The idea of *Callback!* was for unknown talent, like Jeanne, to introduce other unknown talent, like Barry, to the viewing audience. Pamela happened to have caught the show when Barry and Jeanne sang the Laura Nyro song 'Eli's Coming'.

"When I met him in the apartment, I said, 'Didn't I see you on . . .?' and he went, 'Oh!' And then we hit it off, because he liked Laura Nyro, too." It was just the kind of musical bond Pamela had been hoping to find in a new neighbour. "So he got the apartment," she says, "and he moved in next door."

Barry blended in quickly and harmoniously with his new neighbours. Indeed, music was their bond. "We both had studio apartments, Bob and I, and Barry, and Fred had a one-bedroom, because he was like a grown-up, and had a job and everything. And we used to cook these dinners together. Fred would always pay for the most expensive part because he was actually employed and we'd bring salad or something. And we'd have group dinners out in our garden because they all adjoined, out in back there." It was an idyllic time. "Fred used to cook and sing classical music while he was cooking. He made a terrific salad dressing; I still have the recipe."

After his long-time association with Jeanne came to such an abrupt end, Barry filled the void in his professional life by putting more time and effort into coaching singers and picking up accompanist work. One of his clients was a singer-songwriter named Adrienne Artz. Adrienne was, as Barry would later say, "my first experience with wealth". She'd been raised by a wealthy aunt and uncle after her mother had died when Adrienne was very young, and her father didn't think he was up to the challenge of raising a daughter alone. Because of her Park Avenue upbringing, she represented to Barry many of the same sensibilities for which he had earlier expressed to Jeanne an admiration: intelligence, taste, refinement, class. Though Barry had never before held any real regard for popular music, Adrienne began gently nudging him towards an appreciation of some of the better artists and their work. As he put it, "I walked into Adrienne's apartment with short hair and a button-down suit. Within a year, my hair was shoulder-length and my bottoms were belled."

Those around them never observed anything more than a close working relationship between Barry and Adrienne. They did share a genuine fondness and a deep personal empathy for one another that served them well when they began writing songs together, songs they would then make cautious efforts to get published. It was through these efforts that Adrienne met and became romantically involved with Neil Anderson, president of the publishing branch of April-Blackwood Music.

Anderson was a strong-willed music business professional, used to getting his own way. To illustrate the point, Bob Danz recalls an incident during a trip to Neil's house on Fire Island when he, Pamela, Barry and Adrienne were Neil's guests for the weekend. "I remember going to a restaurant with Neil," says Danz. "There was only one slice of pecan pie left in the whole restaurant. And Neil told the waiter over and over again, every time the waiter came to the table, please make sure the piece of pecan pie is saved for us. And of course by the time the meal ended the piece of pecan pie was gone and the waiter came with tears in his eyes to tell us it was gone. Neil became angry and refused to pay the check."

Of course craziness can be an asset in the cut-throat world of entertainment. When Adrienne showed Neil a song called 'Amy' that she had written, Anderson decided the song should be recorded, and he chose Tony Orlando to be the record's producer.

In 1961 Tony Orlando had worked for seven months as a demo

singer for then-unknown composer Carole King. During this time he had had some brief success with two of the demo songs he had recorded, 'Halfway To Paradise' and 'Bless You'. Concert dates resulted from the songs' success, and he even made an appearance on *American Bandstand*. But it wasn't yet Orlando's time, and he vanished from the public eye as quickly as he had appeared.

Orlando joined April-Blackwood Music in the fall of 1963 and quickly rose through the ranks to become general professional manager. When he was given a demo for a song called 'Candida', Orlando tried placing the song with Bell Records, which rejected the record because the lead vocal was, they felt, too weak. The song's producers asked Orlando to re-record the song himself, using the style he'd employed to make 'Halfway To Paradise' and 'Bless You' hits. Though he protested ("Fellows, I don't do demos any more") he finally agreed to record the song himself. Background vocals provided by Telma Hopkins and Joyce Vincent were dubbed in later. The women did their work in Los Angeles, and Tony did his in New York; they never met during the process.

Orlando had been burned by show business once, and was leery of another try. So instead of presenting the re-recorded demo under his own name, he chose the name "Dawn", which held no more significance than the fact that it was the name of their production manager's daughter. Within two months, 'Candida' was a smash hit.

As he had done with 'Candida', Orlando was thinking of recording Adrienne's 'Amy' using a studio singer and releasing the song under a fictitious group name. According to Manilow, though, the night of the recording session, while the background tracks had been completed, Orlando still hadn't decided on a singer. Tony, according to Barry, was having trouble with his own voice that night, but everyone was anxious to hear how the song would sound with vocals. "So," Manilow said, "I was elected to go into the little vocal booth and sing the lead."

It took a little work, but by the end of the session everyone agreed that Barry's voice had a natural warmth and vulnerability that perfectly suited the song. Everyone agreed, that is, but Barry. To Barry, his own voice on the playback sounded odd, nasal, and all Brooklyn. To his surprise, though, Tony took the song to Bell Records executives who agreed with the majority – the song was good, and so was Barry. They okayed the record's release.

On Tony's recommendation, Barry hired attorney Miles Lourie to negotiate the record deal. Lourie was, as one associate put it, "a very hard person, a tough businessman". At the time, that's just what Barry needed. Tony still thought it was a good idea to put the record out under a fictitious group name, so Tony, Miles, Adrienne and Barry brainstormed and came up with the random word "Featherbed". The deal was negotiated, and Barry's rendering of Adrienne's song, 'Amy', was released under this fictitious name.

The song met with enough success that Miles was able to negotiate a new record deal for Featherbed, this time to be credited as "Featherbead, featuring Barry Manilow". Barry wasn't so sure that any deal presenting himself as a singer was such a great idea, but at least it would give him the opportunity to write and arrange new songs for the album. Unfortunately, Barry's favourite collaborator was no longer just a cab ride away. Shortly before 'Amy' was released, Adrienne married Neil Anderson and the couple moved to California. Undaunted, Barry and Adrienne simply continued their friendship and their collaboration, long-distance.

Barry would spend many evenings sitting in his studio apartment on 27th Street, trying out new songs, experimenting with old ones. Pam and Bob would often stop by, as would Fred Norring. For relaxation, Barry and Bob and Pam would go swimming at the pool on 23rd Street and FDR Drive. The group would host parties in their shared gardens that would be attended by more people than could ever fit in any one of the small apartments alone. Since all were musicians – Barry and Pamela full-time, professional musicians, Bob more of a part-time hobbyist between his dental studies, and Fred an informed amateur – there was always something interesting happening musically, as well as interesting guests, other performers Barry and Pamela might be working with at any given time. It was a constant and free-flowing exchange of music and ideas and life that was invigorating for all who passed through the small musical enclave.

One gathering that brought all of their friends to the rooftop garden was Pamela and Bob's wedding. "It kind of spilled over into all three gardens," Pam remembers. "Fred had this old kind of Venetian fountain that he'd gotten somewhere and we put champagne in that. It was just kind of a hippie wedding." Barry played the music for the wedding, and 16-year-old Vicki Sue Robinson sang, as did Peter Allen. Pamela, Peter, and Vicki Sue were appearing together in a Broadway play called *Soon*, the cast of which also included other little-known performers Nell Carter, Barry Bostwick, and Richard Gere.

It was this constant input of creativity that Barry had been longing for. He had successfully made the transition from a nine-to-five office job to making his living solely from music. He was out of Brooklyn, living on his own, in the kind of idyllic setting usually reserved for movie scripts. He had only to walk into his own backyard to encounter others who felt just as passionately about music as he did. If he needed creative input, it was there, just for the asking.

As he sat in the garden one night, sharing a glass of wine with Bob and Pamela, the thread of a melody kept winding its way in and out of Barry's consciousness. He'd been spending time playing a bit of Chopin on the piano that afternoon, and the notes that were writing themselves in his head now seemed to be paying tribute to that composer. When he went back to his piano, Barry turned on his cassette recorder and let the song present itself to him. After spending a little time fine tuning this new creation, he called Bob and Pam back to ask for their opinion. Both agreed that it was something special, though they didn't envision just how special. "I thought it was good," says Bob Danz, "but I didn't think it was going to be a tremendously big hit. I mean, what's the chance of that happening?" Barry decided to call the song, 'Could It Be Magic'.

Barry sent a tape of 'Could It Be Magic' to Adrienne, who responded enthusiastically, as did Tony Orlando when Barry played the tape for him. Tony wanted to record 'Could It Be Magic' along with another Adrienne/Barry tune called 'Rosalie Rosie'. They discussed how the songs would be arranged and, according to Barry, he went away from their meeting thinking that they had come to an understanding on how 'Could It Be Magic' should be done.

Barry's vision of the song was a build-up of tension, as in The Beatles' 'Hey Jude', which culminates, as Barry describes it, in "a musical orgasm". But when he came back to lay down the vocal track, the song Barry heard played back through the headphones sounded, he has said, "more like 'Knock Three Times' than 'Hey Jude'." Again unwilling to make waves, Barry let the song be released as Tony wanted it, complete with cow bells and a dance beat. A listing in the October 9, 1971 issue of *Billboard* magazine notes that with 'Could It Be Magic', by Featherbed, "*Producer Tony*

Orlando of Dawn comes up with a swinging bubblegum group that has it to hit big via Top 40."

What drummer Lee Gurst calls "the pre-disco version of 'Could It Be Magic'" died a mercifully quick death, with Featherbed snuffed out in its wake.

Still, even with this initial disappointment, Barry was in no danger of having to return to his nine-to-five office grind. While it didn't look as though being a recording artist was in the cards for him just yet, his coaching business was thriving to the point that he was turning clients away. So when his client, Sheilah Rae, asked him to be her accompanist for an upcoming audition, he initially declined. But she persisted, and he finally agreed to do one more audition for her. She was hoping to land a gig at a place on 44th Street called The Continental Baths.

Chapter Thirteen

Steve Ostrow, owner of the Continental Baths, was an unlikely hero in what would become the fight for gay rights in New York City in the Seventies. Gay bathhouses were certainly nothing new. But Ostrow was determined to make the Continental Baths a more mainstream and "respectable" place for gay men to come to relax and socialise without being made to feel like criminals though, technically, according to the State of New York, that's exactly what they were. Ostrow himself seemed to represent a perfect fusion of both gay and straight worlds, considering the fact that he was a married man, deeply devoted to his wife, but who also had a male lover to whom he was equally devoted.

Ostrow envisioned the Baths as "a full living cycle, a total environment" which, to him, naturally meant entertainment in addition to the other amenities offered. There was a pool, a steam room, a sun deck, a barber shop (which doubled as a dressing room for the acts that were booked), a massage parlour, a cafeteria and a dance floor. But for all the overt respectability, there were constant reminders that the Continental Baths was, above all, a place for men to meet and have sex with each other. In addition to the small private rooms available for just such activity, there was also a VD clinic on the premises, and the candy machines dispensed tubes of KY Jelly.

If Barry admired what he saw as the elegant lifestyle of some of the prosperous gay men he'd encountered in the past, it must have been quite a revelation for him to walk in and have the shout-out-loud sexuality that permeated the Continental Baths seize him by the throat. Gay men, he'd told Jeanne, really knew how to dress. The first man Barry saw when he and Sheilah entered the Baths was stark naked. No one was ashamed; no one apologised. These men were quite comfortable with who they were, and, within these walls at least, they were free to be themselves, without pretence. To Barry, this was a completely foreign concept, but an intriguing one. "It was," Barry later wrote, "decadent, sexual, and shocking – all the things I wasn't."

Billy Cunningham was the musical director at the Baths, and, after Sheilah's audition, Billy introduced them to Steve Ostrow. Sheilah got the job and, much to Barry's surprise, he was offered a job as well. The upcoming weekend was to be Billy's last playing piano at the Baths. Both Billy and Steve thought Barry would be perfect for the job. Barry hesitated, but the offer of $175 for only two days' work per week – $125 to play one show Saturdays at midnight, and another $50 for a one-hour Thursday rehearsal – was too good to pass up.

With drummer Joey Mitchell, Barry backed a variety of singers and comedians who played to the usually enthusiastic audience of mostly naked men (though they chivalrously donned towels if the act for the evening was female).

The third week Barry worked at the Baths fell on New Year's Eve, a Saturday that year. Barry was still playing for *The Drunkard* Saturdays, and left that evening's performance nicely warmed up from the free beer that was regularly given out to the audience during the show, as well as from the alcohol he'd consumed at the cast party after the performance.

At the Baths, the atmosphere was even more festive than usual. In honour of the occasion, Ostrow had lifted his "no women allowed" rule for the night, and now there was a good representation of naked female flesh scattered among the nude men in the pool and on the dance floor. Everyone, it seemed, was naked – except Barry, still dressed in his staid black suit, white shirt, and skinny tie. From the start of the midnight show, celebrating audience members had been passing drinks and joints to Barry and his drummer, and Barry hadn't said no. Now, as he sat in his proper suit, his chemically lubricated inhibitions wearing party hats and dancing the merengue elsewhere, it all seemed a fine joke to Barry. Get naked in front of a roomful of strangers? Well, why the fuck not? So he doffed his suit and, for the first time in his life, Barry Manilow deliberately made waves.

Chapter Fourteen

"*M*agic is in the air. *Magic that removes the violence of the cold, dark streets. The insecurities, the hates, the fears, the prejudices outside vanish in a haze of camp. It's Mary Martin asking if we believe in fairies. Yes. We Do. Clap harder. And the Jewish Tinker Bell is right there in front of you. Twinkling, glittering, making soft musical chimes of peace.*"

Columnist and critic Rex Reed's ecstatic prose was describing, in terms of great magnitude, a small woman who had begun packing a wallop with her over-the-top performances at the Continental Baths.

Bette Midler had originally come to New York from her family home in Hawaii. Named after movie star Bette Davis (her sisters were Susan and Judy, after Hayward and Garland, respectively), Bette described herself growing up as "an ugly, fat little Jewish girl with problems". Where Barry's father had been absent from the home when Barry was growing up, Bette's father, by contrast, very much dominated the Midler household. "My father was a bellower," she's said. "To get a word in you had to bellow back." It was something Bette became quite good at over the years. It's doubtful anyone has ever had to ask Bette Midler to speak up.

Like Barry, Bette began performing early on, finding a measure of love and acceptance through performing that somehow made up for her father's lack of demonstrative affection at home.

Her doting mother, Ruth, whom Bette adored, did her best to shelter her daughters from the more sordid side of life. "Consequently," said Bette, "I was always fascinated by the seamier aspects of life." When Bette got a bit part in the film of James Michener's *Hawaii,* which was shot on location near the Midlers' home, she was able to earn enough money to move to New York City in

November 1965; she was not yet 20. In New York Bette got to see "the seamier aspects of life" up close and personal when she checked into The Broadway Central Hotel. There was a hole in her bed and the communal bathroom was a good hike away. There were, said Midler, "winos in the hall, whores in the next room, junkies outside". Still, it was life in the big city, and Midler embraced the adventure. "I *loved* it," she later told an interviewer. "My dear, it was my great adventure. So exciting . . ."

Working around a series of the usual odd jobs to make ends meet, Bette worked her way up in the theatre world, eventually landing her dream − a spot in a Broadway play, portraying Tzeitel in *Fiddler On The Roof*. But, as often happens when one's dreams come true, waking reality can be a bit of a shock. "What I thought it was going to be like − legitimate theatre − was nothing of the sort . . ." she's said. ". . . It was cheap, dirty, full of politicking."

Still, Bette stuck with the show for three years, but ended up taking a year off when her sister Judy, recently living in New York and on her way to the theatre to see Bette perform, was struck by a car and killed. After her subsequent retreat, Bette came back on the scene and, with her friend Marta Heflin (who, as Bette's *Fiddler* understudy, had filled in as Tzeitel for Bette during her year's absence) began scoping out other performing possibilities. It was Marta who took Bette to a "new talent" night at a club called Hilly's one evening, and it was there that Bette took the mike, tentatively at first, and then with total command.

"As I was watching her sing," Marta later told an interviewer, "I thought, *Oh, my god. Something is happening here. This is really hot.* Because the audience just was freaked. It was very heavy. I had no idea she could do that." Neither had Bette. But, once she knew, she made the most of it.

It was when Bette was performing at Budd Friedman's Improv club on West 44th Street that she first met Barry Manilow, who, along with his many other gigs, was working as the Improv's pianist once a week.

After the curtain would come down on *Fiddler* each night, Bette would go over to Friedman's club and sing. Friedman, in fact, became Midler's first manager. Marta, in the meantime, had been performing in an Off-Broadway rock musical called *Salvation*. When Marta left New York to do a production of the show in California, she recommended that Bette audition for her part. Bette agreed. Paul Aaron was the show's director, and the pianist for the audition was none other than Barry Manilow.

"He used to do that," recalled Aaron, "play auditions for four or five of the girls and make about 15 or 20 bucks." When Barry saw that the next audition was going to be with the girl he'd seen perform at Budd Friedman's Improv club, Barry turned to Paul Aaron and said, "Wait 'til you get a load of this girl. She's not really what you're looking for to replace Marta – it'd be kind of a strange shot – but give her a chance." When Bette came into the room, Paul Aaron immediately found out what Barry had meant about Bette. "[She] walked down the aisle toward me," said Aaron, "threw herself in my lap and said, 'Well, you may have seen a lot of girls before me, but you ain't never seen one the same.'" She got the job.

The only problem as far as Paul Aaron was concerned, was that Midler was obviously not a team player. "It was very clear to me that Bette was never going to be an ensemble performer," he later told an interviewer. "But whenever that spotlight was on that lady alone . . . she radiated."

Bette continued to make the rounds of New York clubs, and Budd Friedman got her some out-of-town gigs as well. Then one day Midler got an unexpected phone call from one of her former acting teachers, Bob Ellston. Ellston, a friend of Steve Ostrow's, told Bette, "Listen, I know this guy who runs a steam bath. It's a very popular place for homosexuals to go and gather, and he's looking for entertainment. Would you like to work there?" It sounded like exactly the kind of place her mother would have wanted to shelter her from. Bette was definitely interested. Ostrow came to the Improv at Ellston's suggestion to catch Bette's act, and was duly impressed. He offered her $50 to do two shows a weekend. It was $50 more than Bette was making at the Improv. She accepted.

Bette herself has admitted that her repertoire at the time was decidedly down. "I couldn't get up for love or money," she's said. Ostrow would refer to Bette's setlist at the Baths as a "dirge". The audience certainly appreciated Bette's talent, but she was depressing the hell out of them.

Bill Hennessy had been Bette's hairdresser for *Fiddler On The Roof* and he was a regular at the Continental Baths. It was obvious to him, as to everyone who watched her first tentative performances at the

Baths, that Bette simply wasn't communicating with her audience. But Hennessy encouraged her to simply be herself. The scantily dressed men in her audience at the Baths were clearly on her side. Their acceptance and encouragement of her early on helped her to let down her guard and truly let herself be fabulous. "Ironically, I was freed from fear by people who, at the time, were ruled by fear," she's said, referring to the bias against gays that was still so strong at the time. "Be insane," Bill Hennessy encouraged her, and she took him up on it.

She and Bill worked on her show, and soon she was dishing with the "girls", calling them, "My *dears!*" and shooting out raunchy double entendres and self-deprecating one-liners at machine gun speed. Her combination of comedy, camp, and songs belted out with incredible depth of feeling compelled her audience to laugh, cry, and sing along, sometimes all within a single number. They were her dears, and she quickly became their Mother.

James Spada in *The Divine Bette Midler,* wrote of Midler's gay audiences, "They knew that she wasn't entertaining them just to make money; that she thought of them genuinely as soulmates, understood them, didn't snicker at them behind their backs. When she sang Bob Dylan's 'I Shall Be Released' at the Baths, she performed it as though it were a liberation anthem for every oppressed homosexual, stepped-on woman and discriminated-against minority member who ever lived." Midler's appreciation of her audience was just as heartfelt. "As an audience, gay men are spectacular," she told an interviewer. "They're very warm, very responsive. They are the most marvellous audience I've ever had because they're not ashamed to show how they feel about you. They applaud like hell, they scream and carry on, stamp their feet and laugh. I love it." And they loved her right back.

By the time Bette contacted Barry Manilow in September 1971 to schedule an extra rehearsal for a performance at the Baths, Bette had had several successes including two well-received runs at Mr. Kelly's in Chicago, and a very successful first appearance on the *Tonight Show* with Johnny Carson. This would be her third engagement at the Continental Baths, while it was just Barry's third weekend. So, if she seemed to Barry to be rather . . . *pleased* with herself, it wasn't without reason.

"It was hate at first sight," Barry has said. "Two Jews hating each other. But we rehearsed anyway. Bette had shown up at Barry's apartment for rehearsal late and hardly apologetic about it. "I had never experienced anything like her," he later wrote. "She was demanding, her voice was grating, she didn't try to be polite or social. She was downright rude at times." By the end of their rehearsals, it was a relief for Barry to be rid of her. But she wanted two more rehearsals before she returned to the Baths on Saturday; neither meeting was any more pleasant for Barry than the first had been. "By the time Saturday night rolled around," he wrote, "I was counting the minutes until I could say goodbye to this person."

As it turned out, it would be several years before he ended up saying his goodbyes.

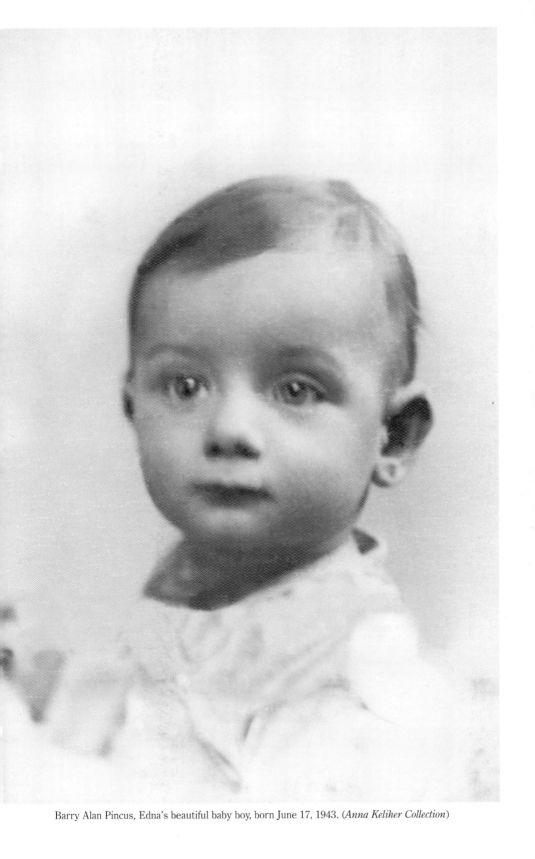

Barry Alan Pincus, Edna's beautiful baby boy, born June 17, 1943. (*Anna Keliher Collection*)

Barry's paternal grandmother, the former
Anna Sheehan. "A real Irish beauty."
(*Anna Keliher Collection*)

Harold Lawrence Pincus, Barry's father, with his
mother Anna. He would later adopt the surname
Keliher, the name of his mother's second husband.
(*Anna Keliher Collection*)

Harold in army uniform during the early Forties.
(*Anna Keliher Collection*)

Barry, aged around 18 months, with his father Harold
on the streets of Brooklyn. (*Anna Keliher Collection*)

Barry and his mother Edna, pictured after her performance at the Lincoln Center, New York, in Jerry Herman's musical *Tune The Grand Up*, December 19, 1978. (*Michael Ochs Archives/Redferns*)

Harold with the former Anna Price, who would become his second wife, pictured together before their marriage. (*Anna Keliher Collection*)

Barry aged 12. (*Anna Keliher Collection*)

At the Eastern District High School in Brooklyn: Barry (top left), Maxine Horn (top right),
Susan Deixler (bottom left), who would become Barry's wife, and Larry Rosenthal (bottom right).
"We were always, always laughing," says Maxine. "If you ask me what I remember, that's it - always, always
laughing, having a good time." Inset: the school as it was in 1961.

Barry and Susan with three friends at Susan's 'Sweet Sixteen' party, in 1960.

Mrs Delise's class at High School, with Barry (centre, back).

The Jazz Partners in 1962, left to right: Jack Wilkins, Fred Clark Billy Fagan and Barry.
(*Photo courtesy of Jack Wilkins*)

Barry in the studio with singer Jeanne Lucas, his first serious musical partner.
"He is the most gifted arranger I have ever known on the planet," says Lucas. "And everybody knew it and
people really wanted him to arrange their material." (*Lee Gurst*)

Barry and Bagel in 1967 at the upstate New York home of Bob Danz and Pamela Pentony, with Linda Allen (above) and swimming with their friend Fred Norring (below). (*Courtesy Pamela Pentony*)

Chapter Fifteen

In his usually earnest way, Barry Manilow set about trying to provide the discipline that Bette Midler's frenetic act was lacking. It was just this interaction of Barry's calm, controlled yin set against Bette's fiery passionate yang that served the two of them so well professionally, and could make them so miserable personally.

"We used to fight," Bette later told an interviewer, after Barry himself had become a star. "It was two ambitious Jews in one room. Such *bitchiness*. We would bitch at each other all the time." While Bette acknowledged that Barry was a better musician than she, it still irritated her that he was so consistently right, musically, at all times. "We would mostly bicker about which song should go where and how the show should be paced," she's said. It annoyed her that Barry wanted to wear white tails sometimes. His habit of sitting on phone books in the absence of the proper height bar stool when he played the piano got under her skin, as did the fact that he was constantly waving his head as he played.

Of course the irritation worked both ways. Barry agreed that he was a better musician than Bette, but that often seemed to be the extent of their accord. "I would lose every argument not because I was wrong," he later wrote, "but because I didn't know how to fight with her. She would try every which way to bully me into seeing musical things her way. But in that area, I was confident and strong."

While, by her own admission, Barry rarely did an arrangement Bette didn't like, still, she would take his disagreement with her ideas personally, even if she knew he was right. "It's true," she's said, "that he would insist on something that I would take to heart and get real spiteful about."

The constant tension was difficult for Barry to take. After all, he'd gone his whole life trying to avoid conflict, to not make waves. Bette's histrionics reminded him, he's said, of his mother, grandmother, and all of his female relatives rolled into one or, he summarised, ". . . every Jewish boy's nightmare come to life". After several weeks working, and fighting, together at the Baths, Barry had worked up eight new arrangements for Bette, and each made an enormous hit with the ever growing audiences, which now often included such luminaries as Mick Jagger and Andy Warhol. Bette's bathhouse reputation had spread far and wide. She was a "happening", and Steve Ostrow was now allowing anyone in to see her perform, though discreet signs asked that ladies please remove themselves from the premises after the show was over.

During this time, Bette was invited to do a two-week gig at Downstairs at the Upstairs. For Barry, it was "been there, done that", as he and Jeanne had performed there for two seasons with Joan Rivers. Even though he considered a return to the club "a step backwards", in his words, he agreed to stay with Bette through the gig. After an unfortunate incident in Chicago during which the venue's house band had nearly ruined her act with their incompetence, Bette had put together her own trio of musicians to prevent the same thing from happening again. She'd met Michael Federal during the same Chicago trip. He would remain with her during that stay in Chicago, then return to New York with her as her lover, and her bass player. Kevin Ellman was the drummer, and, of course, Barry Manilow was at the keyboard, and now acted as Bette's official musical director, doing all her arrangements and keeping the show musically on track.

Opening night at the Downstairs was a disaster – literally. In addition to a hurricane which had hit the east coast, wreaking havoc on people and property, it was also Rosh Hashana. There were eight people in the audience. Bette, trying to cover her distress at the situation, opened by saying, "I want to thank all eight of you for braving the wrath of God to come out and see the dirty Jewish girl from Honolulu."

The next few nights the turnout was only marginally better. So Bette decided to take things into her own hands. She knew that if the gig were to be salvaged, she needed to reach her own people, the kind of people who'd shown her such magnificent support during her performances at the Baths. So, with her own money, Bette took out a full page ad in *Screw* magazine saying simply, *Bette from the Baths*

— *at the Downstairs!* under her picture. By the sixth night, the place was packed and Bette was getting standing ovations. Barry's friend, drummer Lee Gurst, was among the appreciative audience members to see Bette perform at the Downstairs. "I remember," says Gurst, "she was doing 'Friends', and I got up in the middle of the song and went back to the maître d' and made a reservation for that weekend to bring my girlfriend in. I mean I was just blown away! I'd never heard anybody like her, and I'd never seen anybody like her." It was only later Lee realised that this ball of fire was the same actress he'd seen give such a subtle and moving performance on Broadway as Tzeitel in *Fiddler On The Roof* years before. Gurst would go on to do occasional percussion work for Bette during Barry and Bette's remaining performances at the Baths.

Just as at the Baths, word spread and soon the standing room only crowds at the Downstairs contained such celebrities as Truman Capote and Johnny Carson and, perhaps most importantly, Ahmet Ertegun, President of Atlantic Records. The two-week gig turned into ten.

With the success of Bette's run at the Downstairs apparent, the club's owner offered her trio, Barry, Michael and Kevin, an extra $50 if they would play a few songs to open Bette's shows. With Bette's approval, they agreed, and worked up a four-song act with Barry singing, sometimes joined by Michael.

When Bette had finally performed the last of what had become her nearly weekly "farewell performances" at the Continental Baths, a trio of backup singers was added to the trio of instrumentalists because, as Bette observed after all the offers she was receiving from every conceivable venue, "Oh my God, I better get a show together!" Now Bette's show consisted of herself, Michael Federal, Kevin Ellman, Barry Manilow, and The "Harlettes": Melissa Manchester, Gail Kantor and Merle Miller. In addition, Bill Hennessy was still working with Bette, helping her develop the seemingly spontaneous chatter that was often painstakingly devised and rehearsed.

Barry had become more to Bette than just her piano player, more than a musical director. He was also a trusted friend and a respected colleague, not to mention a frequent sparring partner. She had become a regular at his 27th Street apartment. "We'd fight, we'd laugh, we'd gossip," Barry later wrote of those afternoon practice sessions. But between the fighting and the laughing and the gossiping, Barry was helping Bette to evolve her style into something not only unique, but cohesive and professional in that seemingly random, non-professional way that only constant work over a long period of time can produce.

Her performances ever more polished, thanks to her own explosive talent, but tempered by Barry's knowledge and discipline, Bette and her troupe of musicians had made personal and television appearances all over the country. She'd become a pet of Johnny Carson's, not only appearing on the *Tonight Show* again, but also opening his act in the 500 seat Congo Room at the Sahara Hotel in Las Vegas in April 1972. The surprisingly staid Vegas audiences found Bette's raunchy humour a bit shocking for their tastes ("The ladies in the room opened their eyes wide and swallowed hard," wrote a reporter from *Oui* magazine. " 'Tits? Did she say . . . *tits?* ' ") but the reviews were good. They got even better when Bette and her band returned to home turf for venues like Manhattan's Bitter End, where they sold out every show. The mainstream media weren't quite sure what to make of this Midler, a paradox who was at once a throwback to the torch singers of the Thirties and Forties, but at the same time something completely new. It was unlike anything they'd ever seen before, "Yet," declared *Newsweek* magazine, "somehow it all comes together to make her one of the freshest, most captivating of the new girl singers." The piece went on to proclaim, "Bette Midler is – to use one of her favorite expressions – 'hot'."

In fact, Bette and Barry decided that their act had been getting such an overwhelmingly positive response across the country that they were ready for the big time. How do you get to Carnegie Hall? Why, you rent it, of course.

Barry and Bette reserved the main stage at Carnegie Hall for June 23, 1972. The Isaac Stern Auditorium seats over 2,800. After playing the Continental Baths and small clubs, renting a venue the size of Carnegie Hall seemed the ultimate show of *chutzpah*. "Can you dig it?" Bette said to columnist Rex Reed. "From the steam baths straight to Carnegie Hall." Despite Bette's professed fears that no one would come, tickets for the show were sold out within days.

While Barry was busy hiring an orchestra and preparing arrangements for the Carnegie Hall concert, Bette was in the studio recording her first album. Ahmet Ertegun, president of Atlantic Records, had been so impressed by the reaction of the crowd to Bette the night he'd seen her Downstairs at the Upstairs that he'd immediately signed her to his Atlantic label. Roberta Flack's producer, Joel Dorn, had agreed to produce the first album, a choice Barry felt was a mistake. "I was confused," he later wrote. "Roberta Flack's records were *sooo* tasteful . . . Delicate as crystal, cool as a cucumber, controlled, serious – everything Bette wasn't. It made no sense to me that she'd picked him." Barry was even more troubled when Dorn, introduced to Barry after a show at the Downstairs, asked Barry if his arrangements were written out. "I could see that I was going to have very little to say in this project," said Barry.

He was right. Dorn called Barry to ask him to bring his arrangements of 'Superstar', 'Do You Wanna Dance', and 'Friends', three of Bette's most popular songs, to the studio. When Barry inquired about some of the other songs he'd so carefully arranged for Bette during their time together, he was told that those numbers had all been rearranged by someone else. "I was very disappointed," said Barry. "I had worked on perfecting those charts for Bette for months." Any further pleas by Barry to be allowed to finish his own arrangements were met with a dismissive smile. "Joel considered me a lightweight," Barry later wrote, "and he made sure I knew it."

It's curious to note at this point that, when writing of Bette's Carnegie Hall debut in his 1987 autobiography, *Sweet Life: Adventures on the Way to Paradise*, Manilow inexplicably fails to mention that this night would also mark his own Carnegie Hall debut, not just as Bette's pianist, arranger, and conductor, but as a solo performer, opening Bette's second act. While some have suggested Bette was coerced into letting Barry open the second act of her Carnegie Hall debut, Barry has always insisted that his performance during the Carnegie Hall concert was merely a natural offshoot of the trio's opening numbers for Bette when she was working Downstairs at the Upstairs. "She generously allowed us to do our four-song set after the intermission," he's said. Of course he does say that she allowed, not that she offered. For those who knew Bette best, the thought of her happily sharing the stage with anyone on this night of all nights was rather doubtful.

Even wisecracking Bette Midler was awestruck by the enthusiastic reception she received when she first walked out onto the Carnegie Hall stage and faced the sold-out crowd. "Oh, my dears," she said to the audience in a tremulous voice, "your mother is *freaking out!*"

Everything she did was greeted with roaring approval from her fans. Everyone who had loved her at the Continental Baths or Downstairs at the Upstairs or the Bitter End was there, and this time the venue was large enough that they could bring all their friends, too. On this night the music was the star; Bette's usual rambling comedy bits, while still present, had been cut back to a comfortable minimum. It was typical Bette, but not. It was Bette, but grown up.

"And it was [Barry]," says Pamela Pentony, who was in the audience that night. "It was his brain that pulled that together. He was a great accompanist and a great orchestrator and a great arranger. He did all of her arrangements, all the vocal arrangements, got everybody to be in that show." And, as Pentony puts it, "He put on a real good show."

Barry had rented a suit for the evening and was, he has said, so nervous about his featured spot at the top of the second act that he threw up backstage. "I was convinced the audience was going to kill me the moment I walked on stage," he later told an interviewer. "I thought they'd throw tomatoes or drift out for drinks." But he shouldn't have worried because the audience was packed with friends and family members, assuring him an enthusiastic response. If Ahmet Ertegun could sign Bette Midler to a record contract based on the audience reaction he'd seen at the Downstairs, what might an enthusiastic response to Barry's spot at Carnegie Hall do for him? Barry didn't want to miss the opportunity to find out.

In addition to his neighbours from the 27th Street apartment, Barry had invited his high school friend, Fred Katz and his wife, who sat with Edna Manilow and Willie Murphy, along with Barry's grandparents. Of course a good portion of the audience also knew Barry from seeing him perform with Bette at various venues for the past year, as was evidenced by the enthusiastic greeting they gave him at the beginning of the second act.

Barry acknowledged the applause, explaining, "Miss M. has given us this part of the evening to do some original stuff. And so we have Melissa Manchester, Merle Miller, and Gale Kantor on vocals – that's good," he added, acknowledging the applause for The Harlettes, "– as well as Kevin Ellman, Dick Frank and Michael Federal. So we'll just get to it. Thank you."

They then launched into Barry's song 'Sweet Life', Barry taking the lead, with Michael taking a solo in the second verse. Barry's vocal sounded strong, confident, and pleasing. The difference between his voice and Michael Federal's was marked when Michael came in to take over the second verse. While Federal's voice was pleasant enough, still his brief solo after Barry's strong start seemed nothing more than the space of time one had to wait before hearing Barry take over the lead once again.

The response to the number was electric. The audience, clapped, cheered, whistled, and calls of "Bravo!" came drifting up to the stage from all corners. Michael Federal also did a solo of Barry's song 'Buried In The Ruins of Love'. But it was probably Barry's presentation of 'Could It Be Magic' that brought the house down. It was a reaction, some said, that had Midler livid.

"He brought a claque down there of people," said a friend. "And when he sang, they all screamed and yelled and clapped and got on their chairs, so much so that in the reviews the next day, they were talking about how Bette was great and everything, but how the audience had reacted to Barry. She was fit to be tied."

If so, she gave no evidence of it when, clad in a sarong, she reclaimed the show from Barry, who reintroduced her as "The Pearl of the Pacific". Obviously it was still Bette the audience loved. The show ended with a curtain call and two standing ovations.

Luckily Barry had had the foresight to pay Carnegie Hall's sound engineer to make an illicit recording of the show using the Hall's own sound system. Barry played the tape for Bette a week later when, depressed over the continuing arduous creation of her first album, she called him to commiserate. "I listened to the tape and couldn't believe it," Bette said later. "It wasn't the people, it was the *big*. It was just so huge . . ."

While the show was big, in many ways, it seemed it would turn out to be little more than a personal milestone for Midler. It certainly didn't seem to do anything to help the dismal state of Bette's first album, which was still struggling to be born. Ahmet Ertegun had heard Joel Dorn's efforts with Bette, and he wasn't happy. Drummer Lee Gurst had first known Joel Dorn as the brother of a childhood friend. "Joel is probably one of the finest jazz producers in the world," says Gurst. "But Joel was probably coming from an Aretha Franklin model, and that wasn't right for Bette."

As Barry had feared, Dorn had wrung the life out of Bette's performance, leaving behind a perfectly pleasant but completely bland shadow of the Bette Midler whose frenetic power attracted audiences.

It was the Bette Midler who'd gotten two standing ovations at Carnegie Hall those people knew and loved. What Dorn was proposing to present to them was, as Manilow later put it, "delicate as china, cool as a cucumber, boring as shit".

Taking the Carnegie Hall tape to Ahmet Ertegun's office, Barry watched Ertegun's reaction as he listened to most of the tape. Finally, according to Manilow, Ertegun said, "That's what Bette Midler should sound like! That's the performer I signed."

Ertegun wanted a record that reflected the Bette Midler who'd had audiences howling and standing on their chairs that night at the Downstairs. Hadn't Barry been instrumental in creating that frenzy? Barry could feel it: once again, a golden opportunity had walked up to him and taken him by the hand. All he had to do was follow. It didn't matter what he had – or hadn't – done before. All that mattered was what he knew he *could* do. And he knew he could do this. So, casting aside any personal doubts he might have had, he told Ertegun, "I can produce the album for her."

Though Barry had been upset when Bette hadn't fought for his inclusion in the beginning of her album's creation, being handed the project now seemed even more sweet. "The fact was," says Lee Gurst, "it wasn't going well and they finally said, All right, get Manilow. And it was not an act of desperation, but driven by need. Nobody knew what to do the way Barry did. So he went in."

Indeed, Barry had worked with Bette long enough to know that nothing turned her on like performing in front of a live audience. Unlike her stage performances, recording a song in a studio can be a lonely experience. Often all the instrumental tracks have already been laid down by musicians, sometimes days before the singer comes in to add the vocal. Then the vocalist, standing in a small booth and wearing headphones to hear the instrumental tracks, sings the song to a lone microphone rather than performing it for a reactive human audience. Given the process, it's no wonder that Midler, whose energy was derived from the response of her audiences, came off sounding, in Dorn's production (and in Barry's words), "boring as shit".

To remedy this, Barry did all he could to recreate in the studio the feel of a live performance stage. He hung theatrical lighting and invited an audience of friends into the studio. Perhaps more importantly, he got rid of the dozens of outside instrumentalists and vocalists Joel Dorn had used on 'Do You Want to Dance?',[3] 'Hello In There', 'Am I Blue', 'Friends' and 'Boogie Woogie Bugle Boy' and replaced them with Bette's own troupe of musicians – Barry on piano, Michael Federal on bass, and Kevin Ellman on drums (with the sole addition of Dickie Frank on guitar), along with The Harlettes – Melissa Manchester, Merle Miller, and Gail Kantor. With this assemblage of old friends, Bette performed 'Chapel Of Love', 'Superstar', 'Daytime Hustler', 'Leader Of The Pack', 'Delta Dawn' and 'Friends'.

"From the outset, we knew it was going to work," Barry later wrote of the session. "As soon as Bette could feel and react and play to a live audience, the previously missing energy was there. Ahmet, who was in the control booth, kept giving me the thumbs-up sign. Even Bette was having a good time."

Barry would later go back and add horns and strings to 'Superstar'. Hearing his arrangement of the song, with the additional instrumentation, played back to him, complete, for the first time, was the moment, Manilow has said, "that got me into the record business for real."

"I knew then and there," he wrote, "that I wanted to feel that kind of thrill again and again, and that I would do everything I could to make a career for myself in records."

---

[3] It's notable that background vocals on 'Do You Want To Dance?' were provided by Tender Loving Care (Renelle Broxton, Deirdre Tuck and Beverly McKenzie) fronted by Cissy Houston, Whitney Houston's mother.

Chapter Sixteen

The *Divine Miss M* was released in November 1972 and, that same month, Bette gave her *final* final performance at the Continental Baths. Midler was upset because she felt that Continental Bath's owner Steve Ostrow had taken advantage of her recent celebrity by overcrowding the venue. "When I looked out and saw how many people that bastard Ostrow had packed into that place, I was sick," Midler was quoted as saying in a February 1973 article in *Rolling Stone*. "It must have been a hundred degrees the way he packed those boys in. At first we couldn't even get through the crowd to get back to the dressing room."

Ostrow insisted that it was Bette who came to him and asked for the date at the Baths, not the other way around, and that she would have been even more upset if the place hadn't been packed for the occasion. But Midler's new manager – and lover – Aaron Russo, stated quite plainly that Ostrow's motivations had nothing to do with any consideration for Bette. "[Bette] needs the Baths like a hole in the head, right?" he told the *Rolling Stone* reporter. "But we agreed to do one last show as a favour. So what does Ostrow do? He decides to make a killing. He throws us to the lions."

Midler's new association with Russo was not a happy one for anyone, including the two at the centre of the storm. Russo had set his sights on Bette when he'd first seen her on *The Tonight Show* in 1970, but it wasn't until he – and his wife – saw Bette in person at The Bitter End that he was able to meet her. He was, from that moment on, said Bill Hennessy, "conspicuous by his presence". Looking back on their meeting later, Bette would recall, "Aaron was very forceful. And at that point in time, I just wanted to be looked after." Russo proceeded to look after Bette to the extent that he nearly suffocated her, and certainly alienated all those around them.

In October 1972, just before the release of *The Divine Miss M*, Barry was asked to provide some music for a Shasta Cola commercial, on which he would also sing. Melissa Manchester, still one of Bette's Harlettes, and Valerie Simpson, later of Ashford and Simpson fame, also provided vocals for the commercial, as did seasoned singer/musician Ron Dante.

"I was a jingle singer in New York City at the time," recalls Dante, of his first meeting with Barry Manilow. "I'd had a bunch of hit records before that, and I was basically doing a lot of jingle singing, a lot of oohs and aahs. I was booked on a session for the company called Gavin and Wallershcein, and Barry was working for them; I'd not met him."

In fact, Dante's career at that point, beyond mere jingle singing, had included dozens of singles and albums, among which was the smash hit 'Sugar, Sugar', a song which had ridden the crest of the Top 40 charts for weeks and had been voted Song of the Year in 1969. While the song was credited to the cartoon group The Archies, it was actually Ron's voice providing every vocal part for the record.

"It was great!" says Dante, of the Shasta recording session with Barry. "We sang the commercial; it was a really good spot as I remember it. Barry's arrangement was terrific. He was a really good arranger, and a super nice guy – just a really nice musician, friendly, talented." Barry mentioned to Ron that he was working with Bette Midler, whom Ron hadn't yet heard, but had certainly heard of. But Barry made it clear to Ron that he had ambitions beyond Bette's purview. "He knew me from my previous work," says Dante, "so at the end of the session he said, 'I want to be a recording artist. Would you come over and listen to some of my songs?' And I said, 'Absolutely.'"

A couple of days later Ron gave Barry a call and arranged to meet at Barry's West 27th Street apartment. With the recent addition to his household of his first grand piano, Barry had outgrown the studio apartment with the shared gardens, and had moved instead into a larger, two-bedroom apartment directly across the street. "It was very nice," Dante recalls. "It was a nice building, nice apartment, he had his piano there, and he seemed to be ensconced. He seemed very happy there at the time."

Barry's poise in the studio during their first meeting had made a deep impression on Ron. "I was impressed with him as a person. I thought he was a terrific guy, and he was just bursting with talent, there was no doubt about it," Ron says. "He had something. I had come across lots of piano players and arrangers and singers in my career who said, *I'm great! Listen to me!*, and most of them are okay. But Barry definitely stood out."

During that first visit to Barry's apartment, Barry played and sang for Ron 'I Am Your Child', 'Could It Be Magic' and 'Sweetwater Jones'. Already an experienced producer, Ron immediately started envisioning what they could do with the songs in a recording session. "I said, these are great!" Dante recalls. "I loved 'I Am Your Child', I loved 'Could It Be Magic'. I said, 'This could win a Grammy.'"

For fun, Barry also played for Ron a recording that his Grampa Joe had made for a quarter at a Broadway Record-It booth when Barry was four or five years old. "It was just a goof," says Ron, of Barry's motivation for playing him the old acetate recording. "He said, 'First record I ever made as a kid!' He thought it was very funny." Ron could hear Joe Manilow, with his Yiddish accent, trying to persuade the uncooperative child to "Sing, Barry, sing!" His constant pleas for Barry to sing 'Happy Birthday' to his cousin Dennis were met alternately with stubborn silences and squeaky refusals – "No! No!" Finally, his recording time running out, Joe had been forced to sing the song on his own. "[Barry] said, 'Yeah, my grandfather's quarter was running out and I would *not* sing,'" says Dante. "I thought it was hysterical. And I said to him, 'The first record we do with you, we should use that. If we ever do an album, we should start it off with that cut.'"

Barry asked Ron, "Do you think I could be a recording artist?" Dante had no doubt at all. "After listening to him sing, I said, 'Of course you could.'" So Barry said, "Let's go in and make records together." Within two weeks they were in the studio.

While Ron Dante does agree that Barry had not originally envisioned himself as a singer, by the time Barry and Ron booked a recording studio to make some demos, there was absolutely no doubt in Ron's mind who the star of the sessions would be. "Barry's often said that in interviews, that there was a toss-up between him singing and me singing," says Dante. "But I was never in doubt that these were his songs, his tracks and his career, and he was going to sing it. I not for a second thought that I would sing 'Sweet Life' or 'I Am Your Child' or 'Could It Be Magic'. It never entered my mind, and he never mentioned it to me. I always felt that, right from the beginning, he was going to be the artist." Dante's career as a vocalist had often kept him quite anonymous, either singing jingles, uncredited, or providing vocals for fictitious groups, like The Archies. Even so, he'd been quite successful at these endeavours. But what Barry was after was something else. "This was a different type of career," says Dante, of Barry's aspirations at that point. "This was something different. I knew Barry was something very special in what he was going to be doing."

When it came time to shop the completed demos to record companies, it seemed a toss-up between going first to Bette's label, Atlantic, or to Barry's former label, Bell. Barry and Ron both knew Irv Biegel, vice president of Bell Records – Barry from his experience with Featherbed, and Ron from his previous dealings with the music business in general, which had brought him in contact with Biegel many times. But Barry had worked most recently with Ahmet Ertegun of Atlantic Records when Barry had stepped in to finish producing *The Divine Miss M*. It was for this very reason, however, that Ron recommended against approaching Ertegun with their demos. "I thought Barry's career would be squashed for the sake of Bette Midler's career," says Dante. "I said let's go somewhere where you're the king of the record company, where if you succeed, they're looking to build you. I like Bell Records, and they like you."

So the two went to see Bell president Larry Utall, and Biegel, both of whom loved what they had done. "He could see the future," says Dante, of Biegel's reaction to their demos. "And he saw that Barry had talent. He said, 'Let's go cut some singles, let's go put out some of these things you're cutting.'"

Barry was understandably excited to be offered a singles deal, this time more on his own terms. Explains Dante, "He was finally on his way with a legitimate producer who was not forcing him into a role he didn't want to be in, like Featherbed, or doing pop confections."

After ending 1972 with a rollicking New Year's Eve performance at Lincoln Center's Philharmonic Hall, during which Bette had risen to the stage, via elevator platform, wearing nothing but a diaper and a strategically placed sash proclaiming the new year, Aaron Russo had taken Bette away for a much needed vacation. Barry took advantage of this down time to put together an exhibition for himself to promote the singles he and Ron were doing with Bell, with the end goal of convincing Bell that, in Barry's words, "I could put on an entertaining show of my own." The venue Barry chose was one that had worked so well for Bette in the past – The Continental Baths.

Barry put everything he had into producing the showcase. He hired studio musicians to back him, paid for a sound system, and again took advantage of Bette's absence by hiring the temporarily idle Harlettes to back him. He prepared six songs, including the newly arranged 'Could It Be Magic' and a slightly altered version of 'Friends', as a nod to Bette. Ron would do an updated version of his Archies hit, 'Sugar, Sugar', and they put together a medley of some of the commercial jingles both Ron and Barry had either written or performed. "I reasoned that the music would be so strong and solid that the executives at Bell would never even know that I had no idea what I was doing as a performer," Manilow later wrote.

"We invited the fans, of course, and the music community to come down," says Ron Dante, "especially the heads of Bell Records, at the time, Larry Utall and Irv Biegel. I think Ahmet Ertegun was also in the audience that night. Barry did basically what he was going to turn into his first album of material. And it was a smash show."

Over 700 people packed the Baths to see Barry's showcase, which the crowd greeted with overwhelming enthusiasm. "The show was so successful that night," Dante recalls. "There were lot of people, and they were all having a great time. It was a wonderful musical set. I remember thinking, this is magical how good this came out, and how well Barry came off. He was really prepared to come out as a solo artist that night. And he did. And the people recognised it."

Proof of that recognition was soon made evident. Attorney Miles Lourie called Barry the next day to let him know that Bell was offering Barry the album deal he'd been hoping for. And even though this was, indeed, the goal he'd been set on achieving, now, when it was within his reach, Barry hesitated.

Manilow has stated that he initially decided to turn the offer down, feeling that, soon to be 30, he was "too old to begin another career". Indeed, there's a big difference between being part of a larger act – Jeanne and Barry, Bette and Barry – and being the centre of attention. It's an enormous responsibility to know that the livelihood of dozens, sometimes scores of people rest upon what you alone do, and whether or not you succeed in doing it. But what had Barry been working toward all these years, if not this? In retrospect, it seems hard to imagine it was a chance Barry would let pass by. "They predicted such huge success for me," wrote Manilow, "that even I began to become a little excited about performing and singing . . . How could I turn this opportunity down?"

Manilow also dealt with the problem of feeling "too old" for a new career by simply turning back the chronological odometer a bit. "When all of this started," explains Lee Gurst, "and it began to look like Barry was actually going to have a career and some visibility, it didn't seem appropriate to be into his thirties, he decided. And so he picked 1946 and he knocked three years off his age." Journalists began faithfully reporting the amended birthdate, which is to this day often listed in official publications as Manilow's actual birth year. "Year after year these things get reported as gospel because they all go back to the same one or two sources," laughs Gurst. "Every June 17 on television I hear, *Today's birthdays — Barry Manilow is such and such,* and I go, *No, he's not!*"

Everything seemed set to move forward. And then Bette returned from vacation, ready to take her troupe of musicians out on tour.

Chapter Seventeen

It wasn't just his anticipation of Bette's angry reaction that made Barry dread giving her the news that he was going to be unable to go with her on tour. Barry had now been working with Bette for nearly three years and felt – quite justifiably – largely responsible for the success of her show. It was, of course, Bette's talent and raw energy that drew in the crowds. But it was Barry who had worked so hard to channel that talent and energy into a smooth, professional stage act. Now that the act was hot, Barry was torn between wanting and needing to strike out on his own, but also feeling the need and desire to stay with the sure thing that Bette, with his help, had become. "It was important to me that she be presented perfectly," Barry later wrote about what would be Bette's first major national tour. "I wanted the music, the arrangements, the band, the background singers, the whole show to reflect all the effort I had put in for three years."

As he'd feared, Bette's response to what should have been seen as good news for Barry, was less than enthusiastic. "But you *can't* sing," she reportedly said to him when he told her he was planning to do an album for Bell Records. "They'll laugh at you, Barry. Take my advice, just play the piano." Bette had also asked Barry to co-produce her second album, as his first effort for her had been such a huge success. It was another powerful inducement to stay in Bette's orbit rather than striking out on his own.

But Barry was obligated to Bell Records to not only make an album but travel to promote it as well. Bette was doing all she could to persuade Barry to tour with her instead, something that Barry actually wanted to do. Unfortunately, he'd yet to master the art of being in two places at once. Failing a major revision of the basic laws of physics, something had to give.

Barry told Ron Dante that Bette was offering him larger and larger sums of money to go out on the road with her. Ron suggested that Barry counter-offer a compromise. "I suggested to him that he should actually take *less* money, but try to do something in the middle of her act," says Dante. Ron said to Barry, "She's very hot; this would be very good for you to get on the road."

As with his Carnegie Hall debut, Bette was not thrilled at the thought of sharing her stage with Barry. "She didn't like it," says Ron Dante, "but she wanted to keep him. She really loved the way he played piano and did arrangements. He was really crucial to her musical success in the beginning." Once again, Bette didn't seem to have much choice. She needed Barry as her music director, and Barry needed the audiences Bette could provide to help him promote his own work, as he'd promised Bell Records he would do. So it was agreed that, on this tour, Barry would open Bette's second act with a few of his own numbers. "I think she did it begrudgingly," says Dante. "She didn't do it with an open heart."

Melissa Manchester had left The Harlettes rather abruptly some months before.[4] Charlotte Crossley replaced Melissa and was immediately struck by the tension of the situation she had stepped into, tension which seemed to be caused mainly, as far as Charlotte could see, by the highly charged relationship between Bette and the incredibly demanding and possessive Russo. "It was *nutty*," Crossley told an interviewer, of Russo and Midler's relationship. "Continuous drama. We would be rehearsing at Barry's house, and if Aaron knew she was there, he'd keep calling again and again and they'd be *screaming* and yelling over the phone. I don't know how we ever got anything done."

Prior to Russo's appearance on the scene, Bette and her group had gotten into the habit of gathering in Bette's dressing room before performances, just to make sure all were ready and in a good frame of mind to go out and give a fabulous show. Russo put an end to the practice. "He started locking her door," said Crossley, "because he was jealous of that, he couldn't have that – he wasn't part of it, he couldn't contribute to that the way we could. He felt very competitive with us."

---

[4] Gail Kantor and Merle Miller would also depart before the start of the tour, replaced by Sharon Redd and Robin Grean.

Barry had no time for these tensions. He and Ron had worked out a co-producer arrangement for Barry's first album, and Barry was splitting his time in the summer months before the start of Bette's tour between recording his own album, co-producing, with Arif Mardin, Bette's second album, creating and rehearsing a show for Bette and the new Harlettes, and hiring his own representation. Dick Fox, from the William Morris Agency, had worked with Barry and Jeanne in the early days, and now became Barry's agent. Barry also made the decision to retain attorney Miles Lourie as his manager, a decision which caused Ron Dante some concern. "Barry came to me and said, 'I'm going to make Miles Lourie my manager,'" Dante recalls. Ron pointed out to Barry that Miles had never managed anybody before, which could present a problem somewhere down the line. But Barry was adamant. "No, he'll fight for me, he'll be tough for me." So, says Dante, "that was Barry's decision. All I know is Miles is a tough customer to deal with." But tough was what Barry needed. "Barry used to describe Miles as 'my son-of-a-bitch'," says Manilow's friend, drummer Lee Gurst. "Barry could be a nice guy, and Miles was out there intercepting, the one who would say no, so that Barry could always just say yes. And that's not unusual. Lots of managers do that. So Barry was always the nice, sweet guy and Miles was always the one to make demands."

The tour started in August, and Barry quickly learned that he was going to have to struggle for his solo time on stage. The first venue they played, the Merriwether Post Pavilion near Washington DC, was packed to its 15,000 person capacity. The piano was so far back on the stage that Barry knew he would be out of the sight of most of the audience during his spot at the top of Bette's second act, and he and Aaron Russo got into a heated argument in front of everyone over having the stagehands move the piano farther downstage during the intermission. In the end Russo grudgingly acquiesced, but, to Barry, it seemed a bad omen for the rest of the tour.

The ongoing tensions between Bette and Russo were taking a toll on Bette and affecting her behaviour with the rest of her group, making for a highly charged atmosphere. "There was constant fighting, frequent screaming matches," wrote author James Spada in his book *The Divine Bette Midler*, "between Bette and Aaron, The Harlettes and Aaron, Barry and Bette, even Bette and The Harlettes." Sometimes Bette would change the order of his carefully constructed show, onstage, in the middle of a performance, which made Barry squirm. "Oh, Mr Music," she'd taunt him. "Let's not do 'Surabaya Johnny' tonight, let's do 'Superstar'. On the spot, Barry would have no choice but to go along with Bette's wishes. But after the show, writes Spada, "there would be a screaming match backstage, with ashtrays thrown and threats of strangulation from Barry."

While the audience, too, sometimes became the victims of the constant stress Bette was feeling, the shows were, for the most part, smash hits. While in Los Angeles the group again visited *The Tonight Show*, during which Bette, Barry and The Harlettes performed a live version of 'Boogie Woogie Bugle Boy' which brought the audience to their feet in a thunderous ovation. Comedian David Steinberg, scheduled to appear after Bette, reportedly turned to the person next to him and said, "She's the worst thing that can happen to you in show business. It's like following a moonwalk."

Barry himself certainly found this to be true. If Bette had initially been afraid that Barry's spot at the top of her second act would steal her audience, she needn't have worried. "It's like opening for the Statue of Liberty," Barry told Ron Dante. Says Dante, "For anybody to try to get up and sing in the middle of her act was impossible. When Barry came on, people went to the restroom. But the quarter of the audience that stayed really enjoyed his three songs."

In Denver that balance began to shift a bit. Bette and her group were playing at the Red Rocks Amphitheater, an outdoor venue carved into the side of natural red rock mountain. Visually the setting was beautiful. But it wasn't the kind of venue that worked well for Bette. For one thing, the Denver audience was very mellow, sprawled out across the vast property, many sitting on blankets spread across the ground, some toting picnic baskets and drinking wine they'd brought with them. But the main problem was that it was difficult for Bette to gauge audience reaction to what she was doing onstage, as any sound the audience made was diluted by the open air setting. "It's really hard to work to a crowd when you can't hear their reaction," Barry later wrote of that performance, "especially if you're counting on laughs for your timing." By the end of the first act, Bette was, as Barry characterised her, "a wreck".

Though Barry had agreed with Bette early on in the tour that he should not sing the relatively long (nearly seven minutes) 'Could It Be Magic' during his performances, at Red Rocks he changed his mind. The decision had been made originally because it was felt the song took too long to build, and Bette's typical audiences would probably not be held through the entire thing. But the Red Rocks audience seemed, to Barry, to be the perfect group to appreciate the song's slow build, crashing climax, and gentle denouement. Though Barry hadn't been performing the song during the tour, he had rehearsed it with the band and The Harlettes, so he knew they would be ready for it. He informed the stage manager that he would be changing his last song and instead performing 'Could It Be Magic'.

"I sang it to the sky and to the mountains and to Brooklyn," Barry later wrote of that performance, "and I was lost. Lost in the song." When he finished, Barry took his bow and tried to start the music signalling Bette's reappearance for the second act, but the crowd wouldn't let him. They continued applauding and cheering, bringing a dazed Barry back to his feet for another bow. And then the audience started getting to their feet. "I figured that they were coming back from the restrooms," Barry joked. But instead they were giving him his first standing ovation.

It was probably a good thing Barry had his Denver triumph to carry him through what was to come in San Francisco.

The San Francisco show had gone well, and the group was expecting to get a rave review in the paper the following morning. Instead, John Wasserman of the *San Francisco Chronicle* savaged both Bette and Barry, and even had some rather nasty things to say about their audience.

"*Mass Mince-In for Midler – Every Gay Blade's Fantasy,*" was the headline that topped the truly devastating piece. "*It was amazing,*" wrote Wasserman. "*The Divine swept from one end of the stage to the other, waving giant fans of pink feathers and hurtling along like a rag doll on speed, her various appendages sprawling in four directions simultaneously, her eyes rolling like marbles in a vacuum, her bountiful breasts, which resemble ostrich eggs dropped into a pair of panty-hose, springing up and down like yo-yos. 'Oh,' she cried in mock melodrama, throwing her hand to her forehead, 'Gross us out, Miss M, gross us out!' And so my children, gross us out she did for the ensuing two hours.*"

Inexplicably, Manilow would later characterise Wasserman's words as a "rave review" for Bette. One can only assume he meant in comparison to what Wasserman had to say about Barry's set.

"*And lastly,*" wrote Wasserman, after he'd finished with Bette,

"Barry Manilow has got to go, at least as a featured part of her performance. He is a fine musician, but somewhere along the line someone made the mistake of telling him he could sing. Toward this end, he had a new album out on Bell and treated us to four solo numbers to open the second half."

Under the heading HALLUCINATION, Wasserman went on to deconstruct not only Barry's act, but Barry himself, piece by piece.

> *"Manilow, who has his hair done at the Clip and Snip Poodle Salon, apparently thinks he is a potential star. To underscore this hallucination, he has a piano stand-in, like a movie star, has a lighting and blocking stand-in. This fellow comes out first and hits several notes on the piano to make sure it's working. It was.*
>
> *"To open the second half, Manilow swept out on the stage in an all-white Nehru jump-suit. 'May name is Barry Manilow,' he gurgled, 'and I am the captain of your flight tonight.'*
>
> *"Tell that to the Graf Zeppelin.*
>
> *"His opening number guaranteed instant obscurity and he went down hill from there. The second tune was, incredibly, 'Cloudburst,' accompanied by the Harlettes. 'Cloudburst' is, of course, the Pointer Sisters hit. For a third-rate singer to come into the Berkeley Community Theater and render 'Cloudburst' is approximately equivalent to peddling near-beer in Munich. The third tune ['Could It Be Magic'] was pathetic. The fourth was titled, apparently, 'Mama, Can You Hear Me?' Which needs no comment, save mama's, which is, 'Yes, son, and you should wash out your mouth with Black Flag.' "*

Writer Bruce Vilanch had joined Bette's entourage some months prior to the 1973 tour, and provided comic bits for her onstage act. When Ron and Barry had completed recording their first album, Barry had sent Bruce a demo pressing of it. Bruce loved the demo, and sent Barry a note in San Francisco to tell him so. Bruce's note just happened to arrive on the same day Wasserman's vicious remarks appeared in the *Chronicle*. A grateful Barry called Bruce and said, "Thanks, Bruce, your note was the only thing that kept me from the gas pipe."

Unfortunately, Bruce's feelings about Barry's first album were not universal. "We thought we were cutting a Grammy award-winning album," says Ron Dante. "We were just intent on doing the best album possible on a really average budget at the time." Indeed, Ron brought to the project his years of experience and Barry brought unlimited talent and enthusiasm. But still, it didn't seem to be enough. "I used all my expertise and my experience in how to make it sound good," Dante says, "and Barry used all his wonderful arranging abilities to make it sound great, and of course he sang everything beautifully." Barry was on the road with Bette, promoting the album to huge crowds around the country. But somehow, even with all the right pieces present, they simply weren't falling into place.

"We got that album put out," says Dante, "and it was a failure." The album's failure to take off was especially frustrating to Barry, who had taken on so many simultaneous roles – producer, arranger, performer, musical director – just to see the record created and still accommodate Bell's desire for him to promote it and Bette's desire for him to continue working with her. At one point Barry called Ron from the road and said, "I'm so disappointed this isn't going well." Says Dante, "We didn't know what was going on."

But the album was meeting with just enough critical review to keep Bell interested. As Ron had once pointed out, Bell's Irv Biegel was a visionary, and Irv still saw great things in Barry's future. His feelings were bolstered by the growing enthusiasm Bette's audiences were showing for Barry's 20-minute spots leading Bette's second act. More attention was being turned on Barry, who now had his own press agent who was getting Barry more and more interviews. Irv Biegel flew out to see one of the shows during the tour and was impressed enough to offer to support Barry should he want to go out to do his own tour. "I began to feel important," Barry later wrote, "which is dangerous."

Bette's tour was to conclude with a much anticipated run on Broadway at the Palace Theater beginning December 3. When tickets for the show went on sale in mid–October of 1973, Midler set a Broadway record for one-day ticket sales at $148,000. It was as if the previous four months of touring had merely been an extended rehearsal session for the real show at the Palace. "We set out to see America," Bette told the opening night Palace audience, referring to the tour they were now concluding, "and it *disintegrated* before our very eyes!"

Barry wore a white tux with tailcoat for the occasion. The next day *New York Times* reviewer Ian Dove, a British jazz critic, wrote of Barry's performance, "*He showed, during his three songs, talent in his own right and was genuinely received by the audience. He has also been with Miss Midler since the very beginning and so, for him, too, it was a return to familiar ground."*

Familiar ground landmarked by familiar faces. Barry had invited his old high school friends, Larry and Fred, and their wives to attend. Edna and Willie were there as well, as were Barry's grandparents, Esther and Joseph Manilow. In a 1976 article for *Seventeen* magazine, Barry told the interviewer, "Grandpa saw the whole thing, and he got [my] album. Opening night at the Palace, he gave me a standing ovation. My grandmother was sitting next to him and took his hat off when he stood up. I saw that. I was watching. He was a great cat."

It was important for Barry that the article mentioned Joseph Manilow hearing his grandson's album and seeing his performance at the Palace because, within two weeks of the December 3 opening, Grampa Joe died. To Barry, it was a devastating loss. "He was the most alive man I ever knew," Barry later wrote. "He was funny and witty and kind. That's my Gramps. That's who I'll always sing to. That's who I'll always remember."

As Ron Dante had suggested that first day he'd visited Barry's apartment to listen to his songs, the first cut on Barry's first album is the scratchy recording of Joe Manilow trying to get Barry to sing 'Happy Birthday' to his cousin Dennis. "Nobody was doing that on records at that time," says Dante of his idea to include the recording on Barry's first album. "I said, that would be unusual, something different. Start an album off with something very personal, from your childhood." What turned out to be, as Dante characterised it, "just a goof" ended up standing as a loving tribute to the one steady male influence Barry had known through his life up to that time. Decades later, listeners can still pop in a CD and hear Joseph Manilow urging his grandson, "Sing it, Barry! Sing it!"

Chapter Eighteen

Barry's parting with Bette Midler at the end of her 1973 tour was, in the end, an amicable one, though Bette would later say of Barry's decision to leave her show, "I was mad as hell at him!"

"When Barry left," Bruce Vilanch later told an interviewer, "[Bette] was very much at sea musically. He gave the ballads a texture that was missing after he quit. She's had wonderful people who've worked with her, but she hasn't had anybody who's given her what Barry did – she has had to do it for herself."

Even Don York, who took Barry's place as Bette's musical director, conceded that it was nearly impossible for anyone to really fill Barry's shoes in Bette's act. "It was difficult for Bette to lose Barry. They had a strong communication worked out. It was hard for her to accept someone else's presence."

Bette herself spoke wistfully at the time about Barry's absence. "I *really* miss Barry," she told an interviewer, "but I think his success is fabulous." She did, however, still manage to work a barb or two into the tribute. "I was a little surprised . . . in fact I was *very* surprised because there were times when he was working for me –" then she hastily corrected herself, "working *with* me – when he would bring me some of his songs that I didn't like. I would say to him, 'Why are you singing "Come to where the stallions meet the sun"?' I can't *stand* that! Don't sing that! I must have thought, of course, that I was the final arbiter of taste. Obviously I wasn't."

While Barry was no longer fighting with Bette, he now had to fight with her memory. Bell had provided a generous advance for Barry to prepare and launch his solo tour. But the audiences for which he found himself playing were either completely inappropriate for his type of music, or they were expecting a show similar to Bette's manic performances, something Barry couldn't have

112

managed even if he'd wanted to, which he certainly did not.

"He was playing joints where he was opening for jazz people," says Ron Dante. "And the people would come and not like what he was doing, because he was doing a little jazz but a lot of pop music." In fact the first show of Barry's tour was opening for jazz trumpeter Freddie Hubbard at a small club called Paul's Mall in Boston. The booking was a disaster, from top – a ceiling with holes in it that dripped rain on the performers – to bottom – Freddie Hubbard refusing to go on if he had to follow someone who played commercial jingles. Barry persevered and eventually discovered that his shows seemed to work best at the times when he made an effort to step out of himself, to step out from behind the piano, and engage the audience directly. Still, Barry later wrote of that "depressing" first engagement, "I'll never forget trying to hold the small audience's attention during 'I Am Your Child' while fighting the noise of the bartender's blender."

Things were better in Philadelphia, where glowing reviews helped sell tickets. In turn, Barry used the increased revenues, along with his own savings, to hire a sound mixer and shore up the production with a better sound system and stage lighting. "I was still determined to put on a first-class show even though we were playing less than first-class places," Barry has said. The efforts paid off as the tour continued, winding up back in New York City with a scrapbook's worth of solid reviews to show for the effort. The final date of the tour in New York was the Bottom Line, where, on opening night, Barry had to appease the audience with some piano music as he found, when he tried to sing, that he'd lost his voice entirely. The problem was cleared up within a day, though, and he was able to complete the engagement to standing ovations.

Things were once again looking promising. Encouraged by Barry's successes, Irv Biegel and Larry Utall gave the okay for Ron and Barry to begin recording a second album. Barry was excited about the project, and had been busily working with some of his favourite collaborators – Marty Panzer, Enoch Andersen – to create new songs. "I knew exactly what I wanted the album to sound like," Barry said. "I wanted it to be smart, I wanted it to be musical and inventive. I wanted to say things that affected people."

But, behind the scenes, there were other events taking place at that moment that were going to profoundly affect a great many people, including Barry and Ron.

PART IV

In Clive We Trust

"It is important to remember that the saccharin side of American pop music has always been and always will be. Although what the purpose of 'Mandy' by Barry Manilow possibly could be remains a mystery to me."

— *Rolling Stone* writer PJ Rourke,
to VH1's *Behind the Music*

Chapter Nineteen

Clive Davis was an unlikely figure to rise to a place of power in the music industry. He was not a musician, but a lawyer. Like Barry, he'd been raised in Brooklyn, though in a more prosperous area (relative to Williamsburg), supported by a more traditional family unit. "I was your basic, garden-variety, ambitious, upwardly mobile, hardworking Jewish boy from Brooklyn," he later wrote. "I was *bound* – and so were the kids around me – to go beyond my parents. It was simply the way things were. Our parents had worked hard, but we had to work harder; we had to become doctors and lawyers, professional people, scholars, business executives."

When his beloved parents, Joe and Flo Davis, died suddenly within a year of each other, 18-year-old Clive went to live with his sister and her husband in Bayside, Queens. He commuted each day into the city to attend classes at New York University. To help fill the void that had been left by his parents' deaths, Davis threw himself into his studies and into campus politics. "The result," he wrote, "was to be a full-tuition scholarship to Harvard Law School."

During his time at Harvard, Davis took a copyright course that required him to read the entertainment industry daily trade paper *Variety*. "I just loved it," he said, "and after the course ended I *kept* reading it."

After graduating from Harvard in 1956, Davis began working for a small law firm that eventually had to cut back its staff, including Davis, who quickly landed a spot at a larger, more prestigious firm. After Davis had been there a couple of years, one of his colleagues, Harvey Schein, left the firm to take a job as General Attorney for Columbia Records, a division of CBS Entertainment. Columbia's legal office was only a two-man operation at the time, and, when

Schein's fellow lawyer at Columbia vacated his position, Schein contacted Clive Davis to see if he might be interested in filling the vacancy. He definitely was. Clive joined Columbia as legal counsel in 1960 and, within seven years, had risen to the presidency of the Columbia Records Division.

Davis's 1973 dismissal from Columbia was even more dramatic than his rise and tenure there had been. By the time he was ousted amid rumours, scandal, and accusations of wrongdoing (of which he was later cleared), he'd been instrumental in adding to Columbia's roster of talent such best-selling pop artists as Bob Dylan, Paul Simon and Janis Joplin, to name but a few.

Almost before security officers had had a chance to escort Davis out of the Columbia building, rumours were racing through the entertainment world speculating on his comeback. "I kept reading press stories that I was about to take over this or that company, make a variety of deals to do other extraordinary things," Davis wrote in his 1974 biography, *Clive*. "I was mentioned, for example, as the upcoming president of a new Sony, USA record company; of a new American Express-owned record company; and of RCA Records. Other stories said that I was forming a new company with Bob Dylan, The Beatles, and Simon & Garfunkel. Most of these stories were printed as *fact*. I never understood this; nobody bothered to check with *me* about them."

Had anyone bothered to check, they might have found out that Davis was actually in negotiations to take over Bell Records, which would henceforth be known as Arista.[5]

Barry and Ron, in the midst of producing Barry's second album, were understandably anxious about the sudden changes taking place at the top. Their champions at Bell, Larry Utall and Irv Biegel, were now out, as were many of Bell's roster of talent. "Ninety-nine per cent of the artists on the label were let go," says Ron Dante. "And I

---

[5] Clive Davis has always remained exciting and controversial – and successful – as evidenced by this Fox News item which ran on December 14, 2000: "*Here in the real world, [Clive] Davis was ousted from his post as founder and grand poobah of Arista Records on June 30th after nine months of public wrangling. He started J Records on September 1st, and now he's got a No. 1 single. The two executives who forced him out were themselves forced out of parent company Bertelsmann Music Group last month. And you know, with Clive, this is only the beginning.*"

remember hearing stories about how Clive didn't like Barry's first album, and he wasn't crazy about Barry in general."

In an "it's a small world" twist of irony, Schaefer Brewery – where Barry's father and stepfather and (very briefly) Barry himself had toiled – sponsored a series of summer concerts in Central Park each year, and Barry played a date there during the summer of 1974, opening for Dionne Warwick. Melissa Manchester sang with Barry, and Barry's friend, Lee Gurst, was their drummer. Clive Davis came down to the Wolman Skating Rink, converted into an outdoor amphitheatre during the summer months, to take a look at Barry in action. "He really loved what Barry had to do," recalls Ron Dante. Indeed, Davis came backstage after the show and told Barry he was happy to have him on the Arista label.

It was a relief for Barry to know that he still had a home at Bell, now Arista. Before Utall and Biegel's ouster, with things going so well, and in anticipation of another tour, Barry had already hired a band, backup singers and a crew, putting himself in debt. Things would have been pretty bleak if Davis had decided to bounce Barry along with all the other artists he had cut from the Bell roster.

Lee Gurst had worked with Barry on and off since they had first met when Barry was hired as musical director for an ill-fated stage production called *Now* in the late Sixties. During his time at CBS, Barry had picked up work as musical director for the local TV show *Callback!* on which he had appeared a few times with Jeanne Lucas. Gurst remembers one instance when Barry had been able to cleverly get around the CBS brass in order to throw some work his friend's way.

"After we did *Now* together, Barry wanted me to do *Callback!*," says Gurst. "But CBS said no, we have our staff orchestra, and we pay them, and they're going to do your show; Barry had worked with them before." Barry had worked at CBS long enough to know that there was no arguing with executive minds with an eye on the bottom line. So, instead, he presented them with a dilemma. Says Gurst, "He said to the producers, 'By the way, Sunday is the only day I can have the whole day free, so we have to tape on Sundays.' And, what do you know! That was the day the CBS orchestra had to do the Sullivan show." The executives had no choice but to use the musicians Barry had hired. "He actually set it up so that I could be on that show," Gurst concludes.

119

At the end of Lee's time working on *Callback!*, Barry sent Lee a note which said in part, "I feel like I'm writing a thank you note to my brother." Barry went on to tell Lee that everyone who'd worked on *Callback!* thought highly of him and, if Barry had anything to say about it, he and Lee would be working together again soon. "So that was the beginning of life after *Callback!*," says Gurst. "Barry thanked me for my contribution and said, we'll do it again. And we did."

In fact, during the ensuing years, Barry and Lee became close friends and worked together often. Lee had filled in on drums and percussion several times during Bette's performances at the Continental Baths, and he'd also appeared in her shows at the Palace. Gurst had just returned from touring with Lorna Luft while Barry and Ron Dante were in the midst of putting together Barry's second album. Gurst, a gifted photographer as well as musician, was happy to pitch in to help in any way he could with the album's production.

"I went up to Barry's and did [several] rolls of pictures," Gurst recalls. "We were trying to get some publicity-type pictures." Barry tried then to persuade Lee to go on his next tour with him, but the decision proved problematic. "I went to the auditions and watched him trying out people," says Gurst. "We talked a few times. Initially I couldn't afford to go – I mean he was just paying nothing. And then I said, gee I really want to do this, I mean I love the music. But then Miles said no, I don't want you to have any friends on the road."

Not only had Bette Midler's personal relationship with Aaron Russo caused professional complications during her last two tours, but, at the same time, one of The Harlettes had gotten involved with one of the musicians, a relationship that went sour and caused additional tensions on the road. Miles had taken a lesson from that experience and was now insisting that Barry, who'd worked with friends his entire professional life, keep his personal relationships entirely separate from his professional dealings.

"I took some other work," says Gurst. "Then I went in one day to play drums for Barry when he was auditioning bass players." In the midst of the auditions, Barry was called out of the room to take a phone call. When he came back, he put a piece of sheet music on the stand in front of Lee and said, "Here, you might as well go ahead and learn it, you're going on the road with me." The call had been from Alan Schwartzberg, the drummer Barry had hired in Lee's stead.

Alan had been offered a spot playing for a Broadway show. He thought the show was a good one,[6] and he really preferred staying in New York to going on the road. Schwartzberg asked Barry if he would consider releasing him from his commitment. "So," says Gurst, "the following part of my career I owe to Alan Schwartzberg being a very good drummer who was offered a very good show."

Since he was definitely going to be travelling with Barry, Lee was now glad that he'd been around for the auditions for backup singers, held previously, when Lee still thought he wouldn't be going on the tour. Among the singers auditioned had been a dark-haired beauty named Lorraine Mazzola, who performed under the stage name Reparata. "I kind of put my vote in for Reparata," says Lee slyly, "because, I figured, well, you know, maybe I'll show up on the road and want to take pictures or something, and it would be nice if there was somebody to try to hit on." Barry did, in fact, hire Reparata, undoubtedly more for her singing ability than Lee's leering assessment of her date-ability. But it would still turn out to be a professional decision on Barry's part that would end up having a dramatic affect on Lee's personal life before too long.

Lee's relationship with Barry had grown close over the years, a fact which, Lee felt, caused some concern with others working with Barry at that time, including Ron Dante. "Ron and I weren't buddies," says Lee. "I had a personal relationship with Barry that some people, whether they should have or not, perceived as a threat to them." While Lee understood the concern, he didn't feel it was warranted. "Ron didn't know it, but Barry was not going to take a step without him at that stage," says Gurst. "Barry wouldn't take a step without Ron there by his side in terms of studios or a television show where Ron would be there next to the mixer making sure it came out right, things like that. Ron didn't have to worry." Lee noted that Barry had similar feelings about Miles Lourie.

"But," says Gurst, "Barry and I had a comfort and a musical communication and a shared sense of humour; we just connected. And Miles and Ron, for two, kind of didn't like that." Miles, says Lee, was overt in his dislike of Lee's personal relationship with Barry, while Lee and Ron tended to simply steer clear of each other. "We

---

[6] He was right. The show was *A Chorus Line* which opened on Broadway in 1975 and closed 6,137 performances later, in 1990.

had different territories, if you will," says Gurst. "I liked him well enough, but we just didn't click, we weren't buddies, we didn't hang out together."

Ron had taken special care with the production of this second album, and he was justifiably proud of his efforts. With years of recording experience behind him, between his own records and scores of commercial recordings, Ron had become acquainted with the best singers, musicians, engineers, and arrangers New York had to offer, as well as the best recording venues. "I knew there were one or two studios in town that you could get a great vocal sound in," says Dante. "And I knew Media Sound, which was a converted chapel in Manhattan, would be a great place to record Barry."

Media Sound was located in what used to be a church, and it had a 60-foot cathedral ceiling. "You put a microphone in the middle of that room and you put a vocalist in there," says Dante, "and for some reason, the room sound carries into the vocal sound and makes it just a beautiful, angelic sound. It just helps the sound enormously. There are only a few places in the country you get a sound like that. Barry was ecstatic." To serve as engineer, Ron brought in Michael DeLugg, with whom he'd worked on numerous commercial recordings. "Out of the hundreds of people I'd worked with," says Ron, "he was the guy."

So, after all the care and attention they'd put into the production of this second album, it was with understandable pride and enthusiasm that Barry and Ron went to see Clive Davis to discuss the album as it neared completion. The pair were optimistic about the record's commercial chances, certain that the Manilow/Panzer-penned 'It's A Miracle' could well be a hit single. Davis, however, wasn't so sure.

By the time they left Clive's office, Barry had received a crash course in Hitmaking 101. Music was a business, Clive explained. It wasn't enough for Barry to produce songs, or even to produce good songs. He needed to produce *hit* songs, songs that would sell records. A successful album needed a hit single, something highly commercial, to make it sell. Without that, it didn't matter how good the album was musically – no one would hear it. "If you have a big hit single record, your career is made," Davis told Barry.

From the time Barry received his first transistor radio, he'd never been interested in the popular music of the day. With Bette, the songs she sang seemed almost incidental to the way she communicated them to her audiences. Now Barry was being told that it wasn't the quality of his music that would make him successful, but the quantity of it he could sell. "So I turned on my radio and listened to what the kids were buying," he later wrote, "and I started writing."

As it turned out he needn't have worried about writing a song that would fill Clive's commercial expectations. Instead, Clive brought the song to Barry.

'Brandy' had been a minor success in the United Kingdom in 1971 for British singer-songwriter Scott English, who had written the song with partner Richard Kerr. It was a harmless song, a paean to a rather sad girl who came and gave, yet neither demanded nor received anything in return except, apparently, a song to commemorate the coming and the giving. It was a sweet enough tune, though English's voice was a bit harsh and grating. As he listened to the recording Clive had sent over to him, as a producer and arranger, Barry could hear the song's possibilities. As a performer and a songwriter, however, he wasn't sure that he was ready to take the path down which he was certain this song would lead. Barry's most frequent songwriting partner, Marty Panzer, later wrote of Barry's struggle over the song, "Barry thought that if he recorded the song, none of his friends would ever speak to him again. I told him if he changed the song title to 'Mindy', as was suggested, I for one would certainly never speak to him again."

It was the same struggle artists had faced from the beginning of time: stay true to your creative integrity and risk obscurity, or compromise those creative impulses just enough to gain a foothold on that slippery ladder to success. "The truth was," Barry wrote of the outcome of his own personal struggle, "that I needed Clive Davis's support, and I reasoned that if I recorded something he was excited about, I'd get it." So Ron and Barry went into the studio and began trying to faithfully recreate the sound of Scott English's single, just as Clive wanted them to.

But when Clive dropped by the studio late that night to check on their progress, he hated what he heard. "It's exactly like the record you sent me," Barry told Davis. "Well," Davis replied, "it's all wrong. I hate it."

Tired and a bit desperate, plagued by nagging doubts about his choice to record the song in the first place, Barry asked Clive to come out of the control booth and join him at the piano. "You know, Clive, this afternoon, while I was learning the song at home, I played it as a ballad." Clive closed his eyes and listened to Barry play and sing a ballad version of the more upbeat English-Kerr tune, and he smiled. "That's it."

When the song had reached the top ten charts in England in 1971, Scott English had been the brief focus of intense media attention. During that time, English was summoned out of bed early one morning by a reporter phoning, wanting to know just who "Brandy" was. Sleepy and annoyed by the intrusion, English had blurted out, "It was a dog like Lassie and I had sent her away. Now you go away!" and hung up on the hapless journalist. Ever since English's sarcastic comment, though, the song has been dogged, so to speak, by the story that it was, indeed, written for a dog. "I guess I'll have to live with that story," says English.

A name change did seem in order for the song, though for different reasons. In 1971 Clive Davis, who was then head of Columbia Records, dropped by a New York City bar to watch the band Looking Glass perform after the group had sent him a demo tape. Among the songs in their set that night was one called 'Brandy'. Davis liked what he heard, and signed the group to Columbia's subsidiary, Epic Records. 'Brandy' had not been Epic's first choice of song to release as a single from Looking Glass's first album, but the tune had caught the attention of a Washington DC deejay whose constant on-air promotion had built up a strong local demand. It took a while, but 'Brandy', or 'Brandy (You're A Fine Girl)' to give it its full title, finally peaked at number one on the charts in August 1972.

Now, with the English-Kerr song, as recreated by Barry Manilow, Davis was facing another hit 'Brandy', which could prove confusing. "We decided to change the name from 'Brandy' to 'Mandy' right then," said Barry.

"So we did 'Mandy' during those sessions," says Ron Dante. "And I remember Barry saying to me, after we'd completed that album, 'I'm not sure I want to go in this direction.' I said, well, this is what you do very well. I don't know what else you want to do."

★

Perhaps even Barry no longer knew just what it was he wanted to do. But as 1974 turned into 1975 and 'Mandy' began racing its way up the charts, it seemed that the time had arrived for him to figure out just where he would go from here. 'Mandy' still came, and she still gave. But maybe this time, for Barry Manilow, the coming and the giving would no longer be without a price.

Chapter Twenty

By the mid-Seventies, American culture was ready to roll over and play placid, if not dead. And why not? The country had travelled over a rocky road of late, and the nation as a whole was weary of the bumpy ride.

While the Sixties had given the country "free love", "free love", in turn, had given the country a nasty case of venereal disease, with Federal health officials reporting some 2.3 million new cases of gonorrhea in 1972, as well as 100,000 new cases of infectious syphilis, the biggest increase for either disease since the introduction of antibiotics. Free love, it seemed, wasn't quite so free after all. And, as though confirming the price that must be paid for all pleasure, Jim Morrison, the last of a rock and roll trinity rounded out by Janis Joplin and Jimi Hendrix, tanked in a Paris bathtub in 1971, the victim of a good time which had proven itself just a bit too good.

Nineteen seventy-three saw the official end of the Vietnam war, and what looked to be the beginning of the end of President Richard Nixon. Nixon's insistence that "I am not a crook" would ultimately prove to be somewhat less than truthful after the Supreme Court forced release of tapes and transcripts of Oval Office conversations which revealed a cover-up first broken by reporters Bob Woodward and Carl Bernstein in the *Washington Post*. Five days after release of the tapes, Nixon resigned in disgrace, replaced by Vice President Gerald Ford, a man so bland and non-threatening as to make Mickey Mouse look like Mack the Knife. Nonetheless, Ford boldly, though unconvincingly, declared, "My fellow Americans, our long national nightmare is over."

Comedian Chevy Chase, on the new late-night comedy show *Saturday Night Live*, made an immediate hit with the show's audience by skewering the clumsy new president, who had an unfortunate habit of often tripping over his own feet. "I didn't need to do much to make him look silly," says Chase. "But he was also not a helluva lot brighter than a bundt cake."

Proving Clive Davis's admonition to Barry Manilow that a hit album needed only a hit single to make it sell, there were 35 different number one pop singles in 1974, the most ever for a single year. Reflecting the difficult transition from the "you say you want a revolution" attitude of the Sixties to the "please, god, just let it stop" surrender of the Seventies, the singles being sold were all over the spectrum, from teeny-bop pop tunes like the musical soap opera 'Billy, Don't Be A Hero' by Bo Donaldson & The Heywoods, to Bachman-Turner Overdrive's polished hard rock 'You Ain't Seen Nothin' Yet', to John Denver's nearly comatose 'Sunshine On My Shoulders'. With so many hit singles to choose from, it's no wonder that the most popular albums being snapped up by the American record buying public were "greatest hit" type collections, such as Elton John's *Greatest Hits*, the top selling album of 1974.

While the Vietnam war had ended on paper in 1973, the true end for Americans came when US helicopters evacuated 1,373 Americans and 5,595 Vietnamese from Saigon, ending a "conflict" that had cost 1.3 million Vietnamese and 56,000 American lives, leaving Cambodia and South Vietnam to Communist forces. For the first time in its history of marching confidently off to war and marching home again, unfailingly victorious, Americans this time couldn't really answer the question, *What were we fighting for?* Asked of Vietnam, the only answer seemed to be, *For about fourteen years.*[7]

"Nineteen seventy-five was probably the tipping point," says *Rolling Stone* writer P.J. Rourke. "We're finally realizsing the Sixties didn't work out, and that we have given up previous beliefs but

---

[7] Manilow himself was drafted in August, 1964. According to his Selective Service records, he was given a 1-Y classification, which essentially declared him basically fit for service, but in some way undesirable. It was a popular classification for homosexuals and others the government considered undesirable yet difficult to categorise in an accurate yet acceptable way. The 1-Y classification was abolished in December, 1971, due in part to pressure from gay rights groups. After that time, those who were previously classified as 1-Y were switched to a classification of 1-H: "Registrant not currently subject to processing for induction or alternate service."

haven't acquired new ones that are worth anything."

Even the Jefferson Airplane, who, in the Sixties, had admonished the world to "Go ask Alice" in their psychedelic heyday had now decided to flow with the more mellow times, dubbing themselves the Jefferson Starship and finding a hit with their laid-back ballad 'Miracles'. Band member Paul Kantner is defensive about the group's decision to roll over and play dead rather than actually being dead, a victim of changing times. "I'm a musician," Kantner told VH1, "and I get to play whatever the fuck I want. And if you don't like it, well, fuck you."

"People were tired of the bad thoughts, the depressing thoughts, the cynical thoughts," says Toni Tennille. Tennille, with her husband Daryl Dragon, formed the successful duo Captain & Tennille, whose sugary song 'Love Will Keep Us Together' was the single biggest hit of 1975. "I still think that in a lot of people's hearts they wanted to feel good, one more time."

"It was so contrived!" protests author Legs McNeil, co-editor of the chronicle *Please Kill Me: The Uncensored Oral History of Punk*, of the fizzy Seventies sound that was rapidly rising from the ruins of the Sixties. "It was crap! There wasn't an authentic emotion in any of that."

But the people of America were surrounded by harsh reality, and the last thing they needed in the mid-Seventies was more "authentic emotion". They had just limped through a disastrous war; one out of every ten Americans was unemployed; inflation was increasing by 12% a year, the fastest rise since the Great Depression. Gas stations were running out of fuel; the price of meat had rendered the Sunday pot roast a luxury item.

"The American people are turning sullen," said Diane Christensen, Faye Dunaway's character in Paddy Chayefsky's movie *Network*. "They've been clobbered on all sides by Vietnam, Watergate, the Inflation, the Depression; they've turned off, shot up and fucked themselves limp and nothing helps . . ." It's little wonder, then, that a weary nation, clutching their Pet Rocks, frequently consulting their mood rings, and desperately begging each other to "*Have a Nice Day!*", was ready for the reassuring placidity of Barry Manilow.

Barry's act now consisted of Alan Axelrod, who augmented Barry's keyboard work, Sid McGinnis on guitar, Steve Donaghey on bass, and Lee Gurst on drums and percussion. Bette's Harlettes had been replaced by Barry's own singers, Debra Byrd, Ramona Brooks, and Lee Gurst's favourite, Reparata, a.k.a. Lorraine Mazzola. "The Flashy Ladies", as they were first dubbed, hadn't been born without a bit of drama.

"Sharon, Robin and I went out with Barry while Bette was in Europe," says Harlette Charlotte Crossley. It was no secret that Barry had taken advantage of The Harlettes' down time during Bette's vacation to use the backup trio for his own show. But after Bette's return and the group's final tour with Barry as pianist/musical director, Barry needed to put together his own group of backup singers and musicians. "So," Barry told an interviewer, "I figured as long as I had decided on that type of group for Bette, I decided on that type of group for me because they sounded best behind me." So Barry approached Harlette Charlotte Crossley. "Later on," Crossley told an interviewer, "Barry was putting together another backup group of his own and he wanted me to join it. Bette was putting together her new show, and she wanted me, too."

Apparently Barry wasn't one for the hard sell. Recalls Crossley, Barry said to her, "'I really want you, but I know that [Bette's] gonna offer you a lot more money. I respect that – and I know that you love her.'" Charlotte promised Barry she'd get back to him that day.

After her discussion with Barry, Charlotte arrived home to find that Bette had been frantically trying to reach her. "I sensed that as soon as she found out Barry wanted me, her attitude was, 'I'm not gonna let her go!'" says Crossley. Charlotte got Bette on the phone and told the desperate diva to calm down, Charlotte would be right over to talk with her. "Why can't you tell me over the phone?" said Bette. Charlotte said, "I'll see you in a little while." When she arrived it was a difficult confrontation but Crossley's commitment remained solid. She went on to perform with Bette on Broadway in Midler's hit *Bette Midler's Clams On The Half Shell Revue*.

Despite his efforts to woo at least one of The Harlettes into his act, even as 'Mandy' hit the number one spot on record charts nationwide, Barry was still struggling to gain recognition as Barry Manilow, solo performer, rather than as an appendage to Bette Midler. In the fall of 1975, when an interviewer asked Barry if there was any possibility of Barry and Bette working together again in any capacity, Barry's immediate answer was a blunt, "No." Then he softened his answer by citing his lack of time since 'Mandy's success, then added, "It's too soon for me to go out with Bette as a duet. There's not enough people who know what I do and she still wants to do it by herself. Maybe. I don't know, in a couple of years we'll wind up with Bette and Barry." Then, alluding to his often rocky relationship with Bette, Barry outlined the shape of a heart in the air with his finger and added, "In a little heart, they get in the middle of a boxing ring . . ."

There's no doubt it was difficult for Barry to let go of Bette. There might have been some residual feeling of unworthiness on Barry's part to carry an act on his own, but, by his own admission, he'd gotten more comfortable with performing and interacting with the audience as the success of his second album had made it necessary. "I was thrown out from behind the piano!" he laughingly told an interviewer. But his strength, he still felt, was in being a strong arranger, someone who could put together such a solid show that, as he put it, "if I fainted on the stage nobody should know it. The act would be so good, so strong, that nobody would realise that I was just dying up there if it happened."

For all Barry's self-deprecation, co-producer and friend Ron Dante never doubted Barry's ability to carry a show. "He's a consummate stager," says Dante. "Every time you see him perform, he's designing the way it looks, the way you're being exposed to it. He'll bring in people that do the dances and do this and that, but basically he's controlling most of it." In fact, early on in their collaboration Barry said to Ron, "I have a third eye; I can see what I look like on stage, and I will design it so I look like the star." Says Dante, "I thought it was very interesting that he could actually step outside of himself and look at what he was doing. I said, that is a great quality. If you can do that and be talented and fix it and make it better, that's a quality that'll take you far."

Barry's vision for staging his show didn't end with himself. He was involved in every aspect of what went on both onstage and off, right down to his backup singers' make-up and dress. "Barry wanted glamour in his show," says Lady Flash member Debra Byrd. "When he would get ready to do shows, he would say, 'Debra, your make-up is too tasteful. You have the look of a secretary.'" Barry himself had been using stage makeup since he worked the smallest dives with Jeanne Lucas in the mid-Sixties, and he showed his girls how to apply the proper amount of colour to their faces. "We were in the dressing room having this tug of war," says Byrd. " 'More red!' *'No!'* 'YES! You need *MORE RED!* ' "

But his backup singers soon learned to trust Barry's instincts about such things as make-up and clothing. "Barry knows how to anticipate trends," Reparata has said. "We saw it when he would say to us, 'Those shoes with the spike heels that you don't want to wear, everybody's going to be wearing them soon.' And sure enough, the next thing you know. He did that with music, he did that with his whole, entire act." As though confirming what Barry told Ron about his "third eye", Reparata went on to say, "He's also the first person I've seen, as far as live production, who can *see* a song on stage, as well as how it's going to sound."

"So we put it together," Barry explained, of his early stage show, "and it came out real strong, and it gave me a foundation to be able to make mistakes as a performer, because the basis was so strong, the music and the girls singing and the band, even if I did get lost in it, the act would still look powerful. I didn't want to give the whole burden to me, because I'd never done it before, and yet here I was headlining in Philadelphia, and headlining all over the place. I had never done that before. Little by little, I got into it. Now I really enjoy it; I really enjoy performing. I like the music, and I like *making* the music, and I like the audience reacting; because I'm doing it for them. So it's a nice trip."

At this stage of the game, it was a nice road trip. Arista wanted to make the most of the success of 'Mandy' and, by association, the success of *Barry Manilow II*, as the second album had been cleverly dubbed. So the record company sent Barry and his group out on the road. The show was received enthusiastically in 1975 as it made its way from the midwest to the west coast. The tour's success had Barry flying high. But the return to New York and an appearance at the Westbury Music Fair would quickly bring him back to earth again, with a thud.

Thanks to the corrosive effects of time and the vagaries of perception, there are differing accounts of exactly what happened at Westbury in May of 1975, but all agree on the main fact: Harold Keliher, the father Barry hadn't seen in over 15 years, arrived backstage wanting to see his son.

Friend and drummer Lee Gurst tells his version of the incident: "It was very awkward. Not openly angry, but very, very strained. The road manager came to the dressing room after the show – it was on Long Island – and said, 'Your dad's here and wants to say hello.' I was going to excuse myself. I thought, this isn't something he'd want anybody around for. And he said, 'No, no, no, stay put.' Not in the sense of, 'You don't need to bother,' but 'It's not going to get intimate and personal and I have no reason for you not to be here; I want somebody around.' And they met at the door for maybe a minute. His father said, 'Congratulations. You did a good job.' And Barry said, 'Thanks.' And 'Well, take care.' 'Yeah, you too.' And that was it. Barry would often, if there was a meeting or a talk or something, and that person would leave the room, then Barry would make a comment under his breath, like, 'what an asshole' or something like that. And as I recall he said some kind of remark about his father. It was 'what a something or other' – I don't remember the word; it was certainly dismissive and perhaps even very . . . Barry was being tough. And he could make the statement this wasn't going to get to him, and that's how it went. As briefly and quietly as all of that, and then it was over. I mean I don't think it lasted sixty seconds. There was no tearful reunion."

Manilow's account of the incident was quite a bit different. While Lee Gurst remembers several people being present during Barry's meeting with his father, Barry has said that it was only himself and Linda Allen who were in the dressing room at the time.

Barry had met Linda Allen many years previously, when he was working as musical director for *Callback!* at CBS, and Linda was working as production assistant for the same show. Though frequently identified as Barry's romantic interest ("Linda was very enamoured in the beginning," says Jeanne Lucas), in truth the two had developed a trusting, platonic friendship over the years, often living together. According to friends, the arrangement provided not only stability and companionship for Barry, but also a convenient cover story for those who would insist on questioning his sexual orientation. "Linda was a good friend who I think was supportive in the extreme, who didn't want anything in terms of his work," says Lee Gurst. "Linda didn't want to go on the road, Linda didn't want to be a musician or a writer or be in the spotlight. You know, she was just there to be supportive and not looking to get anything in terms of a career. She had her own work and she did very well with that. She was occasionally around on the road, though not very often. You know, a big concert, a special event, something like that. Nice, bright lady." Ron Dante concurs. "They were really close. She was a hoot. A very funny lady, a pleasure to be around. One of those people you meet when you go, 'Loved her, hated him.' You loved her. She was one of those girls. I thought she was the best thing for Barry. Great sense of humour, very comical, very sensitive to him. He adored her."

According to Barry, he and Linda were alone in his dressing room after the show, Barry in the middle of undressing, when an older man opened the door and stuck his head in and announced he was Barry's father. ("That wasn't likely to happen at a Barry Manilow concert," says Lee Gurst, in response to this part of Barry's account. "Security was very tight.")

"I just wanted to see ya one more time. You did a good job out there," Harold said, according to Barry's account of the incident. Then, Barry says, he thanked his father and invited him in, an invitation Harold declined. "Nope. Don't wanna bother you." In his autobiography, Barry wrote, "We stood and stared at each other like that for a long minute. Then, 'Gotta go. Bye.' And he was gone."

"No, no, no, no!" says Harold's widow, Annie Keliher, when she hears Barry's version of the incident. "Barry *threw* my husband out that night. He did *not* welcome him. I'll swear on a bible. His attitude was *Who needs you? You're never around! Get out!* And that's when I understand Linda, the way my husband put it, she was saying, 'Please, Barry, talk to him,' and Barry more or less said to her, 'Keep out of it.'"

Both seem to agree on that fact that the encounter upset Linda. (Lee Gurst doesn't remember Linda being in the room at all.) "Watching Linda cry made me want to get emotional, too," Manilow wrote of the incident, "but I couldn't. I didn't feel anything for this man."

This much Annie Keliher doesn't doubt. "Of course. That I can understand. Absolutely," she says. In all the years since Barry was 16 and he and his father had briefly worked together at Schaeffer Brewery, Harold Keliher had never made any attempt to contact his son, nor had Barry made any attempt to contact his father. As Barry pointed out, to do so would have upset the family and he "didn't want to make waves", the exact same phrase Annie Keliher uses to explain Harold's reasons for not pursuing his son. Barry's grandmother, says Annie, was so violently opposed to Harold's presence in Barry's life, that Harold eventually caved in to her pressure. "When Kelly would bring up Barry," Annie says, "he would always say he had to get away from Edna, they had to drop it because of her mother. The friction was terrible, terrible, terrible, terrible." Instead Harold had simply resigned himself to the loss of his first son, pouring everything he had into loving Tim, the son he and Annie had together, as well as fathering Annie's son and daughter from her previous marriage. "I often wondered how Barry must have felt," says Annie Keliher. *"Here my father is leaning toward three children and he neglected me."*

Now here was Harold, showing up after all these years, trying to horn in on his son's success. At least, that's how Barry viewed Harold's sudden reappearance. "I think he had great bitterness toward his father," says Ron Dante, of Barry's feelings about the Westbury incident. "He was insulted by his father showing up, I think. I just got it second hand, but I was there that night, and I know his face was ashen and he was like in shock that this person had showed up, now that he's a big success, he's on TV and radio and all that stuff."

The timing was, indeed, unfortunate, but for entirely different reasons than Barry imagined.

Esther Manilow, the formidable force that had both kept the Manilow family together and torn the Pincus family apart, died from a heart attack in January 1975. "When she died I knew I had lost something very profound," Barry later wrote. Harold, on the other hand, saw Esther's death as his first opportunity to reclaim his son, something that had never seemed possible as long as Esther was alive. But by the time Harold got word of Esther's death, Barry was on the road promoting his second album, a tour that continued into the spring. The first opportunity Harold had to approach his son was after Barry's return to New York, to perform at the Westbury Music Fair. By then Barry's success seemed firmly established, and, for that reason, Harold's motives for wanting to see his son were questioned.

"I didn't blame Barry," says Annie Keliher, of Barry's doubts about Harold's motives. "In other words, *Here you are when I'm rich; why weren't you there when I needed you?* But my husband used to say,

'It isn't that; I want to wish him luck.' I'd say, Kelly, it's too late, love. It's too late."

What Annie does take exception to, though, is the self-pitying tone Barry seems to take over his lack of information about his father. "There are still dozens of questions unanswered," Manilow wrote of his father in his 1987 autobiography. "So he should ask them!" is Annie Keliher's immediate response. "I'm sorry," she says, "I don't want these damn excuses. He's a man. No reason he couldn't pick up the phone."

Barry had, in fact, kept in contact with Annie over the years, rather pointedly excluding his father from the communication. Annie fondly recalls, after she and Kelly had moved away from New York, getting a call at their Las Vegas home from Barry's assistant, at the height of Barry's success, inviting Annie – and only Annie – to attend Barry's concert at the Sahara Hotel and Casino.

"My husband picked up the phone," Annie recalls, "and Kelly said, 'It's for you.' It was Barry's secretary – very nice young man – saying that Barry would like me to attend the show." Annie was reluctant at first, but Barry's assistant was persuasive. "Please, come, Barry will be very, very disappointed. Just say you are Anna Keliher when you come up to the door."

Though undoubtedly hurt at not being included in the invitation, Harold Keliher encouraged his wife to attend. "My husband told me to go and enjoy myself," she says. "He always talked that way."

Annie's name at the door did, indeed, get her VIP treatment. She and her guests (she doesn't now recall exactly who she ended up taking in lieu of her husband) were escorted to one of the reserved booths at the front of the room, near the stage. Edna was seated at a nearby booth just behind them, with three men, one of whom Annie recognised from their old neighbourhood in Brooklyn. "Edna is making signs she wants you to turn around," one of Annie's guests said to her, which rather confused Annie. "What the hell does she want from me?" she responded. When she did turn, Edna gestured for her to come over to their booth. "Stupid, stupid me," says Annie, rather chagrined now by her response then. "I said to [my guests], 'I'm not getting up, let her come to me.'" By the time the show ended, Annie had changed her mind but, when she turned, Edna's booth was already vacant.

As Annie and her guests waited for the crowd to diminish so they could leave, Annie felt a tap on her shoulder. It was Barry's assistant who said, "Anna, Barry would like to see you backstage." Annie said no. "I said, 'I'm not going – I don't like this,'" Annie explains. "And I meant that this is too much celebrity, I wanna go home." But the assistant again persevered. "Please, Barry insists that you come backstage." But Annie was just as adamant. "Look, give my love to Barry and tell him no thank you, but I appreciate the show."

The assistant retreated, only to return moments later. "We're still sitting because the place was packed with people," Annie recalls. "Barry was just starting to get famous. [The assistant] comes back again. He says, 'Please, please, don't disappoint Barry.'" This time Annie agreed, leaving her guests and following Barry's assistant backstage.

"Ever go backstage?" she asks. "It's eerie. It's actually eerie, the curtain, the things. And we're walking and walking, and we hit a certain area, big security guard comes. I guess that was his job. And I'm with Barry's assistant who tells the guard, 'This is Barry's mother.'" Either the guard didn't know Edna or he didn't see it as his place to question Barry's assistant. Either way, he let Barry's assistant and Barry's "mother" pass.

"And Barry came out," Annie recalls. "And he ran to me and he picked me up, kissed me." Barry had changed quite a bit from the time he was a boy in Brooklyn, playing the accordion with Harold's grandmother in their one-bedroom flat on Sundays. Now his hair was bleached blond, and, at the moment he kissed Annie, his face was covered in stage make-up. "I said Barry, you look like somebody put your head in cement!" laughs Annie. "Brick colour. Everything was orange!" And he was barefoot, which Annie couldn't help commenting on in light of Barry's newfound riches. "I said, 'Oh, Barry, can't you afford a pair of slippers? I'm going to get you some.' And he laughed, 'Oh, Annie!'"

Annie was invited into the dressing room where she was introduced to the others there. Barry and Annie exchanged pleasantries for a while, then they said their goodbyes. "And that was the last time I spoke to him," says Annie. He never inquired about his father during their visit.

In his autobiography, Barry writes: "I hear my friends calling their fathers Dad, and I wonder how that word would sound on my tongue. Sometimes I say it to myself and it feels funny. Hi Dad. Hey

Pop, I'm home. Happy Father's Day, Daddy. I wonder sometimes what it would have been like to play ball with him in the park. I wonder what ails him. Does he have the same kind of sensitive stomach I do?"

"No," says Annie, in answer to the question. Then she goes on to answer all the other questions Barry poses to the general public, though never to the one man who could have answered them the best.

"Does he tan well the way I do?"

"Yes."

"Is he moody like me?"

"No, my husband was funny as hell."

"How musical is he?"

"Very! My husband had a voice . . . if we were out, like at a wedding, and he got up and sang, he'd get a standing ovation. And so was his grandma, Harold's mother, Anna. Music, music, music – it had to come out on Barry."

"I stood looking at the empty hallway and trying to think of what I needed from him. I needed him to have been there when I was growing up. And he couldn't give me that back."

No, he couldn't. But he tried, efforts Annie discouraged, knowing them to be futile. When, some time later, Harold decided to attend another of Barry's appearances at the Las Vegas Hilton, security somehow became alerted to his presence on the ticket line, and guards approached him and told him that Barry had asked for him to leave. "My husband was always with his mouth bragging," says Annie, "and I just would want to hide in a closet because it was embarrassing, and partly not true. You wouldn't be standing on line if you were a guest of Barry's. And something must have gone through security or back to Barry, and security came over and said – this is my husband telling me, like as if he's sitting here – says, 'Mr Keliher, please leave, you're making Barry very, very nervous.' Politely, they escorted him, but they actually threw him out." One look at her husband's face when he came home that day, and Annie instantly knew what had happened. "I used to say, boy, Kelly, you're a glutton for punishment."

Then Annie stresses a point that she has stressed before. "I am not siding with my husband," she says, though she adds in his defence, "You make mistakes in life, and boy, did he make mistakes, where his son was concerned anyway." They were mistakes that he couldn't alter, nor could he let go. "I went through hell with this baloney with Barry and him," says Annie. "It was ugly, ugly, a lot of times."

Annie Keliher similarly cautioned her son, Tim, the few times he expressed interest in kindling some sort of relationship with Barry. "I always hollered at my Timmy – *stay out of it!* Barry will never acknowledge you as a half-brother. Stop making a fool out of yourself." But Tim's curiosity about his half-brother was too strong. "He met Barry going backstage somewhere," Annie recalls, "and that was it, it was very casual. I had warned him, I said, 'Timmy, why are you starting with Barry? If he was interested in you and it was meant to be, on given occasions you would have met him. But this is stupid. What do you want Barry to do?' And he went against my wishes. Barry, I understand, was very polite. But it didn't mean anything."

But for all his outward indifference toward his father, obviously Barry's feelings for Harold ran deeper than he wanted to admit. When Harold, already ailing with cancer, was admitted to the hospital in the mid-Eighties for brain surgery, somehow Barry found out.

"I don't know how Barry found out," says Annie Keliher, still puzzled. "My husband had tumours removed from the brain. And he was still in intensive care, and the family – my sons and daughter – were in. I remember standing around the bed, and I just happened to turn, and I saw somebody carrying a big vase of flowers. And it was like a – how would you say it? How do you mean when you have a couple of senses?" Somehow, despite the long silence from Barry, Annie instantly knew who had sent the flowers. "I had that card for years," she says, "and it just said, 'Kelly' – it didn't say dad – 'Best wishes, Barry.' That's when I turned to my daughter and I said, 'Look at this. How are you supposed to answer to this?' And it was sad."

It was a gesture that would have meant the world to Harold Keliher who, as fate would have it, never recovered from his operation, though he lived for several years after. "He never came out of it," says Annie. "He never knew those flowers were there."

Harold Keliher died on June 11, 1993. Barry was performing at the Teatro Fundidora in Monterey, Mexico at the time. If he knew of his father's passing, he never acknowledged it either publicly or to Annie Keliher and her children. In the obituary that ran in the Las Vegas *Review-Journal* two days after his death, Harold Keliher's survivors were listed as his widow, Anna, his son, Tim, his stepson, Walter, and his daughter (actually, stepdaughter) Carol. Barry Manilow's name was not mentioned.

Chapter Twenty-one

With 'Mandy' going gold just weeks after its release, Arista quickly released another single from the *Barry Manilow II* album. Barry's long-time collaborator Marty Panzer co-wrote the song with Barry, and likes to tell this story of the song's impetus:

Barry called from somewhere on the road and said, "I have an idea for a song, but I stole the title from you."

"Oh, really?" I said.

"Well, every time I call you and tell you about some incredible thing that's happened, you say the same thing. EVERY time," he said. "So I'd like to use it as the title."

"You wrote a song called 'HOLY SHIT!'?"

Actually, the song was 'It's A Miracle', and its up-tempo optimism was the perfect counterpoint to the slower, more poignant 'Mandy'. While it didn't do as well as 'Mandy', 'It's A Miracle' still did well, quickly landing in the top ten. It was enough to make Barry start rethinking his first album, which hadn't done at all well when first released. Now, fuelled by the success of the second album, perhaps the first album could be reworked and re-released with more success.

Toward this end, Ron and Barry went back into the studio in April 1975 and concentrated on four songs from the original album. With new versions of 'One Of These Days', 'Oh, My Lady', 'Sweet Life' and 'Could It Be Magic', Arista released the slightly altered version of *Barry Manilow* as *Barry Manilow I*. 'Could It Be Magic' was selected as the magic single to make the album move. While Barry had loved the song since it had first presented itself to him in his studio apartment on 27th Street so many years before, he felt it was a

140

long shot for single success. Again, though, he relied on Clive Davis's infallible instincts.

"We sold like 35,000 copies of my first album," Barry told an interviewer in 1975, "and it was sold on the basis of 'Could It Be Magic' Everybody kept showing it to their friends on the basis of 'Could It Be Magic' and then the second album came out, and 'Mandy' and 'Miracle' [were released], and Clive heard 'Magic' and said, 'You know, you should have done something with that.'" But, as Barry pointed out to Clive, what were the chances of radio stations playing a seven-minute cut, let alone one based on a Chopin prelude? But Barry and Ron were busy working on Barry's third album so, he reasoned, if 'Could It Be Magic' tanked, people would be too busy paying attention to the third album to notice another single from *Barry Manilow I*. "I think it's time to try it now," Clive told Barry. "You can't lose anything."

As always, Clive's reasoning was sound. By the time the third album, *Tryin' To Get The Feeling* was released in October, the single 'Could It Be Magic' had already achieved gold status and was well on its way to platinum, as was *Barry Manilow I*.

Even though Barry had come to rely on Clive's instincts, still, Clive's suggestions regarding use of outside material wreaked havoc on Barry's already sometimes shaky self-esteem. "My strength as a songwriter was continually challenged," Barry later wrote. "Clive and I played the game of *his* hit songs versus *my* hit songs after 'Mandy' became number one." As a result, Barry had vowed that 'Mandy' would be the last outside song he recorded. Clive, however, had other ideas.

Just as he had plucked 'Mandy' from obscurity to serve as Barry's vehicle to the number one spot on *Billboard* charts, for *Tryin' To Get The Feeling* Clive presented Barry with another unlikely number he was sure would be a hit.

'I Write The Songs' was written by Bruce Johnston who was best known for having taken over from Brian Wilson as The Beach Boys "touring" bass player. But Johnston was more than just a mere session man, he was a songwriter too and had contributed to The Beach Boys' song catalogue over the years, most notably with the evocative 'Disney Girls' on their *Surfs Up* album in 1971. By the time he wrote 'I Write The Songs', he'd officially left The Beach Boys, though his services would be called upon again from time to time, but the song had done nothing for the three acts who had already recorded it.

Clive sent all three versions to Barry's apartment. Barry listened as the song's creator, Bruce Johnston, sang the song. He then heard pop idol David Cassidy's version, and, finally, he listened to Captain & Tennille's take on it. Barry felt he could sympathise with the song's lyric, "*I am music, and I write the songs.*" It was, he understood, a tribute to the power of music to manifest itself through the song-writer, who became simply the tool of the music itself. Barry under-stood the concept because he lived with it on a daily basis. "Sometimes when I'd listened to my own work, I'd been surprised at what I'd been able to do," he explained. "Sometimes it had felt that I really had nothing to do with the writing." But the average record buyer would not have had such an experience to draw upon. Without it, the song could come off as an egotistical paean by a song-writer praising himself for his own magnificence. Barry still often felt as though he had one hell of a nerve expecting people to pay good money to see him pretend to be a singer. He certainly didn't relish the thought of thousands of people thinking that he felt he was, as Bette used to call him, "Mr Music". Barry told Clive he didn't want to do the song.

Clive didn't make suggestions lightly, nor countenance opposition to his proven wisdom. "You're being foolish and childish," he told Barry, who was taken aback at the vehemence of his response. "You're a terrific arranger and producer. With the right elements, this could be a number one record for you. They don't come along easily, Barry. You really shouldn't turn this down."

Manilow says that he continued to decline while Davis contin-ued to press until Barry finally weakened and, reluctantly, agreed. *Tryin' To Get The Feeling*[8] went gold two weeks after its release. Of course Clive's instincts were proven once again dead on: 'I Write The Songs', the first single released from the album in October

---

[8] *Tryin' To Get The Feeling* would mark a subtle shift in the production credits on Barry's album. For *Barry Manilow/Barry Manilow I* and *Barry Manilow II*, the produc-tion credit read "Produced by Barry Manilow and Ron Dante". Starting with *Tryin' To Get The Feeling*, the production credit, at Barry's suggestion, read "Produced by Ron Dante and Barry Manilow", an order that continued until their collaboration ended.

1975, shot up the charts. Just as 1975 had started with 'Mandy' in the number one position, January 1976 saw 'I Write The Songs' in the top spot.

"I think he was awestruck by the incredible power of a few hit records," Ron Dante speculates. "And the incredible power of a good performance to thrust him into the public limelight and make him the number one artist for the next two or three years, he was the number one recording artist in America. When *Cashbox* and *Billboard* would come out with their year-end list, there would be the top male solo singers, the top guy – Barry Manilow."

It was true. When lists were released in early 1976 for the year just ended, Barry's numbers were staggering: he'd sold over four million singles in 1975, and over 1.6 million albums. Both *Record World* and *Cashbox* had voted him the Top New Male Vocalist in both the "Singles" and "Albums" categories. *Music Retailer* named him the Top New Male Artist for the year, and *Radio & Records* proclaimed him the Pop Artist of the Year. And, when it seemed nothing more could be added to the pile of accolades, the nominations for Grammy Awards were announced. Not surprisingly, 'Mandy' was among the nominees for Record of the Year.[9]

"I think he was not prepared for the enormous success that came," says Dante, "and the adulation and the people and the money, and the TV shows – I don't think he was prepared for the onslaught of people wanting a piece of him, and wanting to just talk to him. He was like the background guy; he was the piano player, he was the arranger. And all of a sudden he was the focal point of every place he walked in. People would point and say [whispering] *Look, there's Barry Manilow!* The type of records we started to make, other producers would say, 'let's Manilow-ise this record.' His kind of record became a thing that people copied. Personally I think he was not prepared for the success."

It would seem not. "*Am I going crazy?*" Barry scribbled in his journal in November, 1975. He had surpassed his hopes, surpassed those under whom he used to subordinate himself. After years of hustling, years of juggling the different pieces of his life in order to

---

[9] Other nominees in the category were Janis Ian's 'At Seventeen', The Eagles' 'Lyin' Eyes', Glen Campbell's 'Rhinestone Cowboy' and, the Grammy winner, 'Love Will Keep Us Together' by The Captain & Tennille.

accommodate his musical dreams, suddenly it was all coming true – not gradually, but all at once. And, as was true with Herman Hesse's *Steppenwolf*, "what he strove for with the deepest and most stubborn instinct of his being fell to his lot, but more than is good for men. In the beginning his dream and his happiness, in the end it was his bitter fate."

Chapter Twenty-two

In the fifty-two weeks of 1975, Barry had made over forty concert appearances in thirty-six cities, appeared on the popular television shows *American Bandstand*, *Saturday Night Live*, *Don Kirshner's Rock Concert*, and *The Midnight Special* – twice. He released two albums, both of which he co-produced, and three singles, all of which were smash hits. He'd been honoured and awarded and named and cited by just about everyone who had the power to officially do so, and a few who didn't. In short, it seemed he had achieved everything he'd ever dreamed of achieving, and so much more.

So why, then, wasn't Barry Manilow happy?

"Suddenly my life was out of control," he would later write. "Success had literally exploded over me, wrenching me out of what had been a normal life and thrusting me into something quite different. My roots were pulled out of New York and I felt like a wanderer. Now there were limousines, hotel suites, people taking care of my every whim. I was accepting awards right and left. Of course it was flattering, but it was terrifying, too." *Beware what you wish for,* wise men have said, and for good reason. "The shows got bigger and the crowds got bigger . . ." Manilow has said. ". . . It was wonderful and terrible."

"Barry Manilow was becoming something much bigger than he had ever started out," says Lee Gurst. "That put a lot of pressure on him. He couldn't just go out and eat after a show, and he couldn't just go for a walk in a shopping centre if he wanted to. He didn't have the freedom he did before. When you lose that freedom, you begin to feel the pressure of the fans . . . and being well known and recognisable. It's hard to adjust to."

"I didn't know what to do to alleviate the agony of this pressure," Barry would later tell a reporter for *Rolling Stone* magazine. "At that point, most people turn to drugs, and I can understand it, believe me. Instead, I hollered. I was abusive: bratty, throwing tantrums, being selfish, temperamental, inconsiderate. I was pretty much of a total asshole. I really believed that I was better than others, but in my heart I knew I wasn't. And the danger was that the people around you want to keep their jobs, so they indulge you."

Another journalist who visited Barry in his 27th Street apartment just after the Grammy nominations were announced in January 1976 noted this strain, which seemed to be manifesting itself physically. "Up close, Manilow looks somewhat older than the 30 years to which he admits . . ." the reporter wrote. "Dark baleful circles underline his eyes and weariness is visible through the Gulden's-mustard tan. Manilow looks like a Holiday Inn lounge pianist who has been asked to play 'Misty' too many times." The interviewer does go on to charitably note that on the day of their visit, Barry is not in top form. "For a New Year's present," Barry told his visitor, "God decided to give me a Grammy nomination for 'Mandy' and the most miserable cold in the history of the human race."

Apparently Barry recovered in ample time to attend the Grammy awards on February 28, 1976, having survived the additional crisis of finding a tuxedo for the evening that would fit his skinny behind. "Can't you take them in or something?" he'd snapped at the tailor, who was busy working on the tuxedo trousers during the reporter's visit in January. "There's enough room for another ass in here." Assuring Barry that he'd take care of the problem, the tailor had gathered up his things and made a hasty exit. Then Barry had rolled his eyes to the ceiling and said to the reporter, "Now there's the most startling fact you could write about me. If Barry Manilow is supposed to be so fuckin' slick, if he's supposed to be such a putzy, schlocky, slick guy, how come he still doesn't even own a freakin' tuxedo?"

The white tuxedo he wore to accept the sixth annual *After Dark* Ruby Award as "Entertainer of the Year" in April seemed to fit him just fine, as did the honour. Broadway star Chita Rivera, her false eyelashes giving the appearance of a pair of wild tarantulas trying to seize control of her face, presented the award to Barry who, she said, "can write the songs, and he can also sing them". It seems fitting that Bette Midler had preceded Barry as a recipient of the Ruby Award, which she had received from the magazine in 1972. At the time Bette had been going through her own identity crisis brought on by

146

her then burgeoning fame. That night she'd ended up fleeing to the kitchen of the restaurant where the award party was being held and refusing to come out for photographers, leading to a screaming match between Bette and one of the *After Dark* staffers, who ended up slapping the singer in the face. A tearful Miss M spent the remainder of the evening drinking whiskey with Lucille Ball in the back seat of a limousine in the restaurant's parking lot.

But that was Bette, whose life was made of drama. For his part, Barry told the audience of show business luminaries, "I had this terrific speech all prepared for the Grammys which I never got to make." He then proceeded to make use of the speech, thanking everyone from Clive Davis to Ron Dante to Miles Lourie and everyone in between, including Lady Flash (as the backup trio had come to be known by the third album). "I've been doing what I have been doing for ten years and nobody cared, until I teamed up with the right people to do what I do best." The evening was capped off with a surprise from Clive Davis, who presented Barry with a platinum record for *Tryin' To Get The Feeling*, certifying the sale of one million copies of the album.

Asked by an interviewer once if he believed in God, Barry answered, "Yes. His name is Clive Davis, and he's the head of my record company." In many ways it did seem as though Davis was Barry's creator, though, some of his associates have said, not to the extent that might be believed. "Barry manages Barry," Lee Gurst once told an interviewer. "Barry is the one who plans his career. Barry Manilow is a Barry Manilow production."

In fact, Barry was adamant that, after succumbing to Clive's insistence on including outside music on *Barry Manilow II* and *Tryin' To Get The Feeling*, his fourth album would be all his own. Indeed, nine of the songs released on the fourth album, *This One's For You*, were songs Barry had co-written with long-time friends and collaborators Marty Panzer, Adrienne Anderson, and Bruce Sussman. But, again, Clive had a suggestion.

'Weekend In New England' was written by Randy Edelman, who had released the song on his own album for 20th Century Records in 1975. The song had come to Clive's attention, and he contacted Randy to let him know that he wanted to pass the song on to Barry. When Randy called to discuss the matter with Clive, Clive immediately began telling the song's creator precisely what he felt was wrong with the song and what he should do to make it better. "I really couldn't believe it," said Edelman. "I mean, most record company presidents don't even know what's going on their albums even after they're out, and here's Clive Davis giving me suggestions about how to rewrite a song when the guy who's going to record it hasn't even heard it yet." But with Clive's suggested changes, 'Weekend In New England' became just the kind of song Barry had wanted to make when he tried to explain to Tony Orlando how 'Could It Be Magic' should start out small, then build to a "musical orgasm" before gently easing the listener back down again. 'Looks Like We Made It' followed a similar pattern, a slow build to a grand release or, as co-author Will Jennings puts it, "another of those beautiful, over-the-top-don't-spare-the-melodrama melodies." Each of these songs would become major hits for Barry.

If Barry had a third eye for making himself look like a star on stage, Clive had what might then be termed a third ear for making Barry sound like a star on his albums. With Clive's unfailing instinct for picking the hits, and Barry's sometimes reluctant acquiescence to Clive's wishes, Barry's first three albums had all gone platinum. And, based on the strength of these successes, demand for the fourth album was so high that it "shipped gold", meaning there were already orders for half a million copies of *This One's For You* before it was even released in July 1976.

The instantaneous success of *This One's For You* and its associated singles seemed a perfect springboard into a monster tour that was being planned for Barry and his group. Ticket sales for the nation-wide tour echoed the pre-release success of the fourth album. Venues were reporting that their shows had been sold out within hours, with enough demand for additional tickets to warrant several days of additional shows.

"People were acting like I was the second coming," Manilow later said of the frenzy over him at the time, "and it was impossible to deal with." But with everything that was now riding on him, Barry had no choice but to deal with it, if sometimes badly.

The tour was scheduled to begin in Pennsylvania on July 31, 1976. It would encompass 98 cities, culminating in a two-week stint at the MGM Grand in Las Vegas. It would be an eventful and often painful nine months that would not only mark Barry Manilow's absolute arrival at stardom, but, like a classic Barry Manilow arrangement, in many ways would also prove to be the crescendo before the fall.

Chapter Twenty-three

"**M**y *very personal thanks to my friend, drummer, photographer, conductor, art director and confidant, Lee Gurst, for his enormous support and talents through the years. Lee, this one's for you.*"

The gruelling national tour that started in July 1976 met with phenomenal success across the country. The "Live" album, recorded at the tour's midpoint during a sold-out, week-long run at the Uris Theater on Broadway would be Barry's sixth[10] and best selling release to date. Lee Gurst was touched and a bit shocked to discover, quite by accident, that *Barry Manilow Live* would be dedicated to him.

"Ironically, I knew about the text on that cover before Barry showed it to me," says Gurst. Lee had taken many of the best-known photos of Barry, including the shot of Barry and his dog on the back of *Barry Manilow I* that made Bagel the beagle the most famous dog in America at the time. On the *Live* album, Lee was credited with "Photographic Supervision" of the album, in addition to his musical work. It was this photographic supervision that led to Lee's premature discovery of the album's dedication in the midst of the tour.

"Shortly before we left town one day," says Lee, "I went up to the record company to take a look at the colour proofs on the photography, and in the envelope I saw Barry's text, and I saw what was going to be there. And I was floored!" Not wanting to take away from Barry the pleasure of telling Lee about the impending honour, Gurst kept his new-found knowledge to himself.

If there had been any doubt at all in Barry's mind that he had

---

[10] Including both releases of his first album, *Barry Manilow* (1973)/*Barry Manilow I* (1975).

"arrived", the sold-out crowds at the increasingly large venues on the 1976/1977 tour should have proved it for him. It had only been a short time since his last tour had seen him playing college and high school gymnasiums. "If you had got up on stage and three years later 11,000 people were screaming your name, you'd be surprised, too!" he told a reporter. But, he told another interviewer, he was too professional to let fame turn his head, even a little bit. Or at least that's what he thought.

"Thank goodness I've had the preparation and discipline of eight years behind me to handle this thing," he told *Songwriter* magazine in 1975. "It's brand new and I didn't expect it, and if it ends tomorrow, I've had a terrific time." But he had worked with too many performers over the years, seen too much of what they'd gone through on their way up, to fall prey to the same demons he'd seen devour the others. "I'm handling the attention, and the interviews, and the audiences all because I was six feet away from it for a long time and watched the whole thing happen. I watched Bette go through the whole trip and saw her freak out and watched her handle it . . . So now it's come time for me to do it and I've had all that experience; all that background. So I don't freak out. If you work your way up to it you don't freak out. You handle the ups and all the praise, and you handle the knocks and become analytical about them. Or amused by them."

But that was before Barry found out just how all-encompassing his fame could become. "I'd never fantasised about the kind of success that was now happening to me," he wrote of that time, from the clearer vantage of hindsight.

If his ego was running unchecked from sell-out concert dates, the success of his first TV special in the midst of the already overwhelming tour didn't do much to remind Barry he was only human. Though there were a few critical jibes (the *Variety* reviewer wrote, "The plain-looking Manilow is not flattered by close-up camera work nor does he possess, at this juncture, much self-assurance and presence on camera . . ."), 35 million viewers tuned in to *The Barry Manilow Special* on ABC on March 9, 1977, to watch the Brooklyn boy strut his stuff.

But, just as Barry had seen happen with others he'd helped to stardom over the years, he now discovered first hand that even those who think they're prepared for success are still "freaked out" by the reality of such overwhelming fame. Fans would later coin the terms

"Good Barry" and "Bad Barry" to identify which sides of Manilow's temperament he might display in any given situation. "I know for a fact I was not the only one who has, at some point in time, encountered Bad Barry," wrote one fan recently. "We forgive him," she added, "but we don't forget."

Manilow himself seems neither to forget nor to completely forgive much of his early reaction to his sudden success. While today he has learned, for the most part, to master these two sides of his temperament, at one point it seemed even to Barry that "Good Barry" was in grave danger of being completely supplanted by "Bad Barry". "I'd tell my staff to empty rooms of people before I would walk in," Barry wrote in his 1987 autobiography, *Sweet Life*. "That went for TV studios and restaurants. This was not an easy thing to do without seeming demented. But I'd carry on and stay in the car or in my dressing room until places were cleared out." Because of his star status, very few people were willing to tell him he was making an ass of himself, though friends sometimes tried. When not immediately given something he'd demanded one evening, he whispered to friend and songwriting partner Bruce Sussman, "Tell them who I am." Bruce replied, "If you have to tell them who you are, Barry, you aren't anybody."

Manilow later tried to explain to a reporter from the *Ladies' Home Journal* that these violent mood swings were partly caused by the huge adrenalin rush of being in front of thousands of screaming fans. As illustration, he recounted an incident that was reported in the *Journal*, as follows:

> *Recently, a TV crew came to tape three numbers during Barry's live show in Philadelphia. When the agreed-upon songs were performed, Barry still saw the cameras with their red lights focused on him from all directions. He became incoherently furious and relives the episode with comparable passion.* "My energy and adrenaline levels are up so high during a performance, I could probably lift a car. There were 20,000 people out there screaming their heads off. I was having a great time, but I kept seeing those cameras and their lights.
>
> "At one point, while I was introducing a band member who was doing a solo, I ran into the wings where one of these guys was and grabbed him by the shoulders and threw him further into the wings and yelled, 'STOP IT!' The guy sorta bounced around.

"Then, when I went back onstage, I saw him crawling around to the other side. So I introduced another band member, ran offstage, shoved him again and said to my stage manager, 'Get this man the [expletive deleted] off my stage! I don't know what he's doing here.' What was coming out of my mouth was energy, not fury, But then they had said they were only going to tape three songs. I blew up like crazy and when the show was finished, I was still the same way. Because when I come offstage, if something is funny it's incredibly funny, if something is sad I'm dissolved into tears, if something is upsetting it's double, triple the upset.

"The director came out and gave me a perfectly logical explanation why those cameramen were onstage, but I was not listening. I went crazy. Slammed the door in his face. I know he must have thought I was a total maniac and hated my guts. The next day the TV show called and apologised and I said, no, don't apologise. I had no right to scream like that. That cameraman was a big person; he could have banged me on the head and killed me. But I was on this energy trip and actually threw him into the wings. I'm not a fighter, it's just this insane energy that takes over."

As much concern as Barry would later express about what he put those around him through as he tried to adjust to everything that was happening to him at the height of his fame, those same people were even more concerned while it was happening, not for themselves, but for what their friend was struggling through. "The one thing I know from the earliest years of touring, the people that worked with Barry really liked Barry," says Lee Gurst. "Nobody was in it just because it was a gig, not in those days. Back in the beginning we really were a sort of family, and we really cared. And everybody really was there and supportive in a very personal way."

Many of Barry's entourage, including Gurst and the women of Lady Flash, were not only colleagues, but close, personal friends. Perhaps because of this, or perhaps simply because of his naturally generous nature, Barry would go out of his way to make sure those he travelled with were treated just as well as he was. "Barry was fair and took very good care of all of us in terms of, at least for the first three or four years, the band always stayed in the same hotel Barry did," recalls Lee Gurst. "He never demanded anything for himself that he didn't insist on for the group as well. That wasn't the way

Barry in the mid-Seventies, just as his career was taking off. (*LFI*)

Bette Middler, on stage in the mid-Seventies. Not exactly a shy and retiring girl, her relationship with Barry was marked by mutual admiration and frequent acrimony, but by the Nineties (below) the barbs were forgotten. (*LFI*)

Barry in the studio with (top) producer Ron Dante, and (below) with backing singers Lady Flash, left to right: Debra Byrd, Monica Burruss and Reparata. (*Lee Gurst*)

Barry poses with Lady Flash by a massive Las Vegas billboard advertising a season at the MGM Grand. (*Lee Gurst*)

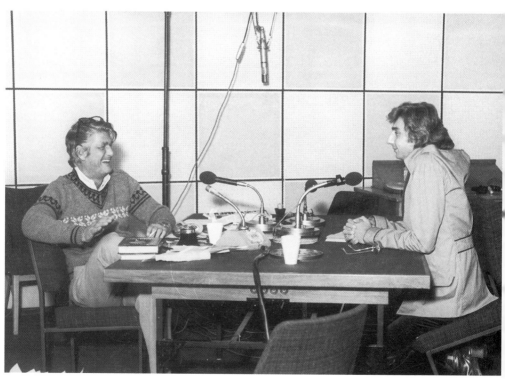

Barry in the BBC Studios with British DJ Pete Murray on a 1978 visit to London. (*Lee Gurst*)

Barry on stage with his friend, musical director, drummer and personal photographer Lee Gurst. (*Lee Gurst*)

Barry with his close friend Linda Allen, in 1982. (*Rex*)

Mr Music through the years. It is largely through his live appearances that Barry has maintained one of the most loyal fan followings in show business. Little has changed over the years, though his stage attire has become more conservative as each Vegas season and national tour rolls by. (*Rex, LFI, Starfile, Bonnie Baisch*)

Barry, the showman of his generation, enters the new century. (*Neil Genower/Rex*)

things were done, but it was the way Barry wanted it."

It was a generosity that his friends appreciated and tried to reciprocate. Barry's fame had made him instantly recognisable in public, which had led to Barry's demands that rooms be emptied before he entered and that people be made to turn their backs when he walked by. "I get very uptight when I go to places with lots of people," Barry told an interviewer at the time. "Even if they don't stop to talk, a lot of people stare . . . it gets to you." A deepening paranoia seized him, and Barry felt he had no choice but to confine himself to his hotel room most nights when he was on the road. "We tried to make life a little bit easier," says Gurst who, with the trio of backup singers, would keep Barry company as much as possible. "At least he wouldn't be locked in the hotel suite alone," explains Gurst. "There was that kind of pressure. There was the pressure of maintaining a quality performance night after night under sometimes gruelling circumstances."

The tour hit Nevada in March 1977, with a six-show run at the Sahara in Lake Tahoe; comedian Billy Crystal was Barry's opening act. The Sahara expressed its appreciation for Barry's visit by running a full-page ad in the March 31, 1977 issue of *Daily Variety* thanking Barry for six sold-out shows. It was enough to make any performer giddy with joy. Wrote Barry of the time, "Alone in my hotel room, I felt as if a huge cloud had descended upon me and that I was walking around in cotton balls all the time. Now and then, I'd emerge and act human and everything would lighten up for a while, but mostly the success and pressure just pushed me further and further into my own confusion."

For all the torment he was experiencing and causing among his inner circle, those who saw the public Barry would likely have absolutely no inkling of the private turmoil he was experiencing. The public admired what seemed to be Barry's down-home, self-deprecating good humour which was, in large part, the key to his concert success. Many other entertainers were equally admiring of Barry's success and what appeared outwardly to be his ability to remain unaffected by stardom. Karen Carpenter was one of these admirers.

During the tour, Barry found himself performing in the same town as Karen and Richard Carpenter. Extending professional courtesy to another headlining act, The Carpenters invited Manilow's group to attend one of their shows on one of Manilow's nights off. Barry went with Lee Gurst and Reparata (defying Miles Lourie's strict "no fraternisation" policy among Barry's entourage, Gurst and Reparata had quietly been married in October 1975; Barry had served as best man). After the show, the trio went backstage to introduce themselves to Richard and Karen Carpenter who, it turned out, had also caught one of Barry's shows. Karen, it seemed, was a big fan of Barry's.

Back in Los Angeles, during a break from the tour, when a special event came up, Barry took Karen Carpenter as his guest for the evening. "There were a few times when they were together in that kind of thing," says Gurst. "I think she kind of liked him. Maybe she didn't know he was gay."

The Carpenters were one of the most musically educated and professional acts in the music business at that time. Richard was an accomplished pianist, songwriter, arranger and producer. Karen, a consummate percussionist, possessed a honeyed alto singing voice that made the most of her brother's imaginative arrangements. Raised in a strict, sometimes stifling, middle-class family Karen, like Barry, had room for little in her life beyond performing with her brother. "I think Karen felt a certain kind of connection with Barry," says Lee Gurst. "I think she probably didn't meet a lot of people who were musically on her level. Barry could be bright and interesting, and she was sweet and talented and probably somewhat naive – I say naive, but I think immature. I think Karen was young beyond her years, in a sense. I don't believe Barry felt anything for her emotionally. I think she did. She never said anything; I wasn't there for that. But I seem to recall she kind of liked him, and I know that, to Barry, she was just a beard for the evening."

It was a side of his friend's character, albeit rarely seen, that Lee Gurst found upsetting. "I was a little mildly pissed that he was, in effect, using her for the short period of time," says Gurst. "I don't think Karen believed Barry was in love with her – I'm not saying she was that deluded. But I think she liked Barry and would have liked to have a friendship with him, and he could not have been less interested other than as someone to show up at a public event with."

By the time the Manilow tour made its final stop at the MGM Grand in Las Vegas in April 1977, everyone was feeling Barry's angst. "My nerves were raw," Barry later wrote. "During the last week in Vegas, I found myself crying or yelling at the drop of a hat . . . I was fed up with smiling and acting nice to radio men and their wives and to the record men and their girlfriends. I was fed up signing autographs. I wanted to be left alone and found it very difficult controlling my frazzled nerves."

Once again, whatever troubles Barry was having offstage were not reflected in his onstage performances. The show, sometimes running as long as two and a half hours, was a non-stop frenzy of dazzle and flash, from the rhinestone studded costumes to the flashing lights and intricate choreography. And – oh, yes! – there was music, too!

Wrote one reviewer, "*Manilow's appeal cuts right across the age barriers. Whether he is singing his own songs or other people's, his performances always have the polish of sheer professionalism, not only in the singing but also in the arrangements and the whole presentation of the music. Ballads are undoubtedly one of Manilow's strongest points . . . But Barry is a long way from being just a ballad singer – he is an all-around entertainer.*"

He was an "all-around entertainer", and he always had been. From his earliest days playing with Jack Wilkins & The Jazz Partners back in Brooklyn, Barry knew what it took to reach an audience, to put a song across the stage with such force and feeling that it not only reached ears, but hearts as well. Not even the worst cynic could leave a Barry Manilow concert unmoved, if only by the sheer force of Manilow's desire to be liked. *I'm here for you*, he seemed to say to each audience member, individually. *There is nothing I won't do to make you smile. Please, won't you like me?* And they did, by the thousands – liked, loved, adored. But, for Barry, it still wasn't enough because, of course, the audience wasn't the problem. Barry Manilow didn't like Barry Manilow.

Barry's crisis of self was nothing new. *For what is a man profited, if he shall gain the whole world, and lose his own soul?* Jesus asked his disciples, according to the Bible. Barry Manilow had, it seemed, gained the whole world. But had he sold his soul to do it?

Between shows at the MGM Grand in Las Vegas, Barry called Lee Gurst into his dressing room and said, "I have a surprise for you." He handed Lee the envelope that contained the cover copy for the upcoming *Live* album, taken from recordings during the sold-out run at the Uris Theater in December and January. Lee, who, unbeknownst to Barry, had already seen the dedication, acted, as he says, "appropriately dumbstruck". But he didn't have to feign surprise at what was coming next.

Barry expressed his sincere gratitude to Lee for his friendship over the years, and for everything Lee had done for him. It seemed a tender moment after a turbulent nine months. Then, says Lee, "at the end of that same conversation, Barry told me that he was letting everybody go and this was going to be the end. *I love you, you're fired.*"

Chapter Twenty-four

If Lee Gurst thought Barry might change his mind by the end of their run in Las Vegas, he was wrong.

The last stop of the tour in Las Vegas would prove to be one of the few times that Barry had separated himself from his band by staying at a different location to the rest of the group. During the nearly two-week stay in Vegas, the band and Lady Flash stayed at a rented condo, while Barry stayed at a rented house some distance away. After the last Las Vegas performance of the two-week run, everyone with the tour threw a big party at the condo to celebrate the end of a long, wearying, but highly successful tour. Barry stopped by to join in the celebration, which lasted through the night.

"I drove him home," says Lee Gurst. "It was dawn, the sun was coming up." Any hopes Lee had had for a change of heart on Barry's part were dashed on the ride back to Barry's rented house. "He said he'd pretty much decided, that's it," says Lee. There was no question about the talent and ability of the friends he'd been working with for the past three years. But, Barry told Lee, "I don't want to work with friends any more. It's too hard."

"It wasn't an angry thing," says Lee. "But it was just a knife in the gut, because I loved what I was doing." During the ride back to Barry's house, Lee tried to persuade his friend to change his mind and keep the team together. "I kept saying, 'I don't get it! This is working so well!' And he said, 'I don't want to work with friends any more.' That was the big thing, was *I don't want to work with friends*."

In retrospect, Lee can see what might have been part of Barry's dilemma. "I think it had gotten to the point where the concerns that he had shown all those years – he wouldn't travel in any better style than the band, whatever he had the band had to have, he got limos, the band had to have limos – was no longer feasible. He watched out for everybody. And it had gotten to the point, I think, where being a star was beginning to occupy a lot of time and energy, and thinking about it, worrying about other people, or worrying about relationships interfered."

It did seem to be a theme in Barry's life. If someone didn't serve some sort of professional function, Barry seemed unlikely to want to maintain a connection. From Lee's perspective, one worked to maintain intimate relationships, to maintain a balance between professional associations that may prove transient, and personal friendships that should span a lifetime. But, Lee observes, "Barry's preference was to not have that kind of relationship. His were intimate in a business sense – he was always in control, he was always the boss. In terms of personal relationships, how many long-term intimate relationships has Barry had? Not that many. It's just not something he's comfortable with."

Barry himself seemed to acknowledge this fact many times over the years, usually stating that he simply didn't have the time to nurture personal relationships. "I can handle today," he said in a 1990 interview. "I can handle getting through this interview. But I can't think about the next year. Futurising. That's what it's called. It's a waste of time and energy. It's just like you can't live in the past. Now is where it's at. You change and when that happens you begin to lose people who related to you when you were something else. So I've had to sever connections with people. It's very painful but it's the only way. I become the more human, humane Barry Manilow and say, Listen, this relationship is baloney now. Our relationship right now is based on old stuff. Unless we can deal with each other now – with these new things that I'm learning – then we're finished. You can't keep dragging me back to how we were because I can't react that way any more. You either renegotiate or you split. If you hang on to that stuff, man, it's going to drive you fucking crazy." People from Barry's past were, it seemed, simply shed as he passed them by. Or was it perhaps they who were moving on – marrying, having children, changing careers – while Barry stayed, motionless, in one very brightly lit place?

Barry scoffed when a magazine interviewer suggested to him that "behind all the flamboyant success there is, in the flesh, one small, lonesome man." In response, Barry simply smiled and said, "If this is 'lonesome at the top', I'll take it." But when it was announced in June 1978 that Barry had won a special Tony Award for his two-week run at the Uris Theater six months previously, he lamented that "the only congratulatory telegram I got, from friends, family or anyone, was from Bette Midler."

At the end of the tour in April 1977, Lee Gurst and Reparata flew to Hawaii for a much-needed vacation, while Barry retreated to Miami to try to rest and try to gain some perspective on all that had happened in the preceding year. His friend Linda Allen came down to visit him, as did his songwriting partners Marty Panzer, with whom he wrote 'Even Now' and 'I Was A Fool To Let You Go', and Bruce Sussman and Jack Feldman, with whom Barry had begun composing 'Copacabana'.

But, according to Barry, he spent the majority of his time in Florida sitting quietly with his dog, staring at the ocean or watching television. He also wrote in his journal, and wrote letters to Lee Gurst and Reparata in Hawaii, expressing some regret at how things had ended. "And we would talk on the phone now and then," says Gurst. "But it was very painful for me." Lee acknowledges that the separation was also hard on Barry. "He was saying he missed the performing, he missed our being together." But even this personal regret wasn't without its professional overtones. "He wrote at one point he'd been listening to one of the last shows," says Gurst, "and he just says, 'Damn, we were good.'"

While Barry enjoyed sitting still in Florida, his career continued to move forward on its own momentum. *Barry Manilow Live*, the double album dedicated to Lee Gurst, entered *Billboard* magazine's Top 20 at number ten. Within six weeks it hit the number one spot on the list, and became Barry's fourth platinum album to date. The arc of the album's success marked a significant moment in pop history. From the time the album entered the chart on May 28 continuing for eight weeks straight, all five of Barry's albums were chart-listed simultaneously, a feat previously accomplished by only Frank Sinatra and Johnny Mathis.

It had been decided that, at the end of his Florida retreat, Barry would spend the next year in Los Angeles, finishing *Even Now*, his seventh album co-produced with Ron Dante, and working on the follow-up to his first TV special, which had been nominated for an

Emmy. He would also use the time to try out new west coast musicians to replace the east coast friends he had just fired. Barry's assistant, Michael Devereaux, went ahead to find Barry a suitable place to live in Los Angeles.

Michael Devereaux, or "Dev" as Barry's friends like to call him, was tall, thin, handsome and, as Lee Gurst puts it, "sophisticated in a way Barry couldn't hope to be." A native New Yorker, Dev was smart, extremely well organised and unflappable, seldom losing his cool. He was unfailingly gracious to everyone he dealt with, showing the same attentiveness and respect to hysterical fans that he would show the biggest names in show business. No matter what the situation, Barry could rely on Dev to maintain the equilibrium of his often roller coaster-like existence.

The house Dev found for Barry was a Beverly Hills mansion that came complete with swimming pool, fountains, a white grand piano, and a butler named Robert. Even Barry's spacious 27th Street apartment in Manhattan with its sweeping balcony terrace paled by comparison to the mansion's pink marble bathrooms, marble fireplaces, and manicured grounds dotted with marble statuary. It was not what Barry had had in mind when he sent Michael to scout for a small, unassuming place to spend his year in Los Angeles. But, Barry later wrote, "Michael's instinct was right . . . The house was so ridiculous that I just couldn't take anything too seriously when I was there. And when the real disasters did happen, the house served to lighten even those incidents."

The disasters started happening almost immediately. To publicise the upcoming album and the second TV special, Barry had agreed to do a cover story for *People* magazine. When the story ran in the August 8, 1977 issue of the magazine, it brought Barry's private life into uncomfortable proximity with his public persona.

The interview with writer Robert Windeler had not been a happy one for Barry. "I wanted to talk about music," he later wrote of their encounter, "he wanted to know who I slept with." Indeed, Windeler seems to casually drop a reference to Barry's sexual preference in the very first paragraph of the article when he follows a quote about Barry's supposed feelings of low self-worth with the attribution, "says a former boyfriend".

The issue of Manilow's sexuality seemed to touch everything he did. Lee Gurst noted that it sometimes even affected their relationship.

"There's no question that, in some sense, in some way, there was always a barrier between us by virtue of our sexual proclivities," says Lee Gurst, "that there was a difference in our worlds that never got bridged. And it wasn't an obvious problem. But on occasion I was aware that there was just that part of life that I didn't cross over into. As open as Barry was – god knows I knew way more than I ever wanted or cared to sometimes – you're not quite in that club. You're not quite there. That was something that was always, not a barrier, but a difference." Others of Barry's colleagues, Lee observed, fitted in because they didn't have to contend with that between them, including Michael Devereaux. "I wouldn't go cruising the gay bars with Barry," says Gurst. "Michael could."

Barry's insistence on frequenting gay bars in Los Angeles seemed an echo of Barry's behaviour when he was working Downstairs at the Upstairs with Jeanne Lucas in New York years before, an unnecessary risk of exposure that could drive his friends to exasperation. Still, Lee Gurst acknowledges, it was a calculated risk. Barry's sexuality, says Lee, "was not a secret in certain circles, and within those circles it was a secret that would be respected." There was also an inherent discretion among patrons of such establishments who, Lee points out, "are going to keep their mouths shut about you the same way they want you, or all the other people in the place, to keep your mouth shut about them."

But obviously someone had not kept his mouth shut for *People* magazine. The article not only made casual reference to Barry having at least one former boyfriend, saying that his busy professional life "has gotten in the way of relationships with either sex", but also exposed the fact that Barry was older than he admitted to being, identifying him as "Now in his mid-30s (he claims to be younger) . . ."

There was little Barry could do about the piece without drawing further scrutiny of his private life. Years later, when he wrote his autobiography, he would get the tiniest measure of revenge by stating that "the interviewer's mind was in the gutter", but ten years had passed in the interim. For all his grousing about what he felt to be the writer's misplaced attentions, Barry never actually publicly denied anything Windeler wrote in the *People* article.

The Emmy Awards, the television equivalent of the Oscars, were presented on September 12, 1977. A flustered Barry went forward to accept the award for Outstanding Special Comedy, Variety or Music for *The Barry Manilow Special* which had aired the previous year. After hugging presenter Jack Albertson, of the sitcom *Chico And The Man* fame, Barry said, "I have nothing to say! I'm freaking out!"

In retrospect it doesn't seem surprising that the first special was such a success, nor that ABC would want more of the same from Barry. A glance at the television line-up for that period of time shows that several of the regular prime time series were variety shows centred around musical acts. Sonny and Cher, whose career had been foundering on the schlock rocks of seedy lounges by the end of the Sixties, had found new life on TV with *The Sonny And Cher Comedy Hour*. The show also foundered when their marriage did in 1974. After attempts at separate careers failed, the couple came back to give the show another go under the slightly altered name *The Sonny And Cher Show*, which was in what turned out to be its last season when *The Barry Manilow Special* aired in 1977.

When Sonny and Cher left the airwaves in 1974, CBS filled their slot with Barry's one-time producer, Tony Orlando and his variety show *Tony Orlando And Dawn*. A summer hit, the show returned in December and enjoyed respectable ratings until it was retooled in the second year and presented as *The Tony Orlando And Dawn Rainbow Hour*. Switching the show's emphasis from music to mind-numbingly banal comedy (for instance, a sketch called "Chinook and the Man", featuring Orlando as an Eskimo, playing on the success of the sitcom *Chico and the Man*) proved to be fatal; the show folded in December 1976.

Hoping to capture the same magic that had made Sonny and Cher a hit for CBS, ABC presented *The Captain & Tennille*. The singing husband and wife team, whose song 'Love Will Keep Us Together' had beaten Barry's 'Mandy' for the 1976 Record of the Year Grammy, provided little substance to build a show around. Alabama-born Toni Tennille was cute, with an inherent southern charm, but she lacked the caustic wit that Cher had used with rapier precision against her husband each week. For his part, "Captain" Daryl Dragon was a master of all keyboard instruments, but had little, if anything to say. The couple's few hits, combined with their limited ability to engage the audience as well, perhaps, as the fact that the only other regulars on the show were their two English bulldogs, spelled an early end to *The Captain & Tennille*, which folded after scarcely five months.

ABC had better luck with another musical duo, the brother and sister team of Donny and Marie Osmond. The *Donny And Marie* show had the odd distinction of putting its hosts on ice skates to open the show. Much fun was made of the Osmonds' wholesome Mormon background. When Donny sang 'Jeremiah Was A Bull-frog', the line was changed to ". . . and he helped me drink my *milk*" to accommodate the church's doctrine against alcohol consumption. So important was family and church to the show's stars that at the beginning of their second season they left Hollywood and moved the entire production to their family compound in Orem, Utah, from where the show continued to air until May 1979. In fact, by the time *The Second Barry Manilow Special* aired on February 24, 1978, *Donny and Marie* was the only musical variety show left on the regular prime time schedule.

Barry's second special lacked some of the spontaneity and wide-eyed charm of his Emmy-winning first special. He looked strained, and seemed to be trying too hard. His performance of the song 'Daybreak' from the album *This One's For You* put together in the space of one song every show-business manipulation ever invented. There were kids singing along while hanging on a set of monkey bars surrounding the piano; old people singing along as they went about clichéd "old people" activities; cartoon characters singing along in helium-squeak voices; and even Barry's dog made an appearance. It all seemed like a good idea at the time but, more than a decade later, the spectacle would make Manilow cringe. "You get up there with the lights and the sound and the make-up, and your first instinct is to be a phony," he told *Rolling Stone* in 1990. "Have you ever seen those old TV specials? Come on – this is an idiot on television! This is just a jerk. But I thought this was the way I was supposed to be: campy, giggly, charming, cute, silly, entertaining, goofy." Mission accomplished.

But if Manilow seemed strained on TV, it may well have been because he was facing much stress off-screen. Michael Devereaux had been in a serious car accident which had landed him in the intensive care unit for two weeks. Barry had taped the special, he said, between trips to the hospital. And something even more disturbing was diverting Barry's attention from the many professional commitments he was trying to fulfil: he'd begun receiving death threats.

The threats at first had seemed mild, nothing more than the usual "craze-os" as Barry called some of his most zealous fans. Barry's manager in New York, Miles Lourie, insisted Barry hire a bodyguard to protect him, as well as a detective to track down the source of the threats. Barry found it impossible to believe that anyone could really mean him any harm. But the violence of the missives escalated, and Barry believed that the upcoming article in *People* would reveal that Barry was recording his new album at the A&M studios in Hollywood, making him easy for anyone to find.[11]

So, an Israeli bodyguard named Shlomo was added to Barry's entourage. Shlomo and his partners took shifts protecting Barry, staying within sight or earshot of him every minute of the night and day until the culprits – "they were just kids and they claimed they were playing a joke on me", Barry later wrote – were apprehended.

Barry had told Robert Windeler that, while everyone in the music business seemed to gravitate to Los Angeles, "I'm not coming. I choose to live in New York. I'm a city kid with soot in my blood." But a year of breakfast served poolside, presumably sootless, by a butler, seemed to have changed his mind. Barry's return to New York near the end of 1977 was simply to pack up his belongings for the permanent move to California.

The album *Even Now* marked not only the end of Barry's days as a New Yorker, but also his reconnection with Lee Gurst, with whom he hadn't worked since they'd parted ways in April 1977. Wrapping up production of *Even Now* after his return to New York, Barry was finding it difficult to get the people at Arista to understand what he wanted for the look of the album's cover. So Barry called Gurst, who was himself now living in California. "They just keep showing me all this crap," Barry told Lee. "Here's my idea – can you shoot it?" Lee knew just what Barry was talking about and was on a plane to New York within the week.

"I got off the plane like 5 o'clock in the morning at Kennedy," says Gurst, "raced to the apartment on Central Park West so I could be there when the sun came up, and shot the cover. Had the proofs back by 10:30, and that was it! It was done." The result was a stunning shot of Barry, in profile in the extreme right foreground of the photo, looking out over the city as the sun rose in spectacular colour

---

[11] The article did not, in fact, reveal any information that would help anyone trying to locate Barry.

over the skyscrapers. It was a perfect complement to the album's collection of songs which included 'Starting Again' and 'Sunrise'.

To Barry's long-time co-producer Ron Dante, *Even Now* represented the best work Barry would ever do. "I think, in terms of creative input of his arrangements, his vocals, some of his songs, the outside songs we chose," says Dante, "I thought that was one of the highlights of his career."

The album certainly came together in record time. "That was the smoothest album ever made," says Dante. "We were hitting our stride, as Barry said on some liner notes at one point. Well we were. We were both flexing; he was flexing as artist and I was flexing as producer. And we were really hitting it perfectly with the sounds and the songs we got to record, mainly because Barry was such a big star then that we were getting great outside songs sent in to us. We had an abundance of great songs." Outside songs included in the album were, indeed, memorable. 'I Just Want To Be The One In Your Life', by Michael Price and Dan Walsh; 'Where Do I Go From Here', by Parker McKee, and the spectacular 'Somewhere In The Night' by Richard Kerr and Will Jennings, a sweeping song that included the dramatic key changes and "big-titty" (as Barry liked to characterise it) orchestrations that had become Barry's signature. But Barry's own contribution, along with his long-time songwriting partners Panzer, Sussman, Feldman, and Anderson, were not to be discounted. "Barry was writing better than ever," says Dante. "I thought 'Even Now' was one of his most beautiful songs."

The entire album had come together in a matter of a few months, "a labour of love," as Dante characterised it. "I thought everything was clicking," says Dante. "I thought we were very on top of our game and I thought that album was our landmark album for that kind of music. It was one of his biggest successes. I think it went triple platinum. To this day it remains one of his best."

In his 1987 autobiography, *Sweet Life: Adventures on the Way to Paradise*, Barry skips from his 1978 move to Los Angeles directly to his 1980 appearance on *The Tonight Show* with Johnny Carson. Far from being unremarkable, this short space of time was actually action packed.

Before returning permanently to California, Barry had turned over his Manhattan apartment to his mother, who was now divorced from Willie Murphy. "They actually date," Barry said in an interview, "and they live together when they feel like it. That seems to me the way to do it."

Apparently Barry had changed his mind about working with friends, as he once again asked Lee Gurst to join him as percussionist and arranger on his latest tour, which would take him to Europe. The tour, unfortunately, was not without its problems.

"The tour was scheduled to be quite a lengthy one," says Gurst. "While we were in Las Vegas, at the Riviera, the whole second half of the tour fell apart. And at the same time they were trying to put together a European tour and a few other things." A Barry Manilow show is always carefully crafted and rehearsed. With the delays caused by problems with tour dates, Barry was afraid he would now lose his musicians and be faced with using unrehearsed replacements at the last minute. Lee, who was in charge of coordinating the personnel for the tour, gathered together crew and performers and explained the situation to them.

"If you can hold on as long as you can before you have to take other work, they're trying to put something together, and we'd really appreciate it if you'd just try and stick it out a little bit," Lee told everyone. As added incentive, Barry promised bonuses to all those who would stick with his show rather than finding immediate employment elsewhere. All agreed to stay and wait for Barry's tour to fill out.

The tour finally did get off the ground, performing at various dates around the country, each more successful than the last. The reception at the Greek Theater in Los Angeles in August was especially ecstatic. The management of the Greek took out an ad proclaiming, "*Congratulations, Barry! Your first week sold out four months in advance! We added four more days, and they sold out in 5½ hours! Now we're adding three more days: September 16, 17, 18! Welcome back to LA!*"

The tour left the States for London in October. The trip started off memorably with a seeming insult. "We'd landed in London one morning after a redeye from Chicago," says Lee Gurst, "and a couple of us had gone out walking around. We'd walked over to Westminster Abbey. And it's probably not even 10.30 in the morning. And Barry and I were there, and I think one or two other people. And a big Rolls-Royce drove by, and from the Rolls-Royce we heard, "Bloody tourists!" It was Paul McCartney, who recognised Barry. It was kind of a nice moment. Wow! I guess somebody knows we're here. And it was, I think, a nice greeting that morning that none of us had our heads on straight as I recall." Upon reflection, though, Lee has to wonder if the remark had been made in as lighthearted a manner as it had been received. "Maybe he meant it seriously!" says Gurst. "You know I never considered that! I always took it as a friendly remark. But now for the first time I'm stopping to think, was he serious?"

If McCartney wasn't welcoming, the rest of England was. A debut at the Royal Albert Hall was followed by a week of sold-out shows at the London Palladium. After brief stops in Holland, Belgium and France, the tour wound up with two days in Germany before heading back home to LA.

The end of the tour would prove to be another ending for Lee and Barry. After promising his musicians bonuses if they stuck with the tour rather than taking work elsewhere during the tour's initial delay, now that the tour was over, Barry seemed to be having second thoughts.

Barry had, according to Gurst, promised each musician a bonus equivalent to two week's salary. So Lee presented Barry with a list of each musician and their weekly salaries so he could approve their bonuses. But instead of approving the funds for each musician who had remained faithful, Barry instead chose to exclude certain of the musicians based on personality. "No, the guy's a jerk," Barry told Lee as he vetoed a bonus for one of the musicians. "Well, he may be a jerk," Lee replied, "but he's done his job, and he's done his job for a lot of years at that." Barry would relent, but only partially. " Well," he said, "I'm just gonna give him one week."

Lee fought for the musician to get the same bonus as everyone else, with Barry refusing. Then, in an ironic echo of Bette Midler's refusal to pay Barry for extra rehearsals back at the Baths because, she said, "He got a salary, so I figured, well, that's enough," Barry now informed Lee that he, too, would only get a one-week bonus because Barry felt Lee already earned too much money. Lee responded by saying, "Well, I earned a lot of money because I did a lot of the jobs. It wasn't like I was overpaid for anything." But Barry still couldn't see it. "Yeah," he told Lee, "I'm just not going to give you that kind of money."

During the tour, the musicians had also performed for several television appearances, for all of which union regulations required them to be paid. Again, there were problems getting the money. As union leader, it was Lee's unenviable job to report the situation to the musician's union. Though this was proper procedure for the situation, Barry saw his friend's actions as a personal attack rather than a professional remedy for a business situation.

Barry and Lee had spent the New Year's holiday together. "When we came back to LA that night," says Gurst, "he found a letter I guess from Miles that the union was after him again. And he called me up and he was very angry. He felt like I'd betrayed him." Lee defended his actions, explaining that it was his job to look out for the interests of the musicians in his charge. "If you needed money, you should've come to me," Barry told him. What they were asking for, Lee pointed out, wasn't a handout or a loan, nor was it a matter of simple need. The musicians had signed contracts and were made certain promises. All Lee was trying to do, he told Barry, was see that those promises were kept. The hell of it was, Lee knew very well that if he had come to Barry, as a friend, in need of anything, Barry would have happily provided it for him, no matter what the cost. At one point in the late Sixties, when times were lean, Lee announced that he was too broke to even send out Christmas cards. Shortly thereafter he received a $100 cheque in the mail from Barry with a note that said, "*I don't want to hear another word about it. You'd do the same for me some day. Send me a Christmas card.*" But to Barry, Lee's actions now, while motivated by business concerns, constituted a personal betrayal, pure and simple. He said to Lee, "Call me when you've got a job and don't need me any more."

Another close personal and professional relationship was about to come to an end as well. *Even Now* had been followed up by two double platinum albums – *Greatest Hits* in 1978 and *One Voice* in 1979. The 1980 release *Barry*, though it eventually went platinum, was memorable mostly for the hit single 'I Made It Through The Rain', which was more than could be said for Barry's collaboration with Ron Dante.

Just as he had done with Lee Gurst and the others in his band at the height of their touring success, Barry informed Ron that their collaboration was coming to an end. "I was kind of blind-sided," says Dante, adding, "It was no big deal. Basically he wanted to try new styles and new producers, and go different directions. We quit at the zenith of our success. It was okay."

"Okay" may have been a bit of an understatement. The Manilow/

Dante combination had produced eighteen top ten records in a row and numerous triple platinum albums. At the time Barry called an end to their partnership, says Dante, "we were still riding the crest of wonderful hits with 'Ships That Pass In The Night' [from the *One Voice* album], and 'I Made It Through The Rain'." But, he adds with a laugh, "Sometimes you go through a midlife crisis. I think [Barry] did. He changed everything. He moved to Beverly Hills, he got a new manager, got a new agent, he changed his lifestyle."

As had happened only recently with Lee Gurst, when Ron Dante made moves to protect his legal interests after the dissolution of the partnership, Barry took personal offence. "The legal problems were nothing important, actually," says Dante. "It's just I had to protect my interest, because we had many albums to do together, and he was walking, wanted to go somewhere else. So I had to protect myself at the time, legally, with papers. It wasn't a suit so much, it was an official thing you had to do at the time. But it's been blown out of proportion over the years that I actually sued him. It was not true. We had to have some papers that said this is what each of us gets. We had a long-term partnership going. We couldn't just end it. We couldn't just walk away. There was too much at stake. I'd put many, many years of my life and my career on hold almost to make these records, to guide the ship. I wasn't just going to let it walk away. But that ended it."

For Barry, it was impossible to separate his professional life from his personal life because, as he'd pointed out many times, there was simply no difference between the two. To separate them, says Dante, "would be very difficult. His career is his life, his life is his career." Further proof of that could be seen in Barry's choice to change his management from attorney Miles Lourie, to Garry Kief, a former ABC Entertainment employee who Barry had begun seeing socially in the spring of 1978. To Ron Dante, Garry was an even less appropriate management choice for Barry to make than Miles Lourie had been. "He was like from ABC Entertainment Center in Century City, I think he booked real estate space or something for them," says Dante of Kief. "He had no background in music whatsoever, so that was a strange choice, I thought, on Barry's part to get a manager who really doesn't know much about managing. But he did it, you know. Garry's another tough businessman. He's the pit bull protecting Barry, so to speak. That's what I hear. That's what he thinks he's doing. That's fine."

Dante felt that it was Barry's new management in Los Angeles that may have been acting as a catalyst for much of the upheaval in Barry's life at the time. "I couldn't stay in that relationship with the power I had at the time," says Dante. "For other people, it was too much influence. And I think other people wanted to influence him more. So they kind of like painted it black. It could not have been just an official paper, it had to be an insult." But Dante has been in show business for a lot of years, and he knows how things work. It's this experience that allows him to be philosophical about the sudden severing of his relationship with Barry. "That's the way it goes, that's the way the business works," he says. "I'm not surprised. We had run a very good road together. I was involved in almost every one of his huge hits. So we had a very good run."

Yes, it had been a very good run. For five years the boy from Brooklyn had ruled the world, with a little help from his friends. But as the Seventies turned into the Eighties, his reign, along with many of the old friendships, seemed to be running out along with the decade. Barry Manilow would go on to have many other triumphs in the years ahead, but none of his successes would ever reach the frenzied heights of those he'd achieved during those last few years of the Seventies. It had all begun so simply, just like a Barry Manilow song – a slow start, a dramatic build, and then the slow release. As he told *Keyboard* magazine in 1983, "Endings are one of my specialities."

PART V

One Man In The Spotlight

"There must be something good in a thing that pleases so many; even if it cannot be explained, it is certainly enjoyed."

– Baltasar Gracian, *The Art of Worldly Wisdom*
(1647)

Chapter Twenty-five

"When I make love with my husband I imagine it's Barry Manilow. All the time. And after, when my husband and I have made love and I realise it's not him, I cry to myself. It's usually dark when the tears flow and somehow I manage to conceal them. It happens to an awful lot of people, too. I didn't realise how many until I got involved with Barry fans. A lot of them are married and around my age and they feel the same way and they do the same thing. It's comforting to know I'm not the only one."

Far from being the only one, Joanne, a 42-year-old housewife, is among a legion of sometimes frighteningly loyal fans Barry Manilow has amassed worldwide over his long career. These followers, comprised largely of middle-aged females, range from those who simply enjoy a Manilow tune when they hear one on the radio, to those who will actually spend their mortgage money to follow Barry to yet another concert date.

Barry's former singing partner, Jeanne Lucas, witnessed some of the fan devotion run amuck when she visited Barry at his mansion in Bel Air in the mid-Eighties. Barry had called Jeanne because he was gathering material for the autobiography he was writing, and he was interviewing a number of his friends to help bolster his memory of past events. It had been a long time since Jeanne had seen Barry, and his opulent surroundings seemed a far cry from the Brooklyn apartment Barry and Jeanne had shared so many years before. But for all the pretensions of his surroundings, Jeanne had to laugh when Barry's houseboy served lunch – bologna sandwiches on white bread. "His tastes in food are very simple," says

Lucas, "very white bread America. And I thought, 'oh, god, he hasn't changed!' "[12]

Among the many things they discussed that day, Barry talked about the lengths his fans would sometimes go to just to get a glimpse of him. "One night a bunch of them found out where he lived and they camped out on his front lawn," Jeanne remembers. "That's pretty scary, you know. He said, 'Oh, they're just nuts, these people.' "

Even Barry's father, Harold Keliher, and his wife Annie became targets of Barry's fans, who saw the Kelihers as conduits to their idol. Annie Keliher recalls an incident when she and Harold were living in California. "Don't ask me how, but they found out Kelly was Barry's father. We were living in an apartment, and the groupies – they had me nuts! I was scared of them. I got up one morning, I thought I heard something; I found a bouquet of flowers on my doorknob from one of the groupies." A card attached to the bouquet said, *To the stepmother of Barry.*

Even after Harold and Anna moved to Las Vegas, intrepid fans would still manage to track them down, trying to forge some kind of connection with Barry, no matter how tenuous. "Oh, it was terrible with them!" says Anna Keliher. "If I had submitted myself, my husband and I, to these groupies, I would be god to them. That's how crazy they were for Barry." But the operative word for Anna was "crazy".

"I used to be afraid," she says. "I said, 'Kelly, one of them could turn angry, you never know if they've got a gun.' He used to think I was crazy, but I said no way do I want these people around me."

Though Barry worked for years in various aspects of show business, when his "star exploded", as he has characterised it, it seemed to happen instantaneously. Almost overnight Barry Manilow went from being a private citizen to being a public commodity who was constantly on the lookout for those trying to gain access to him.

---

[12] Nor, apparently, will he ever. In an internet news blurb dated May 10, 2001, writer Dan Croft had this to report: "Official celebrity sighting, 2001: Today, on a side trip to Palm Springs, a fast two-hour spin from downtown Los Angeles, we watched the Man Who Writes the Songs That Make the People Sing, Barry Manilow, enter a corner convenience store and emerge minutes later wielding what looked to be a package of Hostess Cupcakes. Moral of this sighting: Man, or Manilow, does not live by music alone."

"I'm a very private person," Manilow, in 1977, told a *People* magazine interviewer who went on to note that Barry's success "has made him a virtual recluse, terrified that fans will discover his address or phone number."

It hadn't started out that way. When a reporter with *Oui* magazine came to visit Barry at his 27th Street apartment in New York in 1976, Barry said of his surroundings, "It's the same apartment I lived in for years before I had a hit record and became the number one artist in the country. I was perfectly comfortable here when I was singing commercials and when I was Bette Midler's musical director, so why should I move just because I became a star overnight? I mean, being famous is fun, but it hasn't affected my lifestyle one iota."

Unfortunately, that wasn't true for long. By the time Barry spoke with *Ladies' Home Journal* in early 1979, he'd been forced to move from the 27th Street apartment when *Who's Who* printed his home address, "without my permission, I might add," Barry told the journalist. "First the letters started coming," Manilow explained. "I had no idea how. Then they started piling up in front of the door. Until then I had had a wonderfully private life there. My records were number one yet I was able to lead a normal existence. Then suddenly this *Who's Who* thing came out and fans started to camp outside the door. It was hellish, just hellish, so I had to move."

The *Who's Who* incident would mark the end of Barry's dual life of public star and private citizen. "I live in this building under a pseudonym," Manilow warned the visitor from *Ladies' Home Journal*. "Today the doormen were told you'd be asking for me, but if you come here tomorrow and ask for Barry Manilow, they will shoot you in the nose." Later, when he'd made the permanent move to California, he told another journalist that his Bel Air mansion had been equipped with security devices that would "blow your brains out if things go off".

"I thought he liked it," says producer Ron Dante, of the adulation Barry received from his fans. "I thought he was very happy about all that. He was a little scared. He was afraid they'd get overly zealous and hurt him in some way. But I think anybody who's got a crowd of people around him pushing and shoving would feel the same way."

Barry's former assistant, Paul Brownstein, concurs. "Have you ever been in a limo that people are pushing and shoving on and you're trapped in your own exit traffic? With people pushing and shoving and you feel the car may go over? And he lived on Central Park West and I was working for him the week John Lennon was shot. He's got a very high pressure job. It's not easy to be a star."

In the beginning of his career, the waves of adulation coming from total strangers just seemed to confuse Manilow, who was already going through an identity crisis as his life began changing with his success. "I was getting an acceptance that I'd never dreamed of," he later wrote of the mounds of fan mail that quickly began accumulating from his fans. "They gave me credit for all of their triumphs and gratitude for helping them through hard times. It was as if I was a light in the darkness for them." Barry, from his point of view, was merely doing a job, the same job he'd been doing more or less constantly for years. But suddenly he was doing that job in a blinding public spotlight. "Why were the fans acting so fanatically?" he wrote. "People were acting like I was the second coming and it was impossible to deal with. They felt as if they really knew me. Hell, I was just a musician trying my best to learn how to sing and perform."

It's this ability to make a connection with his audience that is the key to the steadfast loyalty of Manilow's followers. "He has an extraordinary touch for touching people," says Manilow's friend, rock icon Dick Clark. "He knows exactly what they want to hear."

It's this ability to sing to the world, one person at a time, that makes many fans feel that they have a window into Manilow's soul. Having toured with Barry for years, Lee Gurst was a constant witness to Barry's interactions with his fans and the ways in which they invest Barry with their own projected longings. "People create in their minds a relationship," says Gurst. *"He's singing to me, he knows about me. I know everybody else is hearing this, but he really knows about me. That's so much my story, my struggle. I know who he is because he sings about me.* And that's not so. But people make of it what it means to them, and then they live with that as if it's real. And then to feel that seen and that understood when a lot of people don't — I mean, wouldn't you gravitate towards someone who just seems to get you, that personally, that deeply, that intimately?"

But to make that kind of connection with an audience can put a performer in an extremely awkward situation. More often than not the person the audience sees on the stage is not the same person offstage. "I have to make myself *bigger*," Manilow told a *Playgirl* editor who was witnessing Barry's pre-show ritual. I pump myself up like I'm pumpin' air into a tyre. I couldn't go out there otherwise, I don't think anyone would notice me." The problem is, where does a performer draw the line between person and persona?

"Most fans of mine would be very disappointed if they realised I don't walk around in my rhinestone top all the time and do not sing all day long," Manilow complained to a journalist in 1979. "Sometimes I don't even want to meet fans because I'm afraid I'll disappoint them." To illustrate his point, he cited the example of his idol, respected singer-composer Laura Nyro. "Her music changed my life," he said. "I fantasised about her for so long. Then I kept hearing reports about what it was like to work with her, to be with her, what she was *really* like. And it wasn't anything like I wanted her to be. After I heard all that, I didn't *want* to meet her."[13]

Former Eastern District High School teacher Herb Bernstein, after leaving teaching and embarking on his successful music career, saw enough examples of this dichotomy to make him completely sympathetic to Barry's feelings on the matter. He cites one example of a couple he and his wife knew who used to like to attend concerts and stage shows, for which Herb could often get them backstage passes to meet the stars. One day Herb's friend said, "You know, Herb, do me a favour and don't introduce me to any of these people." Herb, nonplussed, asked why. "I love their talent, I love to hear them," his friend explained, "and then I meet them and they're such jerks that I lose it. I can't appreciate their talent."

Herb recalls his own wife's excitement one night when they were able to go backstage to meet a well-known jazz singer, who Ann Bernstein, daughter of Italian singer Jimmy Roselli, greatly admired. Ann breathlessly expressed her admiration to the singer, saying, "I love your singing, I have all your tapes!" to which her idol replied, "Fuck off!"

---

[13] Laura Nyro's cousin, Dan Nigro, has this memory of Barry Manilow: "I met him at one of Laura's Bottom Line shows in '88 – he was with Melissa Manchester. I told him how much I liked his live show I'd attended when I was 13 – he had put on a very good show. He was very standoffish when I talked to him – didn't say one word. Laura could get away without speaking and not seeming rude – Manilow couldn't."

"So," says Herb Bernstein, "I see what Barry means. Unfortunately a lot of these performers you meet are so disappointing as people."

But Barry Manilow's stage persona seemed so personable, so affable, so open, that fans would never suspect it was a well-rehearsed facade, simply that pumped up version of the offstage man. To these devoted followers there could be no distinction between – as Manilow once characterised it – Barry Manilow and BARRY MANILOW. This person singing to all their hopes and dreams and fears obviously knew and understood them so intimately, it was simply inconceivable that they, in turn, didn't know him equally well.

"Some people," says Lee Gurst, "really see it as like a personal connection that is so intensely intimate that it is real and deep, and they will go to great lengths to keep that connection. And they identify with Barry because he obviously knows them, so they assume they know him. And that's just not the case. Performers are performers. They're not necessarily telling the truth about themselves every time they get up and perform a piece of music."

★

Barry and Jeanne Lucas once went to see Judy Garland making one of her final appearances in New York City, and after the show, they went backstage to meet the legendary singer. Both Barry and Jeanne expressed their admiration for Garland's work and for her performance that night, and mentioned that they'd be catching the next show as well. "I wish you wouldn't," Garland replied. Jeanne and Barry were taken aback by the comment, and Jeanne, slightly hurt, asked Garland why she didn't want them to return. Garland explained, "Because I work very hard at being Judy Garland, and everything that seems spontaneous to you won't the second time around." Respecting Garland's wishes, Jeanne and Barry did not return for the second show.

"She didn't want people to know it was all the act," Jeanne says, explaining that Barry would find himself in the same situation after his own success. "Barry works very hard at being Barry. And it's the kind of thing we all do. It's part of your show. Even the things you're trying to make seem as if you just thought of it, it's all part of the show. We're entertaining – it's an act. And his fans who see it night after night must know that."

But if they know it – and, as Jeanne points out, they must – they don't care. Like the constant repetition of prayers on a string of rosary beads, Manilow's truly faithful seem to find comfort in the constant repetition of the same material presented in the same way but at different venues, night after night. It can be a bone of contention, a dividing line between the Manilover elite and those the über-fans see as non-contenders.

"Certainly in most cases it doesn't get into anything pathological," says Lee Gurst. "In some extreme cases it does, and you have stalkers and fans who follow you from town to town, and they show up front row for every show for three weeks in Las Vegas. I can just imagine the kind of money they're laying out to get those seats."

Like drug addicts, there are fans who will go to any lengths to score one more ticket to one more show in one more town, just to be in the same concert hall or arena with Barry, one more time. A British housewife explains what she went through in order to see Barry again:

> *"The first time I saw him was at Blenheim. And when I actually saw him I thought: He's real, that's him. Especially when he stood there after all these fantasies and looking at pictures and videos and things. He was actually there.*
>
> *"I could have burst into tears. In fact I did, but that was at the end when he'd gone. It was an emotion that made me want to cry – that he was there after all the waiting and fantasising and staring at his pictures. I mean, his pictures are plastered all over the bedroom walls. And it was just something that made my heart beat faster. I kept thinking: Oh God, when he goes – what's it going to be like when he goes?*
>
> *"And at the end when he'd gone it was dreadful. I thought: I'll never see him again. I felt: This is it. He's gone. I was really, really upset. I kept saying over and over again: 'I can't stand it. When am I going to see him again?' And my friend said: 'The Festival Hall.' I said: 'Ridiculous! What, at £50–£100 a ticket?!'*
>
> *"That was awful. That really hit me more than anything – that money comes between me and Barry. 'Cos I hate money anyway. It embarrasses me. I'm not interested in having it unless I want something.*
>
> *"So I got this job delivering coupons. I delivered 5,000 coupons to buy one concert ticket! I nearly dropped but I did it. I worked it out – it was 5,000 coupons to buy one concert ticket, and that was the cheapest one."*

It's an extreme the majority of fans would not be willing to go to, though there is intense peer pressure among Manilow fans to rack up attendance points. "I cannot afford to follow him around the entire country," complains one fan. "I cannot afford a weekend in Las Vegas. I've never met Barry or Garry [Kief, Manilow's manager] or Marc [Hulett, Manilow's personal assistant]. I doubt I ever will. They've never heard of me. But I have followed Barry's career for years and I adore him and his music. And that's good enough for me."

But for those not willing to make such sacrifices – and some have even gone so far as to forfeit their marriages and spend their mortgage money – there is a strict caste system that can make those who've not actively devoted their lives to Mani-love (as some fans call it) feel like "untouchables".

"I tell you," says Lynne, from Atlanta, "when I first got on the internet, I could not wait to meet and talk with other Barry fans. But I learned real quick, it's a dog eat dog world with Barry fans. If you hadn't been to over 100 concerts, then you weren't a 'real' fan. I had so many girls try to make me feel 'less than worthy'. I've only been to six . . ."

Another fan agrees that the pettiness has gotten worse in recent years, and can often get out of control. "Everyone knows more, has seen him more, has more of his things . . . You have to understand, I've been a Manilow fan for 25 years and it's never been about the crew, the background singers, the sexuality, the colour of his hair, jacket, tie, etc. For me it's about the music . . ."

But of all the songs in Barry's repertoire, the one that fans have claimed as their own is a harmless little ditty called 'Can't Smile Without You'. For many music lovers who aren't Manilow fans, the song can be like a piece of tin foil caught between the teeth.

"Did I ever tell you that I tried to watch a Manilow special on cable?" rock biographer and former *Rolling Stone* editor Jerry Hopkins recently wrote. "This was about six months ago and I'd never seen him before, didn't know what any of his songs sounded like, didn't even know what he looked like. I was appalled. Trivial lyrics and melodies that all sounded like the same Hallmark valentine, and those fans! The way they giggled and swooned over a man who obviously has no interest in them – or any other females, for that matter – made me want to puke."

Ironically, 'Can't Smile Without You', the song that makes fans giggle and swoon the most, actually got its genesis from a greeting card. David Martin, one of the song's co-authors, says, "In 1975, my wife Debbie was working at a greeting card store. One evening she gave me a card. The card was completely plain except for a small blue badge on the front. On the badge was a face with the mouth drooping at the corners and a tear rolling down the cheek. Across the top of the card were simply the words, 'Can't Smile Without You.'" Thirty minutes later, the song was composed. Nearly 30 years later, it has become the centrepiece of all Manilow concerts.

To an outside observer, the ritual of choosing the "CSWY girl" at each Barry Manilow concert looks like a cross between a Texas cattle auction and *Let's Make a Deal*, with Manilow serving as combination herd boss and Monty Hall manque. By the time Manilow gets around to actually introducing the number, his words are all but drowned out by the shrieks of knowing fans, who've been to so many concerts they have the sequence memorised. Manilow is careful to specify that only women are eligible for the CSWY honour. In turn, scores of mostly middle-aged women leap to their feet, screaming and crying, jumping up and down and frantically waving giant, brightly decorated placards with legends like LET'S DO IT! and BARRY, MAKE ME SMILE! and LAST CHANCE THIS TOUR! A reporter from the British magazine *Q* was in the audience to witness the spectacle one night, and lived to tell the tale:

> "*Tonight, Barry Manilow, the unlikely sex symbol who never quite completed the metamorphosis from frog to prince, is playing Liverpool. Halfway through the tinselly extravaganza – a slickly executed procession of bantamweight jazz numbers and high-cholesterol ballads – Barry enquires as to whether a member of the audience would care to join him on stage for the jaunty duet 'I Can't Smile Without You'. The request is met by a mass unfurling of banners reading:* Choose Me! I'm The One! Please Please Please Please! *Etc. After much hammy deliberation, Barry opts for Anne, whom he instructs, a little patronisingly, to 'sing into the top of the microphone', holding her firmly by the elbow. During the second verse, Barry hops up on to his piano and cheekily positions Anne between his legs. She seizes the moment and places a shaking hand on his shin. 'Hey!' he leers. 'Whoa! She gives great knee!' As the nine-piece band bring the*

*curiously joyous number to its high-kicking, spangly
staircase-descending climax, Barry ceremoniously presents the
trembling secretary with a freshly recorded videotape of their
performance to take home and treasure forever. Chivalrously, he kisses
her on the cheek and, with a smile like a suspension bridge, waves her
back to the stalls. As she reaches the edge of the stage she turns to
blow a final kiss but, alas, his smile has long since evaporated and
he's about-faced and sashaying back to his piano, mentally running
through the words to his next densely sentimental scarf-waver. The
following evening in Blackpool it happens all over again with the same
Rolex-timed precision. Even when the girl bursts into tears, Barry –
prepared for any eventuality – produces a man-sized tissue and dabs
lovingly at the salty streams alternately murmuring words of solace
and pulling amusing faces at the audience over her shoulder."*

For the women who get chosen to be one of Barry's nightly partners, it's an event that ranks right up there with taking their wedding vows and having their first child – though one doesn't dare enquire as to the order of importance of these events. "I've known my wife for about ten years," writes one proud husband of his wife's turn as a CSWY Girl. "We've been married for about seven, we have a cocker that she loves dearly, I cut the cord when Julie [presumably their daughter, not the cocker] was born, but I have never been happier for my wife than the day she got to sing with Barry Manilow."

It's this sort of over-earnest devotion that makes Manilow fans a favourite target of cynics, comics, and the world at large. After all, it's hard to take seriously a group who can engage in a protracted, heated argument in an online forum over the fact that a former CSWY Girl went back for seconds, a flagrant breach of concert etiquette. "Sure hope it pleased you to get up there and sing for the second time with Barry," wrote one poster cattily, incensed at the injustice of it all. ". . . so many haven't had the chance, and you go and do it again, and only a few months apart. And, the way you were all over him was not so very nice, it was disgusting." Battle lines were quickly drawn, some defending the woman's actions, others taking exception not only to the fact that the woman put herself forward twice for CSWY Girl honours, but that she also took advantage in other ways once onstage. "I never called her a slut," said another poster, defending earlier statements she had made about the woman. "I said she behaved slutty. I'm sorry, but you can not tell me that Barry appreciates that sort of behaviour. I was embarrassed for the man."

Barry Manilow is a favourite target for humour columnist Dave Barry, who says he "hates to reveal" that he has spent some time surfing the net and has observed the behaviour on the online fan forums, much to his chagrin. His curiosity has taken him to the alt.fan.barry-manilow and alt.fan.hawaii-five-o newsgroups. "It's fascinating," he writes, "to see this week-long, thoughtful, careful, articulate, literate debate over whether Jack Lord did or did not wear a hairpiece in a certain episode." On the Manilow newsgroup, he says, "Someone will come in and say bad things about Barry, and this will really upset his fans, and violent flame wars will break out – over Barry Manilow. Without the internet, this would not be possible." He does not say this in praise of the internet.

To those who have known Barry the best, the extreme devotion of his fans is simply a mystery. "It's like they feel that Barry needs them desperately," says Jeanne Lucas. "It's not that they need him, he needs them. It's like they'd feel safe with him, and all that stuff, and he's this good guy. But also it's like he's this flawed, needy guy that they have to be there to support. That's the sense that I get. It's really interesting. But these are all people, I think, who need to feel that they belong somewhere. If they were different people they'd join Scientology. I really feel that this is, the whole gestalt of them being the fans and all that stuff, has really got more to do with their needs than it ever does Barry. It gives them a sense of belonging, of camaraderie, of that kind of thing, is what I think."

In her essay *Fandom as Pathology: The Consequences of Characterization*,[14] Jolie Jenson has what most scholars would probably deem the effrontery to cast Barry Manilow fans in the same mould as academicians pursuing a scholarly subject. She puts forth the proposition that the fan, cast as an object of alternate fear and ridicule, is all subject to perspective:

> *The literature of fandom, celebrity and media influence tells us that: Fans suffer from psychological inadequacy, and are particularly*

[14] Contained in the book *The Adoring Audience: Fan Culture and Popular Media*, edited by Lisa A. Lewis, Routledge, 1992.

vulnerable to media influence and crowd contagion. They seek contact with famous people in order to compensate for their own inadequate lives. Because modern life is alienated and atomized, fans develop loyalties to celebrities and sports teams to bask in reflected glory, and attend rock concerts and sports events to feel an illusory sense of community.

But what happens if we change the objects of this description from fans to, say, professors? What if we describe the loyalties that scholars feel to academic disciplines rather than to team sports, and attendance at scholarly conferences, rather than Who concerts and soccer matches? What if we describe opera buffs and operas? Antique collectors and auctions? Trout fishermen and angling contests? Gardeners and horticulture shows? Do the assumptions about inadequacy, deviance and danger still apply?

What is the basis for these differences between fans like 'them' and aficionados like 'us'? . . . Apparently, if the object of desire is popular with the lower or middle class, relatively inexpensive and widely available, it is fandom (or a harmless hobby); if it is popular with the wealthy and well educated, expensive and rare, it is preference, interest, or expertise.

Am I suggesting, then, that a Barry Manilow fan be compared with, for example, a Joyce scholar? The mind may reel at the comparison, but why? The Manilow fan knows intimately every recording (and every version) of Barry's songs; the Joyce scholar knows intimately every volume (and every version) of Joyce's oeuvre. The relationship between Manilow's real life and his music is explored in detail in star biographies and fan magazines; the relationship between Dublin, Bloomsday and Joyce's actual experiences are explored in detail in biographies and scholarly monographs.

Yes, you may say, there are indeed these surface similarities. But what about the fans who are obsessed with Barry, who organize their life around him? Surely no Joyce scholar would become equally obsessive? But the uproar over the definitive edition of Ulysses suggests that the participant Joyceans are fully obsessed, and have indeed organized their life (even their 'identity' and 'community') around Joyce.

But is a scholar, collector, aficionado 'in love' with the object of his or her desire? Is it the existence of passion that defines the distinction between fan and aficionado, between dangerous and benign, between deviance and normalcy?

"I guess the core of it is you've gotta figure out what does Barry mean to these girls?" says Jeanne Lucas. "I mean what is it they fantasise about? If there's some gorgeous singer out there or whatever, we know we're all fantasising about maybe being with them or whatever because they're sexy, etc. But Barry, he's just the antithesis of that. What is it that he's projecting? Safety? Would they feel safe with him? Is that what it is?"

In fact it's the sexual component of the fans' adoration that most puzzles outsiders. One magazine described Manilow as "the unlikely sex symbol who never quite completed the metamorphosis from frog to prince". But Manilow is a frog prince who has always been able to inspire the twin desires – maternal care-giving and drooling lust – in many of his followers. And, as Jolie Jenson points out, it is very often this duality of emotional and physical love felt for the object of obsession – in this case, Barry Manilow – that marks the difference between fan and aficionado.

A case in point was illustrated with frightening clarity in Fred and Judy Vermorel's 1985 book, *Starlust: The Secret Fantasies of Fans*. Far from being the fictionalised titillation typical of lurid "true confession" magazines, the stories found in *Starlust* were gathered by the authors from, according to the Vermorels, "typical pop star fans as we found them in over four years of research. For every story told here there were dozens of similar ones. There are fans like these in every classroom and every suburban street."

Among these stories was that of Rosie, a 43-year-old British housewife, who first found comfort in Barry Manilow's songs, then found companionship through a shared love of the singer with others in her area. Barry Manilow once remarked that his fans acted "like I was the second coming". For Rosie, that became more than just a turn of phrase.

Rosie: Barry and God

"Me and my husband only live together now as brother and sister.

"Because – and this may seem rather silly and stupid – but I just feel unclean with any other man apart from Barry. If I can't have sexual intercourse with Barry, I'll go without. I'll never be unfaithful to Barry.

"My husband understands this. He realises my interests are different to his and he does try to understand.

185

"Sometimes he does say: 'You've got to make up your mind between me and Barry.' But then he knows how much I love Barry and that if he got on to me too much I'd just go and live with one of my friends.

"So I'm really fortunate. We've got a good relationship. I've never felt this way for anyone else even though I've been married three times and I've had quite a number of boyfriends.

"But I really feel for Barry and I think it's because he came when I needed love and friendship the most. What he's done for me only I and dedicated fans can understand.

"I never used to have any friends as such. Me and my mum had been very close. And then she died.

"And about two weeks after she died the BBC repeated Barry's concerts from the previous January and April. I put the television on and it was as if just at that moment Barry looked into the camera and was looking at me through the television. I know he wasn't of course, it's ridiculous, but he seemed to know. He said to me in a private sort of way: 'Rosie, don't worry. You've lost your mum but God will be good to you. He's sent me to help you and I will help you. If you love me and follow me, I'll help you as much as I can. I'll get you friends, I'll take you out of yourself and you can start a whole new way of life.'

"Next day I went into town and bought Pure Magic No.2. And funnily enough there was a girl's address on a sticker on the record. She lived fairly locally, six miles away. I rang her up and she invited me to a get-together at her house the following Wednesday.

"Joanne and I became good friends. She got me videos done, she got me photocopies of Barry which I'd missed.

"Then I joined the official fan club. And about four weeks later I got a letter from Mandy saying she'd heard about me through the fan club and inviting me to a get-together at her place. I made more friends there and then I joined another local club where we all meet Friday evenings – we call Friday evenings 'Barry nights'. And without Barry and all these dear friends I've made through him I don't know how I could have coped with life. I mean no one can take my mum's place, but he's certainly done a very good job trying to.

"And it's not just me. He's helped so many people. Like my friend Joyce who lost her husband and through Barry she's been able to start a new life, make life mean something again.

"Joyce and I have only met once, at the convention last year. But through what we call 'Manimail' we've become very, very close. If *we're upset, if we're sad, if we're happy, we write and tell each other about it. We open our hearts to each other, tell each other all our problems. We understand each other. Because we've got the same love for Barry.*

"*Barry is a lover, a husband and a very best friend. I tell him everything. When I'm happy I tell him. And I cry to him.*

"*But I must admit I do get very frustrated sexually. When I have a sexual urge and I know he can't be there I often have to fight it. Joyce goes through the same thing. It can be very, very frustrating.*

"*I love him. And I'd love to have his child. When he says he'd like a kid I pray to God — I know it just can't be but I hope.*

"*Every night Barry's always here with me. Even if we don't make love he's lying here with me — he kisses me goodnight and that. And I think: 'Oh, if only I could wave a magic wand and make these posters come to life.' And if a fairy godmother said you can have one wish I'd answer: 'Let Barry be here with me — as my husband, or my boyfriend or even a good friend.'*

"*I kiss Barry's photograph every night and I say: 'Good-night and God bless. Have a good night. See you in the morning.'*

"*I couldn't sleep without his posters on the wall. Sometimes I imagine him in bed with me and we're making love. I close my eyes and we kiss and I touch myself and I imagine it's him. And I get sexually worked up . . .*

"*When I wake up Barry's always the first thing on my mind. He's the first thing I see because my bedroom's full of posters.*

"*I say: 'Good morning, Barry. Good morning, Biscuit. Good morning, Bagel [Barry's pet dogs].' I usually get up half-sevenish, something like that, and do a few jobs. Most days I have Manimail. I like to read it over a cup of coffee, to see who's written to me. I usually try and answer two or three letters a day.*

"*My fantasy is that Barry's always here. The house never seems empty and if I feel like talking I talk to Barry. I ask him: 'Do you think I'm doing this right?' or, 'Where have I put this?' Or if I put a spoon down or a tea towel I say: 'Barry, have you seen this? Now, where have you put it?' And I have a fantasy based on the fact that I know he doesn't get up very early. So I always shout and say: 'Are you going to get out of bed? If you don't I'll pull your clothes off you.' So he starts running around the bedroom. And I say: 'Stop acting the fool. I've got my work to do. There's a time and place for everything.'*

187

"And I say: 'Shall we have a cup of coffee now?' I say: 'Now go and practise your piano. I've got some letters to write, and if you want anything, give me a shout.' He says: 'OK, honey, I will.'

"And me and Barry usually do a few jobs together in the morning.

"In the afternoon Barry always practises the piano while I do things for the club, answer letters, arrange sponsoring or just anything connected with Barry.

"And then at night my husband comes in through the door.

"He says it's like entering another world. He says: 'I never hear Barry's name mentioned all day, but first thing I hear in here is always Barry: what letters you've written, what you've been doing, what records you've been playing and all the nonsense you've been saying to Barry.'

"And he says: 'I feel embarrassed to tell people at work what kind of wife I've got. I think you're round the twist.'

"He knows a girl at his work who likes Barry. I've asked him to ask this girl to our house. But he says: 'I'll do no such thing. I don't want to be laughed at.' I say: 'Well, it's no laughing matter. It's real.' He says: 'I know it's real to you.'

"And he says: 'The trouble with you, Rosie, is that you think everybody should be addicted to Barry like you are. When the neighbours come round,' he says, 'you're embarrassing. It's like you've got no other subject: Barry this, Barry the other. It gets a bit embarrassing.'

"I say: 'Well, I understand your sister Hilary's got her interest in the Chapel.' He says: 'Yes, but she don't go on about it like you do.'

"I say: 'Well, I don't think I do keep on about it.' You know, to me I think it's just normal.

"And, as I say, we've got separate rooms now. And sometimes I say to my husband: 'Go and have a look in my room. See if Barry's in there.' And he accepts it.

"But I know girls whose husbands won't let them have a picture of Barry in the house. They rip posters down.

"Quite a number of my friends have had divorces through Barry. Like Elsie and Patricia who run the fan club. Patricia's husband said: 'I think it's quite ridiculous you being so addicted to a man you're never going to meet. You're a married woman, you're grown up, you ought to have more sense.' And he says: 'You've got to choose *between me and Barry.' She said: 'That's not very hard to do.' So they split up.*

"And, of course, I can understand men. I suppose in a way I'm very lucky. It's as if your husband had pictures of Sophia Loren all over your flat and fantasised making love to her and kept saying: 'I love Sophia Loren. I wish she was here.' What would your reaction be? So you've got to like try and see their point of view.

"But me and a lot of my very dear friends have got understanding husbands. They understand they can't do anything about it. It's been like a jigsaw puzzle – I just can't understand it. I think actually it's Manilow magic.

"Because I've only been an addicted fan for two years and I've got closer to him than some of the girls who've been fans of his since '78.

"Like at the Royal Festival Hall I just couldn't believe my luck. I was in the fourth row, right by his piano and in line with his mike stand. And it was just like family – you forgot the people behind you.

"After he'd finished singing his first ballad he put his arm out. I put mine out to him and he saw me.

"And for a few moments our eyes met.

"The person sitting next to me said: 'Hey, you two!' He heard her and he gave her one of his famous chuckles – which was fantastic. And all that night Barry knew I was there, you know, we kept looking at each other.

"I cried for nearly a week after he'd looked into my eyes. Every time I played a record I saw him and I would burst into tears. It took me a month before I could listen to a record or look at a video without tears rolling down my cheeks.

"You have to go to one of his shows to realise the magic and the warmth and the love Barry creates among his fans. When they start singing 'We'll Meet Again' and all join hands you can almost feel the love. Something runs between us like an electric shock. It's just wonderful.

"One day my friend, Hilary, said to me: 'Rosie, if Barry had lived 2,000 years ago who would you say he was?'

"Me and Hilary didn't say anything. We just looked at each other and we knew what we both were thinking. She said: 'Yes, precisely.'

"I think he's the second coming.

"He is a Jew, he comes from that race of people and I think Barry's a very special person. There's nobody else like him. There's other pop *stars but they don't seem to do as much for the fans as Barry does. He's a different sort of singer, different sort of personality. He creates a lot of love and warmth. He helps people through a lot of things in different ways – which no other singer can do.*

"And I quite agree with Hilary. My husband thinks it's blasphemous, but I don't. He says: 'You're putting Barry before God.' I say: 'On the contrary, I don't put Barry before God, he's brought me closer to God.'

"People who aren't fans of Barry, like my husband, think: 'Well, he's laughing all the way to the bank, getting richer and richer and you're getting poorer and poorer.'

"I say: 'No. Barry's getting richer financially, we're getting richer morally.' "

It's interesting to note how often Barry and those who know and have worked with him will employ the same kind of language to describe his effect on others that the fans themselves will often use, though sometimes in a startlingly different context. Like Rosie, who made literal Barry's comment about fans treating him like the second coming, 42-year-old Joanne echoes producer Ron Dante's sentiments when he says, "The world at large takes him very seriously. People travel with him to see his show. Fans in Europe they go from place to place to see his show. Over 60 million fans can't be wrong." And, like Rosie, Joanne, mother of three, married to an often-absent travelling salesman, tells a story of passion and longing that again brings into play Barry's apparent ability to fill a desperate need for companionship and love:

"I suppose it's the same kind of thing people get out of religion. I can't really explain it more than that. But they obviously get something from God to help them through their lives. And Barry is – maybe I shouldn't say it but it's the way I feel – he's the same sort of thing. He helps me through my life.

"But also it isn't just that, because I'm attracted to him as well. I am definitely attracted to him. It's what I describe as a one-sided love affair. He's my lover in my fantasies. He's my friend when I'm depressed. He's there and he seems to serve as something I need to get through my life.

"He's my friend and he's my lover- mostly he's my lover!

"I've been married 20 years. My husband's used to me being a fan

*because he knows what I am now. But when it first happened it
frightened him and it frightened me too because neither of us knew
what was happening . . ."*

She tells of a previous obsession with another star, an infatuation
that led her to the brink of suicide before finally dissipating after
several years.

*"So now with Barry I can cope better because I've been through it all
before. When I felt it coming on I thought: I'm older now, I can cope
with it. I couldn't cope with —— because I'd never felt anything like
it before. And although there have been times when I've been very
depressed and I have the crying fits where I can't stop crying over him,
I've never got suicidal over Barry.*

*"It helps too that my husband accepts it – he accepts Barry. This
time it's easier for him to accept . . .*

*"I've gone over that, trying to analyse it time and time again. I do
love my husband, very much . . . But Barry at the moment is
something that excites me and he's the be all and end all of this
moment in my life.*

*"My husband's away quite a bit, so Barry kind of keeps me
company when he's away.*

*"I imagine he's composing at the piano and I'm just there and I'm
his girlfriend. And he is so deeply involved in composing his music he
doesn't take any notice of me whatsoever. I bring him a cup of coffee
and he kind of says: 'Put it there,' and carries on. And then he's
angry because something won't go right with the piece and he's angry
and in this terrible mood. And I'm just sort of there, but I don't
interrupt him. And then suddenly he realises what he's like and he
comes out of it and sympathises with me, apologises for being that
way. And then we make love and everything's fine.*

*"Usually we make love on the settee or on the floor – or anywhere.
Not very often in bed. Usually where we are. He's very passionate,
very gentle, considerate. I can't imagine that there's any aggression
there at all. He's not that aggressive sort of love-maker. Very
passionate, very romantic.*

*"Sometimes I imagine us having a shower together. It's beautiful.
We're caressing each other and kissing under the shower, our bodies
are pressed together and oh, it's heaven. Always so gentle and loving
he appears to be.*

"*Touch plays a big part in it, it really does. Touching each other is really important. It's all done so romantically and gently. Not just for sex. It's love more than sex. And it's a bit like it's all in slow motion.*

"*I love his lovely, long fingers. I can imagine being caressed by his hands all over my body.*

"*Usually it's in subdued lighting, and in the open air ones it's under the stars.*

"*And it really does help me through my life. It makes life, you know, worth living.*

"*He's the type of man who would buy me flowers. He would be considerate and treat me like a woman and not like a mate, you know, like making me help him shift the settee. I like to be treated like a woman sometimes and have flowers bought for me. So I imagine Barry would be very tender and loving.*

"*And I think that's probably what I'm in love with. Although I'm also attracted to his looks and his body – I'm very attracted to his body! I love touching him all over, every part of him, and running my fingers through his hair. And I'm particularly attracted to his neck. I think he's got the most gorgeous neck I've ever seen. I kiss his neck. And, I'm also attracted to his arms. People laugh at me because he's got thin arms but I find them so attractive. I've got pictures of him in a sleeveless T-shirt which shows all his arms. And he seems to have such soft skin – it's a real-turn on that is! I imagine putting my hand inside his T-shirt and his body would be very soft. I would love to touch his body.*

"*I do get wet thinking about him like that, but I don't ever orgasm. It can be very frustrating. It's handy having a husband! I think Barry has improved our sex life if anything. To be quite honest, definitely, he has improved our sex life. I was quite frigid before but now with this fantasising it's better for me and it's better for my husband. And luckily he never says no, he's always ready for it.*

"*Often I look at a poster and that will start it off. I think he's got the most beautiful body. And certain posters turn me on more than others. Some just make me happy and others I find sexually attractive.*

"*I like to lay in bed at night before I turn the light out and look at them. That's when I start to fantasise.*

"*He comes into his dressing room. I'm aware of him shutting the door and locking it. There's nobody else there. And he's all excited*

192

and sweating from his exertions with the concert. And there's just me and him in his dressing room. And there's no place to lie down so we usually do it standing up.

"Sometimes he unzips his trousers, sometimes I do. Then there's the one in front of the fire, on a fur skin rug. That's after the wine and the soft music and the talking.

"I imagine that we would talk an awful lot beforehand but not actually when we're making love. He becomes silent. He French kisses me and kisses me all over and on my breasts and he touches me here, between my legs.

"I've got no appetite whatsoever whenever I'm about to see Barry. It completely goes. I just don't want to look at any food. I've always got this feeling I'm going to be sick, going to spoil things. It's an odd feeling. It always affects me in that way, the excitement . . .

"I've never known such a sexual element with any other star as there is with Barry. Because the fans all go for these photographs we call 'bum shots'. It's a sort of race for who gets the most bum shots.

"When he was last over here he caught on, because he said: 'Since I've been over here I've seen more photographs of my backside than of my face!' And he sees the funny side of that.

"With all the photographs that get passed around, the more disgusting ones the better. Like one particular photograph I got hold of called 'the headless wonder'. A girl took this photograph of him in a fantastic black satin outfit and she was so thrilled with her efforts because it showed up his manly bulge to a treat! She was so pleased with this photograph it was three weeks before she noticed they never printed his head. She had it pointed out to her: 'Yeah, it is very nice, but where's his head?' She said: 'Oh, I hadn't looked up that far!'

"And that is the kind of fans he's got. I reckon 99 and three quarter per cent of his fans are like that. They do get a great thrill out of that kind of thing.

"But it isn't only that.

"Because I've been to lots and lots of concerts but I've never felt that kind of atmosphere and that kind of closeness. Complete strangers catch hold of your hands. And you are all united, united as one.

"And to think that one man can do that to so many people. I mean, he must be special to be able to do that, to create this atmosphere and this special feeling. He can't just be ordinary, can he? So many people can't be wrong.

"I rarely dream about him. And when I do it's not what I'd like. I rarely dream romantic dreams. They're usually troubled dreams. I often dream I have this concert ticket and I can't get there. There's always something stopping me and by the time I get there it's all over.

"When he was due to come on TV the other day and I was planning to tape it, I had this dream where it had been on the day before and I'd missed it, completely. I was glad to wake up and find it was only a dream. That is a thing I dread anyway. I always make a point of buying two tapes and I have my friend make a copy in case something goes wrong with mine. I'm a neurotic when he comes on TV. I never enjoy it, not the first time I see it. Not until I play it back and know I've got it.

"Last Christmas Eve my husband was away and I was alone and when midnight came I thought: It's Christmas Day, I'm going to spend it with Barry. I'm going to open my presents now and I'm going to have Barry for company. So I sat here all on my own and I opened my presents and played Barry on the video. He was like my friend that was with me, because I was alone. Him being there on television is like he's in the room with me. I don't go as far as thinking he's actually here. But his spirit's here with me.

"When I watch him I sit right up close – I've always got to sit up close. I get a pouffe and sit right up a few inches away from him. The closer I am the better. I get frustrated if I'm not close. Because I feel otherwise I'm going to miss something . . .

"I often wonder whether I would actually give up my life that I'm leading now to go with Barry. It's difficult. I don't really know. You see, I can't hurt people. I find it very difficult to hurt anyone. I tend to put other people before the way I feel myself. I don't think if he came in here now and said: 'Come on', that I would go. Even though I love him so much, I couldn't leave my husband to go with him.

"But I often think that I would give up my life for him. If it was just me, if it was just me to think about, I would give up my whole life for him. I would die.

"I always say: 'If I could spend one night with Barry I would happily die tomorrow.' That's how much I love him. I just know I would be quite happy to give up everything for him. Just to know what he was like, what he was really like.

"I suppose it does sound overdramatic really, but it's not something I've just thought up on the spur of the moment. I've thought about it *a lot of times, many times. That's how deep I love him.*

"I don't know whether it is love. It feels like love. But then I've never met him. So how can you love someone you've never met? It's incredible really. It's something I don't really understand.

"But then I wonder if we ever know what love really is. I mean, there's so many different kinds of love. There's the love I have for Barry, the love I have for my husband, the love I have for my children.

"But this, what I feel for Barry, feels like the biggest love affair ever. I don't know whether it is or whether it isn't but it certainly feels like this is what love should be. It's quite hard to cope with sometimes, this passionate feeling, this ultimate of love.

"Some people might say they fall in love, but I wonder if they really feel what I feel. Do they feel the type of love that I feel? I don't know. I think there's different degrees of love in different people. I don't think many people would say that they'd give up their life and die to spend one night with one man.

"They might be very passionate about a man but I don't think they'd be prepared to die for him."

Are Rosie and Joanne examples of the extreme? Absolutely. But for Barry Manilow fans, the extreme is not all that far off centre. Karin, a fan in the United States, recently struggled to sum up Manilow's attraction:

"He touches us; he always has a song to remedy any situation. He pulls us through life along with him. Together we started out uncertain, hesitant, geeky, and we've matured, gained confidence, and threw away polyester! We emerged as adults, with passions, with dreams, with chutzpah and we all give a lot of credit for whom and what we've become to our leader: Barry Manilow. No one can explain it . . . it's an undefinable mystery of how he captivates us and we can't and won't get off this journey. It's in our blood, in our guts, in our hearts . . . I once took a 'virgin' to a Manilow show in New York City and she, to this day, only talks about the unity of the fans, the way he treats his fans, the way he reaches out and touches us. She became hooked after one matinee ten years ago. But remember, there are different levels of 'hooked'. There are those who relate to his nerdy side, those to his 'up yours' side, those to the simplicity of his words. Some would sell their souls to sleep with him, eat with him, know him intimately, and some follow him around the world. There are total opposite ends of the Manilow spectrum: I like to think of myself as a normal, married woman. I've raised two incredible daughters who are in fields of 'giving back'; they took piano lessons and have been to many Manilow shows. My husband, who has been to his share of shows, doesn't 'get it' and therefore this is *my* canasta game, or *my* sewing day, or whatever the women do these days. I've earned the right to do what I want, when I want."

It is an incredible burden of adoration and expectations to place on the rather narrow shoulders of one fragile human being. So what did Manilow make of all this attention being beamed his way?

" I don't remember him ever expressing to me any problems with his fans," says Ron Dante, of Barry's earliest success. "He was very happy to have them, at least when we were working together. And he would read all the fan magazines to see what they were saying about him, he was very interested in everything. It was a great trip."

But as soon as the novelty wore off and the public adoration began affecting his personal life, Manilow started feeling quite differently about some of his fans, though most clearly meant him no harm.

"It's not about meaning no harm," says Paul Brownstein, Manilow's former assistant. "It's about how much time do you have in the day? He had fans that he was personally pen pals with since his first tour, who he wrote to all the time. I assume he's still in touch with them. There are only a handful. They were VIPs as far as he was concerned. They were just normal, ordinary people, various cities."

But it wasn't the "normal, ordinary" people Manilow came to fear.

"As I began to become more and more recognised," he wrote in his 1987 biography *Sweet Life*, "the public became frightening to me. I'd walk down the street and before I knew it there was a mob of people wanting things from me. I'd get on a plane and soon there'd be people kneeling beside me asking for things. They'd stare and point and take my picture as I tried to have a meal in a restaurant. Little by little I began to become very wary of the public . . . The last straw came when I discovered a few 'fans' had been going through my garbage and publishing their findings in a local newsletter. It turned me off so much that I stopped reading fan mail and had a different view of people who approached me from then on."

Lee Gurst confirms that Barry would do all he could to avoid even brief encounters with fans before and after concerts. "I think there are performers who genuinely like their fans," says Gurst. "I think there are performers who endure their fans. I don't think that Barry respected his fans. Kind of like the old Groucho Marx thing, 'I wouldn't belong to any club that would have me as a member.' In reality it speaks more about Barry than about the fans. Barry didn't like having to see people, he was uncomfortable. He's very private, he was very shy. It was awkward, he was awkward with it. I don't think he enjoyed having to play that part of the game. So generally the rule was he would try not to see people after a show. He certainly didn't set himself up and make himself available easily and comfortably to sign autographs or to do that kind of thing. It was arranged when it had to be."

Barry would refuse to see VIPs after the show. There were always more fans than he liked milling around backstage, so often tunnels of sheets would be erected so he could pass without the scrutiny of prying eyes or, failing that, everyone would be required to turn their backs so Barry could pass by, unwatched. Writes Manilow, "I began to understand why celebrities get a reputation for being creeps. I found myself being rude to strangers all the time and I always wanted to run after them and apologise."

Lee Gurst felt that a part of Barry's refusal to deal with his fans any more than absolutely necessary stemmed from Manilow's own unhappiness with the work he was producing, an admitted compromise from the kind of work he'd started out to produce, and the slicked-back, over-produced music largely suggested by Clive Davis that had made Barry a star. "If you did not really love the music you were making, you wouldn't have the best feelings about the people who do," says Gurst. "First of all you have to resent them because you're doing it for them. If someone likes something you do that you love and believe in, you have a connection with them. If you're pandering to them, then you have to resent them for forcing you to give yourself up. They're the ones who call the tunes. They're the ones who put him through hoops to get their approval; it's not the other way around. And the connection between the audience and the artist is not going to be truly a connection through the work. The artist isn't expressing himself and then connecting with the people who received that communication."

Manilow credits Roberta Kent with helping him to get over his need to isolate himself from his fans and interact more freely with them. Kent was the friend of Barry's assistant at the time, Paul Brownstein, who brought Kent to a Christmas party at Barry's house one year. Barry and Roberta immediately hit it off, and she began working with him on writing his stage show, often travelling with him on tours. It was Kent, says Manilow, who began reading his fan mail and bringing some of the more funny, touching, and compelling letters to his attention. "For the first time," Manilow later wrote, "there was a channel of communication opened between me and the public and it was a revelation."

To this day Manilow shares a connection with his fans unparalleled by other artists. His fan base remains greatly unchanged since his early days; the teenagers who bought his music on eight-track tapes are now 21st-century mothers and grandmothers (and, yes, fathers and grandfathers) who collect his work on compact discs, DVDs, and CD-ROM. When Manilow sings 'I Made It Through The Rain', there is a collective consciousness that sings with him, grateful that they've all weathered the same storms together.

Are Barry Manilow fans just a tad more fanatic than aficionado? Perhaps. But, once again, it's all in your perspective. The New Jersey *Star-Ledger* recently ran a piece on fan clubs in which one female fan expressed her exasperation that her devotion was somehow seen as abnormal. "I've had big burly men laugh at me," she says. "These are men who wear large foam fingers and paint themselves green every Sunday afternoon (for football games) – and they call me crazy?"

It's all in your perspective.

Chapter Twenty-six

It was the mid-Seventies, and Lee Gurst and Barry Manilow were driving from New York to Philadelphia for a concert date; Lee was at the wheel. On the radio, a Carpenters song began playing. The poignant sound of Karen Carpenter's exquisite alto was perfectly offset by her brother's rich and intricate orchestration. As the lush melody began to build, Lee reached over to turn up the volume. In the seat next to him, Barry groaned, "Come on! How *can* you!"

"But he's very, very commercial . . ."

For years Barry Manilow has been inspiring similar expressions of agonised disbelief from critics, comics, journalists, and the public at large. "I don't want to defend him because he doesn't need any defence; he's very successful," says rock and roll patriarch Dick Clark, when asked why he thought Manilow has been such a popular object of derision since even before his solo career began. When Manilow made his first appearance on Dick Clark's ubiquitous *American Bandstand*, it had not yet been two years since John Wasserman of the *San Francisco Chronicle* had sneered, "Manilow, who has his hair done at the Clip and Snip Poodle Salon, apparently thinks he is a potential star." At that point Barry had simply been opening the second act of Bette Midler's show. By the time he played 'Mandy' and 'It's A Miracle' for a studio full of screaming and dancing teenagers on *American Bandstand*, Barry actually was a star, though some folks were still stumped as to precisely why.

"I thought he had a great touch," says Clark, of his first impressions of Manilow, "but I could not envision him ever captivating audiences the way he subsequently did years later. I mean, he's a tall,

199

skinny, not particularly handsome man. And they loved him. Just immediately, there was a warmth and an attraction – great smile, wonderful touch with a song. You listen to his voice, and it's not the best voice you ever heard – nor is Ray Charles' or Jimmy Durante's. But there's a sound and a feel to it. I mean Billie Holiday had like a five or six note range and became one of the most popular jazz singers of all time. If you look at the surface, or you look at the sort of statistics and stuff, it's unlikely. But if you suddenly realise that beneath all that there's a helluva lot of talent and knowledge – Barry knows everything there is to know about the music business and arranging and putting songs together that touch people."

And that, in itself, could be a large part of the problem. There is often a perceived sense of manipulation in Barry Manilow's work that seems to work magic with audiences, but often disgusts critics and other professional musicians. Says Clark, "Barry has an amazing commercial touch, which is a double-edged sword. I think musically he has the common touch; he knows exactly what people want. He produces, he writes, he sings, he performs, he does it all magnificently. But he's very, very commercial."

"Commercial" is a tricky concept in any venture that could be even remotely construed to be artistic. While artists of all types are encouraged to produce good works and explore the boundaries of their creativity, somehow they often seem to be expected to do so without the perceived taint of turning that art into a moneymaking endeavour. Given that attitude, it seems odd that so many of the musicians and writers who look down upon the "commercial" seem to be doing so from the comfort of nice homes and opulent surroundings paid for by the commercialisation of their own artistic endeavours. So why, then, should some artists, like Barry Manilow, be held to a higher standard than others?

"When you become that popular and that successful," says Dick Clark, who's been actively involved in the popular music business since before Elvis had sideburns, "you become the modern day punchline like Lawrence Welk used to be years ago. And that's not fair. Totally unfair." The mere fact that Dick Clark remembers the time when kids even knew who Lawrence Welk was is a testament to Clark's longevity in the business. "In the early days of rock and roll when kids would make jokes about Lawrence Welk," Clark continues, "I'd say, 'Now let me point out something to you. If you can ever pursue your dreams, and do it for 30 or 40 years, and amass a fortune and become as wealthy as he has, and have a legion of fans who adore you, then you've got to think about that before you make jokes. Because your career may be 20 minutes.' That shut 'em up pretty good."

While Clark's words may have put a lid on the teenaged Welk bashers, such logic seems lost on the professional critics, so many of whom seem to see their main job to be not actually giving anything or anyone a serious, thoughtful review, but rather trying to see how clever they themselves can be, often at the very personal expense of their subject. Again, witness *San Francisco Chronicle* writer John Wasserman's review of Bette Midler and Barry Manilow at San Francisco's Community Theater in September 1973. Bette is described as "like a rag doll on speed". Wasserman notes that Bette wore a large orchid in her cleavage "which, in Bette's case, is in the vicinity of her knees". In case folks didn't quite get that image, a few paragraphs later Wasserman writes that Bette's "bountiful breasts . . . resemble ostrich eggs dropped into a pair of panty-hose, springing up and down like yo-yos". Of the five column piece, perhaps two paragraphs were actually devoted to discussing Bette's work. The rest made fun of her appearance, made fun of her audience and, beyond all professional reason, made fun of Barry Manilow who, said Wasserman, "has got to go".

"Oh, it's an easy joke for god's sake," says Clark. "It happened to me in my life. I was synonymous with rock and roll, and I was a comedian's punchline for a while. It didn't bother me particularly because it didn't have anything to do with my abilities, I was just synonymous with this freaky thing that was happening, rock and roll. So they could either end the line with 'rock and roll' or 'Dick Clark' and it was a little more funny if you ended it with a person. Barry has, unfortunately, suffered the same problem because over the years people began to make fun of his work, and it's a cheap shot."

The never-ending cheap shots can be particularly devastating to a performer whose sense of self may already be hanging by some pretty weak threads. And it does seem that Barry Manilow has spent a lifetime trying to please people, first by not making an effort to connect with his father so as not to upset his family, then by being the perfect, enabling son to a suicidal, alcoholic mother, then, ultimately, by allowing Clive Davis to steer his career into the bubble gum and

Clearasil scented waters of pop stardom. In fact, it would seem from Manilow's own accounts over the years that he has been the perfect go-along guy, a rudderless ship tossed on the turbulent seas of commercial success and market demands though he himself, he has said, "was never one to make waves."

But, unfortunately, it's more often than not Barry Manilow who causes the most trouble for Barry Manilow. An incident with Philadelphia disc jockey Ed Sciaky is one of the earliest examples.

"I'm going to be the biggest star . . ."

Ed Sciaky has been a fixture on the Philadelphia radio scene since his student days at Temple University's radio station WRTI-FM in 1966. He joined WMMR in 1970, quickly becoming a rock and roll guru, recognising new talent and helping to launch the careers of scores of artists, including Bruce Springsteen, Billy Joel, and Barry Manilow.

"I met Barry around December 13, 1972," Sciaky recalls. "He was playing piano for Bette Midler at the Bijou Café. I missed the opening night because I had to go to New York to see the American debut of Genesis at Avery Fisher Hall, but I saw the next three nights, 13, 14, 15 – I don't know why I remember the dates, but I do. Bette was awesome, and the Bijou was this little tiny club at Broad and Lombard; my wife Judy and I lived at 17th and Lombard. Barry was just hanging around the bar at the Bijou and I guess I introduced myself, having seen him play or whatever. I don't remember the details of the conversation but, in any case, he ended up coming over to our apartment after one of the shows one night. I don't know whether we discussed it beforehand or when he got to our place, but he was very interested in a record I had called 'Beach Boys Stack-a-Tracks', which was a weird record that Capital put out of Beach Boys backing tracks, with no vocals, so I guess you could sing along with it or something. It's a weird record. Being an arranger and all, Barry found this of interest. So that's how we met and became friends over the years."

When Bette's tour came back through Philadelphia during the Thanksgiving holiday of November 1973, Barry and Ed again hooked up. "It was Thanksgiving night or the night after Thanksgiving," Sciaky recalls. "Barry said, 'I would love a home cooked

meal.' And he came over and had leftover turkey, and loved it."
Barry continued to keep in touch with Ed. While Barry and Ron
Dante were working on Barry's first album for Bell Records back in
New York, Barry sent a reel-to-reel tape with four of the album's
songs to Ed. "He was so thrilled to make that first record," says
Sciaky. "He sent me a tape with a note that said, 'Hot off the presses,
for Ed and Judy!' It was very sweet of him to do that. There are very
few artists that have ever sent me a tape like that, just so thrilled and
proud to actually be making a record."

When the record came out, Barry returned to Philadelphia in
March 1974 to promote it, playing the Bijou Café, this time as the
headliner rather than Bette's accompanist. "We lived our lives at the
Bijou Café," recalls Sciaky. "I spent a lot of my life watching these
artists perform. If Barry did twelve shows in a week at the Bijou, I
was there for twelve shows. In fact I'll never forget the week he did
twelve shows, and the opening act was Andy Kaufman. That was
unbelievable, because Andy Kaufman was insane, and did twelve
completely different shows over the six days. Every single show was
something completely different. The audience had no clue, they
hated him, they booed him. He'd get up and read *Moby Dick*. It was
insane. His whole thing was to get the audience to hate him. So the
Barry audience definitely hated him."

During his run in Philadelphia, Ed had Barry on his radio show. "I
was working at WMMR then, which was a hip, album rock station,"
Sciaky continues. "This was Barry's first-ever radio interview in the
world, he claimed, promoting his record. Because at this point, who
was he? He was nobody. He was Bette Midler's piano player. And I
took a liking to this song 'Could It Be Magic' and played it on my
show. I was music director of the station, I could play whatever I
wanted, and I thought that was a great piece, 'Could It Be Magic'.
And the record label's pushing a piece of crap called 'Sweetwater
Jones' from the record, which was bullshit. So I had Barry on my
show, and he brought a tape of his commercial jingles; we played
that. It was great."

It was clear to Ed that, with his first solo album, Barry hadn't quite
figured out who or what he wanted to be. "If you look at his first
record," says Sciaky, "on the back of it he's wearing a *Screw* T-Shirt –
Screw magazine, which is a New York sex newspaper. I mean that
cover was removed from that album and is not to be seen since.

Basically he envisioned himself a rock type performer, a singer/ songwriter type performer, an Elton John, Billy Joel kind of a performer."

While Sciaky was ecstatic about 'Could It Be Magic' on the first album, which went nowhere, Barry's next album, *Barry Manilow II* came as somewhat of a disappointment. "He got into this produced thing with 'Mandy' which I honestly didn't care for," Sciaky explains. "He didn't write the song – I guess it was a good song because it was a hit and it did what it was supposed to do. But I didn't like where it was going to take him and obviously it took him there." Just as he had been effusive with his praise for 'Could It Be Magic', Sciaky didn't hesitate to tell Barry that he thought Barry had sold out with 'Mandy'.

"Clive Davis got him into this produced sound, which he became known for, for better or worse," says Sciaky. "I mean it made him a gigantic star, one of the all-time biggest. I think he's done great things, but I think some of the stuff he's done has been rightfully categorised as formulaic, through no fault of his own, basically. He got pushed into that super-produced thing, the way they produced his voice, and the way they produced the band. I mean it was in some ways terrific pop music, but it veered away from the kind of serious singer-songwriter he'd hoped to be. So, obviously this is no secret, he didn't get that kind of 'credibility' as a serious rock artist. Obviously he became a brand name of a particular kind of pop music regarded by many as schlock. And I think some of that was deserved and some of that was not deserved. That's where his tastes were and that's where the production led him and so on." It was a disappointment for Sciaky, who told Barry he thought this new commercial direction he was taking with his career would prove to be a mistake. "Maybe not enough people would tell him when they didn't like something he did," says Sciaky. "I have a feeling most people around him were just, *Oh, Barry, you're the greatest! Everything you do is gold!*" At the time it was something that Barry seemed eager to believe.

Ed had also befriended two other little known performers – Bruce Springsteen and Billy Joel. Like Barry, both Bruce, a New Jersey native, and Billy, a native New Yorker, had spent time at Ed and Judy Sciaky's home, enjoying home cooked meals and sometimes sleeping on their couch due to lack of funds for hotel accommodation. It was an odd confluence of events that brought Bruce, Billy, and Barry together one night, with Ed at the vortex.

"Bruce shows up at WMMR, unannounced," Sciaky recalls, "walks in and goes on the air with me, just hanging out. He's on his way to Texas or something, or on his way home from Texas. Meanwhile Tony Visconti is listening to the radio and hears this and calls me and says, 'I heard Bruce is there. Can you get him to come to the studio because David is recording one of his songs.'" Tony Visconti was David Bowie's producer. Bowie was at Sigma Sound recording Springsteen's song 'It's Hard To Be A Saint In The City'. Bruce, however, had headed back to New Jersey immediately after speaking with Ed on the air, so Ed promised Visconti he would call Bruce the next day after he'd had time to reach home and see if he couldn't get Springsteen back to Philadelphia. As promised, Ed placed the call to Bruce the next day. "I said, can you come down here because David Bowie would like you to come to the studio, he wants to meet you," says Sciaky. Bruce agreed, but then missed his bus and had to wait for the next one, which didn't get him into Philadelphia until midnight.

"We pick him up at the bus station at midnight and we take him to the studio," Sciaky continues, "and we hang out with Bowie all night. One of the following nights we took Bruce to the Spectrum to see David Bowie, at his show, then we immediately left there and went to the Academy of Music where Billy Joel was headlining with Janis Ian opening. They were doing two shows, like 7:00 and 10:30 or something; we made it to the second show. So we go backstage after the show and Billy says, 'Let's go get something to eat.' Janis disappears, but Billy and Bruce and [Judy and I] go across the street to the Eagle II Diner, on Broad Street. And in there happens to be Barry Manilow; he had been to the concert. He's promoting 'Mandy' on WIT, on their Leukaemia-thon. So he's there. So we said, 'Well Barry, why don't you join us?' So that's how we had Barry Manilow, Bruce Springsteen, and Billy Joel sitting together having late dinner at one o'clock in the morning in the diner on Broad Street in Philadelphia. And that is where Barry said, 'I will be the biggest star at this table.'"

It was a shocking thing to say, not only in retrospect, but at the moment the words were uttered as well. Indeed, Manilow would tone down the incident considerably when retelling it in his 1987 biography, *Sweet Life*, even though Ed and Judy Sciaky reminded him exactly what happened, specifically for the book. Explains Sciaky, "Years later, Barry called us, he wanted us to come to

Atlantic City to be interviewed because he didn't remember the incident exactly and he wanted us to refresh his memory. So we go down to Atlantic City where he's playing a casino – this is years later – and we refresh his memory. But what he writes is, 'I said I was making the most commercial music of anyone at the table.' But that is not what he said. What he said was, 'I will be the biggest star at this table,' in those words. He doesn't remember saying it, and he reworded it for his book. I guess he didn't want to come off that smacked ass."

Though he put the less "smacked ass" version in his book, Barry later spoke publicly of Ed Sciaky's version of the incident. "Sciaky reminds me that I made an asshole of myself then," Manilow told *Rolling Stone* senior writer Bill Zehme in 1990. "Apparently at one point I said, 'Out of all three of us, just watch, I'm going to be the biggest star at this table.' Ed says he winced, and his wife began to gag. I don't remember this, but if I said it at all, it was because, of the three of us, I was making the most blatantly commercial music. I respected their music more than my own and said, 'Hah! Just watch!' But it just came out wrong, and they never forgot it. To this day, Billy Joel gets pissed off when people mention my name – and I have always been such an incredible fan of his."

But Sciaky is more philosophical about the incident, and less judgmental of Manilow's pronouncement than Manilow himself seems to be. "Really, it was just a statement," Sciaky says, "and what he meant was, yeah, he's making the most commercial music. Because Bruce Springsteen [at that time] is shit – he's got two records out that haven't sold shit, and he's a rock weird guy, totally scruffy – he couldn't afford a hotel room, he was sleeping on our sofa. And Billy Joel had one hit with 'Piano Man' and then had a follow-up album, *Street Life Serenade*, which was a flop. And Barry has 'Mandy' happening and figures he's going to be a big Top 40 star. So, you know, actually he was probably right depending on how you measure stardom. I mean I'm sure there was a time when Barry was the biggest star of the three, you know. But it depends on how you measure stardom. Radio play? Total records sold? Total concert tickets sold? Barry was a big radio artist; Billy was that also, but sold albums like crazy, not necessarily singles, and Bruce didn't sell singles really, but did sell some records, but mainly was a concert attraction. So they actually had completely different niches; you wouldn't confuse them. If anything, Billy is sort of halfway between Barry and Bruce. But they're not the same. Years later, imagine my surprise when there was a magazine – you know one of these fanzine things that come out, these special editions? – there was a magazine called *Barry Manilow, Bruce Springsteen, Billy Joel Magazine.* I swear to god! I've got it somewhere. It's shocking! It was just articles about the three of them. It's so bizarre! Who would put those three together? It's insane!"

Sciaky also doesn't think the statement had the long-term negative impact on Bruce and especially Billy that Barry seems to fear it did, though Joel certainly wasn't happy about it at the time. "It's hard for me to put myself in their shoes," says Sciaky, of the assumed impact of Barry's statement on the other two artists. "But they were basically all unknown artists. Billy Joel did have a hit with 'Piano Man' a year previous, and Bruce had nothing – remember this is before *Born To Run*, this is the end of 1974; he's lucky Columbia didn't drop him . . . so he was in this nowhere period there. But I don't think he knew who Barry Manilow was at that point; I don't think Billy knew either. [Barry] was just a friend of ours who had a record or something."

Still, Sciaky admits, the statement certainly charmed no one at the table, and, at the time, especially angered Joel, who at that moment was probably the most successful of the three. "Bruce and Billy were taken aback by it," says Sciaky. "Bruce is very shy, really. He's nothing like he is onstage, he's a shy guy. I don't know what he thought. I know that Billy was a little pissed off. And years later, Barry was on some awards show, and he went out of his way to praise Billy Joel. I don't know if he was giving him an award or he was just mentioning that he had won an award, but he went out of his way to say, 'I just want to mention how great I think Billy Joel is.' I think he was sort of apologising to Billy."

But Joel doesn't seem to have held a grudge. Says Sciaky, "I think one of the best things Barry ever did was a song called 'Some Kind Of Friend', which was on one of his middle period albums." In fact, Manilow himself has said of the 1983 release, "Up tempo! Aggressive! Rock 'n' Roll! Finally!" Sciaky continues, "I played that for Billy Joel and he said, 'This is great, who is this?' I said, 'It's Barry!' He was shocked and delighted."

When told of the Manilow-Springsteen-Joel incident, former

Rolling Stone writer and editor Ben Fong-Torres doesn't fault Manilow for what he sees as simply a show of bravura in the face of professional intimidation when Manilow found himself sitting down with two other up-and-coming musicians in front of an influential rock deejay like Ed Sciaky. "The kind of bravado that he hopes is going to be able to make it sound like he's cocky, or that he fears nobody, and that gives him an edge that he feels he needs to have as part of his image," speculates Fong-Torres. "There's a lot of stuff going on in the creation and the architecture of a show business venture. So I don't begrudge him for taking that tack and just trying. Because Eddie Murphy did the same thing in some magazine – was it *TV Guide?* – where he said he was bigger than The Beatles. And The Beatles said they were bigger than Jesus – twice. And there was a band that I reported on in *Rolling Stone*, way back, called Bread, who groused that they were not being paid the same amount of respect as Crosby, Stills, Nash and Young. And Credence Clearwater Revival didn't help themselves any, despite their great music, when they did a press junket and party in the Bay area in which one of the undercurrents was that they felt like, with all of their hits over the years, they were still not being seen on the same level as The Beatles. So they complained about it in public, and it was pretty obvious what they were after. And when that happens, then, the critics just pile on you. And so that may well be what's gone on, too, in Mr Manilow's career."

"I've got a swell idea. Let's put on a show!"

It's this sort of personal insecurity masked by professional hubris that often drives Barry Manilow's many critics into a frenzy. One good example was Manilow's first proposed foray into acting.

"Back in 1980 or 81, Barry was salivating at the thought of being an actor and doing movies," says Lee Gurst. "He wanted movies more than just about anything else you could think of." To this end, Barry began taking classes from renowned acting coach Nina Foch. These classes were not only in anticipation of a new facet of Barry's career, but also to help him perform better during his live shows. After observing Foch's class, Manilow told the teacher that while he would like to join, he didn't think he was capable of publicly expressing the kind of emotion he'd seen Nina's other students offering during the class. "What are you saying?" she reportedly asked Manilow. "You do that and more every night. The only difference is that you have a band behind you."

Reassured, Manilow began a series of increasingly frequent sessions with Foch. "Taking acting technique classes from Nina Foch was a turning point in my life," Manilow later wrote. "Although it was difficult and awkward in the beginning, I soon began to get the hang of it. Soon I was studying with her privately nearly every day."

An opportunity for Barry to flex these newly toned acting muscles beyond the concert stage soon presented itself, and in a big way. "There was actually negotiation about his doing a movie with Frank Sinatra, a musical," says Lee Gurst. "And it would have included certainly a large number of songs which Barry was going to write." It would seem an incredible opportunity for Barry, to not only make his acting debut, but with an Academy Award winning actor and a musical legend. But, again, Manilow's hubris got in the way.

"Sinatra's people communicated that Sinatra would want a piece of the publishing," continues Gurst, "and Barry said, 'Hell, no. It's *my* music, *my* songs.'" Gurst still feels exasperation at Barry's behaviour in the circumstances. "That's the way the game's played," says Gurst. "If Sinatra wants a piece of the music, you give him a piece of the music and you get your first movie made and who cares what you give away to do it?" The movie never materialised.

Before long, another opportunity arose for Barry to make his acting debut, albeit on the small screen. Having done four variety specials for ABC over the years, the first of which won an Emmy for Outstanding Special Comedy, Variety, or Music, in 1982 CBS approached Barry about doing the same thing for their network. But the variety genre hadn't really survived the Seventies in the best of health, and Barry felt that he'd done pretty much all he could do in that format for ABC. The idea was temporarily shelved.

Then in the spring of 1984, Manilow got the idea of a movie based on his hit song 'Copacabana', which had had its genesis in a vacation to Rio de Janeiro Barry took with his partner Bruce Sussman in 1977. While strolling on the Copacabana Beach one day, Sussman said, "That'd make a great song title." When they returned to the States, Sussman got together with his collaborator, Jack Feldman, and the two created the musical story of Lola and Tony, a sort of Romeo and Juliet with sequins and décolletage. The words so resonated with Manilow that he was able to put the tune with the lyric in one continuous take. 'Copacabana', included on the *Even Now* album, was released as a single in 1978 and was an immediate hit. But would it make a hit movie as well?

"The plot, like the song, was right out of a 1940s musical," Manilow wrote in 1985, "but I wanted the film to look like a combination of an MTV video and an old Technicolor movie." After writing the synopsis, Barry liked what he had. But CBS wanted an hour-long variety show, not a 1940s musical. "So there I sat," wrote Manilow, "with a very exciting, innovative musical idea, but it wasn't a variety show. What should I do with it?"

What he did was take the idea to his friend Dick Clark, who, in addition to his roles as *American Bandstand* host and overall rock icon, was also a successful television producer. Clark had his misgivings about this untried format, not to mention its untried star; sure Barry could pull off a musical variety hour, but play the romantic lead in a feature length movie? Despite Clark's misgivings, Barry decided to pitch the idea to the network himself. CBS decided to take a chance.

In previewing the upcoming show for the *Washington Post*, Stephanie Mansfield wrote, "Maybe it's my imagination, but I think Barry Manilow must have bounded into the CBS offices sometime last year and warbled, 'I know you're worried about network ratings. I've got a swell idea. Let's put on a show!' How else could the Mickey Rooney of rock have conceived such a gosh-darn root beer float of a film . . . it's been a long time since something so upbeat has burst into our living rooms, leaving out the last Smurfs special." Mansfield goes on to note, "Manilow is cuter than a pet chipmunk in his white tuxedo and sings ten catchy new songs. So what if they all sound like McDonald's commercials – you were expecting Gershwin?"

'Copacabana' was broadcast on Tuesday, December 3, 1985, to mixed reviews and disappointing ratings. "A bit of consciously cornball fluff," said the *Chicago Tribune*. After praising the work of Annette O'Toole, who played Lola opposite Barry's Tony ("Annette O'Toole, a talented young actress . . . brings a combination of sensuality and sardonicism to her part"), the *Tribune* reporter went on to say, "How one feels about 'Copacabana', however, undoubtedly depends on one's own personal Manilow meter. Mine, admittedly, has never even been plugged in. That said, I must admit that my favourite single moment comes during the quiz-show segment, when Barry/Tony tells the host that, no, he didn't perform in the USO but he did fight on Guadalcanal and Iwo Jima, and not a single person in the audience laughs."

It did stretch the imagination a bit to accept the 42-year-old Manilow as the struggling young hero, especially when put up against the youthful exuberance of O'Toole, eleven years Barry's junior. But some were more eager to suspend disbelief than the *Tribune* reviewer. "Thanks to producer Dick Clark and lyricists Bruce Sussman and Jack Feldman," wrote Stephanie Mansfield of the *Washington Post*, "Manilow has managed to breathe new life into the tired variety-show format. There is much to recommend in this big-budget production: the photography is first-rate, the smoky cafes and rain-swept streets a haunting backdrop for the lush string section; even the showgirls look as though they're having fun."

Unfortunately, the majority of the American public was watching ABC that night. 'Copacabana' earned only a 12.6 Nielsen rating and a 20 per cent audience share in the national ratings, tying for 55th place overall.

"For all intents and purposes, Barry never had a movie career," says Lee Gurst. "He studied acting for years and no movie ever came of it, partly because he was a terrible actor. But he just wouldn't go along with the things you do to get there."

"There go my people . . ."

Over the years, *Playboy* magazine has seemed especially quick to cut Manilow down to size if he ever seemed to be getting a bit too full of himself. A bit in *Playboy*'s "Fast Tracks" column was typically disdainful. "*News flash! Barry Manilow admits what we've known all along, that he's a boring guy. Says Manilow: 'There's nothing much to spend money on. I'm not into yachts, Rolls-Royces, drugs or wild parties.' He did, however, compare his music to that of Led Zeppelin. 'It's as important and as good as anything they've done.' Say good night, Barry . . .*" Of course Barry's statements might have carried more weight if he hadn't been, at the time, living in a Bel Air mansion and driving a white Rolls-Royce Corniche convertible with red leather interior. It was just such perceived insincerity that the editors of *Playboy* delighted in.

"I think Barry actually complained to Hef [*Playboy* publisher

Hugh Hefner] at some point," says *Playboy* editor and long-time *Playboy* "Advisor" Jim Petersen. "Like, 'why do you guys beat up on me in the pages of your magazine? You gave me my start.' " Petersen refers to the letter Barry sent the magazine in 1964 asking if he should quit his job to pursue a musical opportunity, something the magazine's editors encouraged him to do, though it was advice Barry actually didn't take at the time. "We did get word down from Hefner," continues Petersen, " 'please don't use Barry Manilow as a fall guy in the music column.' What we liked in music during that period was not what he was doing, so our music editor regularly used Barry Manilow as a measuring stick for a certain kind of thing we thought was uncool."

While Manilow continued to have career successes after shaking off his friends and acquiring new musicians, new producers, and new management, the Eighties would not bring the kind of personal and professional satisfaction that had seemed to gush from a bottomless well during the Seventies. His last album with friend Ron Dante proved to be a bit of a wet end. "The songs are commercials without products – overproduced but underpowering," wrote the *Playboy* music editor, not yet restrained by Hugh Hefner's orders to play nice with Manilow, concluding wryly, "They'll probably be big hits." In fact, they were not.

Released in 1985, the same year as the disappointing TV movie 'Copacabana', Manilow's compilation album, *The Manilow Collection: Twenty Classic Hits* received an even cooler reception. "The songs here are enough to make your fillings ache," wrote reviewer J.D. Considine, who characterised the album as "an anthology that comes at the listener like a truckload of Twinkies." He goes on to note, "Part of it is Manilow's heavyhanded use of sweeteners; from 'Mandy' to 'Memory,' his voice is awash in strings and supportive harmony, an approach that leaves a sugary crust on songs that were syrupy at the start. But his favourite ploy is familiarity, which allows him to build his confections on the listeners' memories and expectations. 'Copacabana', after all, isn't a song, it's a rummage sale of rhumba clichés."

Considine's complaints weren't new to Manilow, who had gotten used to words like "schlocky" and "schmaltzy" being applied to his work. And, as *Playboy* had pointed out, "overproduced" also seemed to have become another constant refrain from Manilow's critics, if not his audiences.

"There's a kind of an unnatural sheen to some of his records," says Ed Sciaky, "they're just so finely produced. Not that he's the only one that ever did it, but he probably did it better than anybody, and more consistently." It was that consistency that seemed to offend. In his early career, and in his work with others, Barry would often take chances, try new things, explore his vast talent and what it could produce. But since first allowing Clive Davis to propel him off into stardom on the wings of 'Mandy', Manilow seemed bent on doing nothing that would alienate the fans who had made him a star. Therefore if "overproduced" pop songs like 'Mandy' and Bruce Johnston's 'I Write The Songs' made people happy, how could he give them anything else?

"I can't believe that Barry set out to have a career writing 'Copacabana'," says Lee Gurst, of the wildly successful 1978 singing soap opera penned by Manilow with partners Bruce Sussman and Jack Feldman. But Manilow has said that it's the audience who should set the programme, not the performer. "I've done that kind of thing once or twice," Manilow told an interviewer in 2000, when asked if he hasn't yet reached a point when he can do what he wants in a concert. "The audience indulges me for the first couple of minutes, and then they get antsy. They want to hear the stuff they've come to hear me sing. And the difference between the response when they indulge me and when I do 'Copacabana' is so huge. Am I here for me, or am I here for them? How self-indulgent can you be?"

Perhaps, say some critics, it's not selfless devotion to his audiences that has held Manilow back, but rather fear of losing that audience by risking something new. Professionally, Manilow became like the French radical who says, "There go my people. I must find out where they're going so I can lead them." Far from breaking new ground, Barry seemed content to follow the well-worn groove forged by the perceived desires of his audience.

"I think the artists who really endure and who are taken seriously are the ones who say, look, I'm creating to express something for myself, and I'm on this journey and I'm eager or at least willing to have you watch and come along," says Lee Gurst. "But I'm doing it for me. When you stop doing it for you and start trying to figure out what the audience wants, I don't think you can ever do that. I mean it's impossible. The audience is looking for the artist to lead, as it were. So you get people who are constantly experimenting and trying new things. A Paul Simon, and Elton John, or Billy Joel. Every album has got at least some degree of exploration, searching. Certainly Paul Simon has been around the world, several times, coming up with new things – and it's from his heart. And with that, the audience says, hey, I want to come along with that – I'm with you. If you try to do it the other way around I think it's not likely to succeed, and I think Barry's been trying to do it the other way around for a while."

It's a conformity that hasn't gone unnoticed by other artists as well. As Gurst mentioned, Paul Simon was a musical trailblazer, and someone that Barry Manilow idolised. In fact, when asked for a high point of his collaboration with Barry, Ron Dante mentions an incident involving Paul Simon.

"I think we were in the studio with the second album," recalls Dante, "and Clive Davis came in with Paul Simon, and they sat down in the booth with us. They listened to like four or five of the songs. And Paul Simon leaned over to Clive and Barry and said, 'I really like what you're doing on 'New York City Rhythm'.' And I remember Barry and I kind of glowed. Here was Paul Simon, one of our idols, and one of the finest songwriters/singers in the world – right up there with Gershwin when they finally write it – and he's complimenting us on a production and a song. We were very, very self-satisfied that day. And I leaned back in my chair next to Clive, and Barry was next to Paul, and I said, 'We have achieved some of those things we started out to achieve, which was to create something good, something with a life of its own, and something that people get to hear and like, and a lot of people. And here's one of our idols sitting here saying they like it.' So I remember that instance was really, really nice."

Nearly ten years later, Simon would undo whatever good feeling he had imparted by denigrating Manilow's efforts during an interview with Tony Schwartz for *Playboy* magazine. Schwartz asked, "Do you have to be an artist to have an emotional impact on people? What about Barry Manilow?" Replied Simon, "No. You might be a liar. An innocent. A sentimentalist. But I question what emotion Manilow touches. People are entertained by him. But are they emotionally moved? By 'Mandy'? By 'I Write The Songs'? I don't think so. I don't believe *anything* that Barry Manilow sings." When Schwartz pointed out that there obviously are many people who do believe what Barry sings, Simon's reply was condescending, at best. "Not everyone has the opportunity to be sufficiently sensitised to what is genuine. If you were raised with a lack of exposure to quality, I think it would be more difficult to recognise it. If you just eat Big Macs all your life and someone serves you the finest French food, I don't think you will necessarily appreciate it."

Of course there are far fewer escargots sold worldwide than Big Macs. In 1983 Manilow played a concert at the English estate of the 11th Duke of Marlborough, Blenheim Palace, that drew over 40,000 enthusiastic fans to the grounds of his ancestral home[15]. The year before, over half a million people had applied for the 21,500 seats available for five Manilow concerts at London's Royal Albert Hall.

Ironically, Simon made his remarks to *Playboy* in 1984, the year after Manilow's enormous success in England, and the very year in which Manilow released what would be, to date, his most critically acclaimed album, *2:00 a.m. Paradise Café*. The album came about, as Manilow has stated, as a result of Barry's apparent recognition of his surrender to pop sensibilities and abandonment of his own creative desires. "I had never imagined that I would wind up being thought of as the King of Commercial Music," Manilow wrote in his 1987 biography *Sweet Life*. "I mean, *me* – with all of my snobbish musical taste. Me – who wanted to be the next Edgar Winter or Laura Nyro! Me – who didn't even like Elvis Presley when I was growing up because he was too commercial! How did this happen?"

Ed Sciaky sympathises with Barry's puzzlement, remembering Barry's comments that he'd always envisioned himself as another Edgar Winter until he sat down with Bruce Springsteen and Billy Joel, and he suddenly saw himself as Bobby Sherman instead. "I think that's important," says Sciaky, "because he doesn't really see himself as Bobby Sherman. He thinks he's Edgar Winter. I guess if you're Bobby Sherman you don't want to think you're Bobby Sherman either. But, you know, he kind of became like Bobby Sherman in a way, although I think that's not really fair because Bobby Sherman was just a teen idol singer and [Barry] produces and arranges, and he became much bigger than Bobby Sherman."

---

[15] When asked by the Duke to play the Palace's house organ, Barry played the McDonald's jingle. Take that, Paul Simon.

But unless you're living in 1969, being bigger than Bobby Sherman is hardly an accomplishment any entertainer wants to be remembered for. "I had set out to make a living at a job I loved – making music by arranging, conducting, and songwriting," Manilow wrote. "When I found myself in the Top 40 arena, I had to learn new rules and compromise in order to survive." But one compromise, he found, often led to another, until constant compromising leads to total capitulation. "Art versus commerce," Manilow wrote. "I was in the middle of the classic dilemma. I'd read and heard about it for years, and here I was, smack in the middle of it. Although I was emotionally attached to my values and tastes, I saw the wisdom in the commercial approach as well. BARRY MANILOW (in capital letters) had become successful, and I needed to keep supporting him, but now I was searching for Barry Manilow."

Lee Gurst echoes Barry's own sentiments about his career choices by this time. Speaking of Manilow's desire to give the fans what they want rather than take chances on what might be more heartfelt material, Gurst says, "I'd say it's a very risky proposition in terms of success, and it's even riskier in terms of your own life and endurance as an artist. It just kills you. And I'm sad to say that I think Barry made a choice a long time ago to be more focused on trying to find that success or somehow gratify the audience. And I don't think that's really what they want. I think they want to be led along on a personal journey. And it's a very gutsy thing for an artist to do, and it's a courageous path to take to let the world observe your own exploration. But if you don't do that, I think no good will come of it ultimately. Obviously Barry's making a very nice living and he's not been abandoned, but nor has he gotten the recognition, and I would be very surprised if he really has the satisfaction that he would like to have from his career."

Manilow would probably agree. By his own account he had, by 1984, lost his ability to play the piano for his own pleasure, and listening to the radio had become, he has said, "a competition: 'Oh, why didn't I think of that drum lick?' I was always trying to catch up. You can go nuts doing that." So, after opening Super Bowl XVIII with his rendition of 'The Star-Spangled Banner', Manilow retreated to his Bel Air mansion and, he has said, began to look into himself for a change, rather than looking around him to gauge everyone else's approval or disapproval at what he did. "It was like the end of the movie," he later told an interviewer. "I didn't know what to do. I felt the credits should roll: 'The End'.

Instead, he conceived the idea for *2:00 a.m. Paradise Café*, he has said, in a dream. "I always know I'm onto something when I get ideas in dreams. These projects always go smoothly," he later said of the album. "*Paradise Café* was composed and recorded in less than two months." In fact, the album was recorded, astonishingly, in a single take. "When we finished," Manilow later wrote of the experience, "it had been 45 minutes of straight playing and singing. Everyone in the control room burst into applause." It was a long way from the "overproduced" pop records he'd been used to making, and it felt good. "It represented taking control of a career in which the light of success had been so bright that it had blinded me."

Of the eleven songs on *2:00 a.m. Paradise Café*, the biggest hit was a Manilow melody paired with a Johnny Mercer lyric, 'When October Goes'. Mercer's daughter, Mandy Mercer Neder, was at first rather puzzled by her mother's decision to offer her late husband's lyrics to Barry Manilow for completion. Mercer's widow and her friend, Mark Kramer, had been going through some drawers one day and had discovered the lyrics. Says Neder, "[My mother] called me up and she said, 'Mark wants to give them to Barry Manilow.' And I said, 'Well, I don't know. Who else would you be comfortable with? Make a list, and who else would you feel comfortable with?'" But Kramer had his heart set on Barry Manilow. "Why he picked Barry," says Neder, "I don't know."

"So they went to a concert or something," Neder continues, "and went backstage and I guess they proposed these to Barry or to his manager. So he took them and said he'd see what he could do with them. And almost immediately he got this one hit, which is a beautiful thing, 'When October Goes'. It's a gorgeous, beautiful song. And he came up with that." Neder had been a bit leery of the idea initially, but hearing 'When October Goes' immediately eliminated any misgivings she may have had over the choice of Manilow. "I thought it was a little odd, but of course he didn't seem to be writing the type of things that my dad wrote, so I thought it was a little unusual. But then when he came out with that song – wow! I think it was very apropos, it was a very beautiful song. I can't say enough about it."

Neither could the critics. In a turnabout of the typical Manilow release, *2:00 a.m. Paradise Café* was given a somewhat cool reception by Manilow's fans, but was lauded by the critics as "a surprising change for the popular Mr Manilow", as Max Preeo wrote in *Show Music*. Peter Reilly of *Stereo Review* concurred: "A very fine album, worth your time and attention."

But after a personal and professional lifetime of trying to please others, it's difficult to be comfortable suddenly becoming an iconoclast. Just as *Barry Manilow Live* would mark the high point of Manilow's recording career in terms of sales, *2:00 a.m. Paradise Café* would prove to be the high point of his critical success. But if Barry Manilow thought it would mark a turning point in the public's perception of him, he was mistaken.

"The guy could be Barry Manilow in five minutes . . ."

In 1986, Phil Collins expressed to *Playboy* magazine a frustration over the negative attention popular music seems to garner simply because of its popularity. But, even while decrying the same treatment that Manilow himself had suffered over the years, Collins managed to do the exact same thing to Manilow in the following exchange:

> PLAYBOY: We've remarked that your biggest talent is being able to speak to the average listener. Do you agree?

> COLLINS: I don't know about biggest, but it does seem that people relate. There's a tendency for people to be cynical about popularity, like you're appealing to the lowest common denominator, which is another term for trash. It's an insulting attitude – insulting to the audience. I mean, sometimes I feel it. Like, God, I wish I were David Byrne, with this small, tight group of fans. The critics would like me. Instead, I've been taken less seriously because I've been more popular – I'm cast aside as some sort of Barry Manilow. I find it frustrating.

> PLAYBOY: How is a Barry Manilow song different from some of your ballads – 'One More Night', for example?

> COLLINS: It has a heartfelt thing in it, it comes from some place deeper, and that comes through in the songs, I think. It hits the chord of truth. People understand it because they have felt it, too.

PLAYBOY: Manilow might say that people respond to his songs for a similar reason.

COLLINS: He might, but I still believe there is an important difference. People are living with the problems that have to do with their homes, their day-to-day lives, their relationships. There are obviously more substantial problems in the world; but from the feedback I get, I think they find compassion for their situations in my songs. Understanding. That's different from gay little love songs. People use music for solace. Somehow, when people are miserable, they put on a miserable song; they want empathy or something. Stephen Bishop writes some of the best love songs because he loves being miserable.

PLAYBOY: We may have caught you being less than nice right at the start. Why the sensitivity over Barry Manilow's sort of music?

COLLINS: Well, it defines a certain area of music to me: soft, spineless music. I never met Barry, so I don't know what he's like, but though the music may be very well produced, polished, smooth and glossy, it has no spine, no edge, no backbone.

In 1997, *Los Angeles Times* music critic Robert Hilburn, managed to slam two singers at the same time when he printed a quote from an unnamed "industry insider" who said, "I don't consider [Michael] Bolton a threat in any way. He could disappear in a minute. The guy could be Barry Manilow in five minutes."

It's important to note here that Manilow has had an unprecedented 25 singles reach the Top 40 in consecutive order; had five of his albums chart at once in a single year — a feat matched, to date, only by Frank Sinatra and Johnny Mathis. He's won an Emmy, a Tony, a Grammy, and was nominated for an Academy Award. He has walls filled with gold and platinum records marking a career which has, so far, spanned over a quarter-century. Yet, given all of his accomplishments, somehow it's understood that, when it's suggested a performer could become Barry Manilow at any time, it's not meant to be a good thing.

The question of why Manilow has always been viewed with such pervasive contempt is difficult to answer, and one Manilow and his friends have been grappling with for years. But Collins' charge that Manilow's work is "smooth and glossy" but has "no spine, no edge, no backbone" seems to hit closest to home. As Lee Gurst has pointed out, a true artist is expected to break new ground, lead, inspire. Manilow's work, however, has, over the years, inspired any number of jokes, but very little serious consideration.

"The criticism of Barry wasn't serious," agrees disc jockey Ed Sciaky, "it was more joking. I've never seen a really serious critic that says there's something wrong with his music or it's bad or some reasoned explanation of what's wrong with it. It just became a sort of an easy, shorthand way to say schlock, basically the new elevator music. People become clichés in a way, and he became the cliché for the schlock pop artist. The elevator music, schmaltzy – I don't know what the real, the underlying cause is other than just taste. He just got branded as somehow either insincere or just lacking in musical credibility. Kind of cheesy pop music like guilty pleasures and so on. But that doesn't do him justice because there's a lot of finely crafted music there."

Dick Clark agrees. "I think it's a combination of envy and misunderstanding. Once they understand that the guy is really good at what he does, then they become a fan. He's a consummate entertainer. He knows the business backwards and forwards. He does it well. I can't put it any other way." Ed Sciaky echoes that opinion. "I don't understand how anybody can go see his concert and not rave," he says.

Jack Wilkins, leader of Barry's first band, The Jazz Partners, like others, sees Barry's problems hopelessly enmeshed with his blessings. "How do you explain a guy like Barry?" says Wilkins. "It's a dichotomy, and that's what Barry is. Everybody's snickering and all that – I don't buy that. It's bullshit really. I like the 'Copacabana' song, I like a lot of songs he's written and all that. I like his voice and I like his charm on the bandstand. I mean the fact that most of the girls that like Barry are in their late 40s or 50s is neither here nor there in a way, is it? He's not exactly attracting the Madonna crowd, is he? So he's got these old housewives who love him. Okay, that's cool. Sure, you could laugh at what he does. But this guy is doing great; he's charming and he does a lot of great stuff. At the same time, I could find the humour in what he does. I could see how people could find it rather amusing. What he's doing is appealing to the lowest basic instincts. But it's not because he's doing that, it's because he hears this. He deals with it. He understands it. He's not trying to attract the 50-year-old crowd. He's just doing his stuff that he does. And people love him. And why not? You have no idea how good that feels, getting up on the bandstand and having 15,000 people screaming at the top of their lungs because they love you. There's nothing like it. So Barry gets up there and sings a song that's heartfelt for a lot of women – screw it! I'm happy about that. You could say anything you want about Barry after that. Hey, man, you get up there and do that, see what you feel."

But perhaps it's not surprising that in a world where television shows need laugh tracks in order for the home viewing audience to know when they're supposed to be amused, people have a tendency to look over their shoulders to make sure that the entertainment they're enjoying is socially acceptable to their peers. Ron Dante is angered by those who feel the need to "make you feel somehow less because you happen to like a certain song or type of music. I don't expect everybody to like what I like, but don't tell me I'm crazy for liking it. Because you don't have the right. They don't have the right."

Manilow found a surprising champion – of sorts – in the acid-tongued critic and columnist Joe Queenan. In his 1998 book, *Red Lobster, White Trash and The Blue Lagoon*, Queenan, while not pledging his eternal love and devotion to Manilow, at least pays him grudging respect:

> *"Here was a guy who knew how to put on a show,"* Queenan wrote. *"Not a show I necessarily wanted to see, but a show all the same. Here was a guy who understood that no performance was complete without dragging some woman who had flown all the way from England up onto the stage for a kiss and a cuddle. Here was a guy who realised that when the public had given so much, you had to give something back. Here was a guy who knew that when six thousand women named Debbie get together with one guy named Barry, there's going to be magic in the moonlight."*

As comedian Dennis Miller once said, "I wanted to get right up to the precipice, pivot, and jeté back to Coolsville." In like manner, Queenan tempered his tribute with a bit of a disclaimer:

"I am certainly not suggesting that after all these years in the business, Barry Manilow had finally learned to sing or dance, or that his songs had miraculously stopped sucking. 'I Write The Songs' was still a crime against nature. Manilow still danced like a spindly Travolta impersonator. And the guy who writes the songs that made the whole world sing still sang like Barry Manilow."

But, as Dick Clark and Ed Sciaky both stated, if one watched and listened to Barry Manilow with an open mind, you just couldn't help but admire the guy, as Queenan discovered:

"I am only saying that his songs were at least songs, not pointless New Age riffing like Kenny G's interminable jerking off. And unlike Billy Joel or Phil Collins, Manilow seemed to be doing material that he genuinely believed in, songs that were appropriate for his personality. 'Memory' may have been pure schmaltz, but Manilow was nothing if not a schmaltzmeister. Like Lawrence Welk or Liberace before him, he knew himself and he knew his audience. My hat was off to him."

Faint praise, perhaps, but at least well reasoned and thoughtful, consideration most critics never bother to give Barry Manilow.

Ben Fong-Torres has been one of America's leading music journalists for over thirty years. He began writing for the enormously influential *Rolling Stone* magazine in 1968, during an incredibly exciting time in music history, and later served as one of the magazine's editors. He has interviewed such musical luminaries as Paul McCartney, Bob Dylan, Elton John, Jim Morrison and the Grateful Dead, to name just a few. Fong-Torres tends to agree with Ed Sciaky's position that, in the music business, image is everything, and the public perception of a performer is far more telling than that performer's commercial success. "Success does not provide a shield from such criticisms," says Fong-Torres on the lack of respect Manilow is given. "In fact, it often makes one vulnerable to that kind of attack. And that's been the case with Kenny G and Michael Bolton, and goes all the way back to any number of people who have tremendous commercial success and not a particularly hip credential, and they get slammed. It goes all the way back to Pat Boone and before. That's just the way it is in popular culture."

But why?

"It's just the nature of people to criticise others and to find targets that are vulnerable and to have fun with them," Fong-Torres explains. "And it's not just in entertainment. It's often in sports and in politics and in other areas as well. So that's just human nature. And certain artists come along and they get to be that target for that particular time that they're around. Sometimes there's substance to it and sometimes there isn't. There certainly are what you might call fabricated artists who are seen to be such by not only critics but by a lot of fans, but still attain success for other reasons, because of their looks, because of a particular song that becomes a hit and that leads to more success, or because of other media exposure, because they're good for television or movies. So they are able to make a name for themselves, but that name is quite often tarred and feathered."

That has certainly proven true of Barry Manilow's career yet, says Fong-Torres, Manilow is certainly not the only performer to live, personally and professionally, through such constant drubbing. "So have many of the others who have been vilified," he says. "They maintain a success. They have somehow a personal strength, they have a knowledge of a core base of fans who are loyalists. They have come up with a psychological defensive shield against those attacks. As you know, there are many artists who don't read reviews or don't look at clippings or don't read books or whatever, don't watch TV shows in which comedians might be making fun of them. And that's how they are able to survive. I don't know Barry Manilow, so I wouldn't be able to say how he has survived, but he certainly seems to have been one that has thick enough skin that he's able to continue with his career and make just enough adjustments every few years to keep things interesting for himself, whether it's tackling a new medium, or tackling a new form of music, or whatever."

In fact Manilow has not always been able to maintain good humour about the attacks by critics and others who just want to get in a good shot or two at his expense. But even his anger at unfair personal attacks simply seems to provide fuel for those who seem to have fashioned themselves his opponents. Ron Dante cites *Los Angeles Times* critic Robert Hilburn as a prime example. "Hilburn doesn't like Barry," says Dante. "He's not the market; nobody cares what he likes. But he's got the *LA Times* as his power, so when Barry first came out he'd write some bad reviews. Barry finally wrote him a terrible note and told him to go screw off or something, and he posted it on his board. He was proud! *Look at what Barry Manilow sent me!*"

Knight-Ridder newspaper columnist Leonard Pitts Jr. is another example. "Barry Manilow knows we've been laughing at him, and he wants it to stop," Pitts wrote in a 1993 article entitled, *Barry Manilow Wants a Little Respect, and He'll Go Toe-to-Toe to Get It.* Using a technique popular with paparazzi, Pitts basically did his best to irritate Manilow, then gleefully reported the results when he was successful. "I'll tell you what," Pitts writes, obviously exultant, "I got into a fight – verbal, folks, verbal – with Barry Manilow." How very thrilling for Mr Pitts.

It's no wonder, then, that Manilow has, over the years, become suspicious of everyone's motives, and, as Bill Zehme wrote in *Rolling Stone* in 1990, when paid compliments "he sifts them for snide subtext."

And for good reason. When Canada's hip music magazine *Graffiti* decided to put Manilow on its cover, it was with tongue firmly in cheek, though Manilow seemed unaware of this fact. "I felt kind of sorry for him," said former *Graffiti* editor-in-chief Alastair Sutherland, who conducted the interview with Manilow, the same interview in which Manilow denied being gay. A one-page addendum to the interview stated, "Nobody polarises music fans faster than Barry Manilow. At the peak of his popularity in 1977, he was simultaneously the biggest selling pop vocalist in North America and a man whose severest critics split into camps of those hating him, those *really* hating him, and those who drove cars over cliffs every time one of Barry's songs came on the radio."

It's not surprising, then, that when British magazine *Q* requested an interview in 1990, Barry's response was, "Why do you want to interview me? Why should I be in your magazine? What's the *slant?*" The magazine made sympathetic noises. "Pressing the British flesh has never been high on Manilow's priority list," wrote Adrian Deevoy. "His press here has been only marginally better than Adolf Hitler. Reviews of his live concerts haven't always been so kind. Subsequently he is ferociously paranoid and has only given a handful of interviews in the last decade."

Of course just because someone's paranoid doesn't mean no one's out to get them. The Adrian Deevoy *Q* article was preceded by the less than flattering introduction, "You are either adored with a frightening intensity or despised with a burning passion. Your closest friends are in your employ. You are cosseted, isolated, deeply embittered, yet every night you're high-kicking down the spangly staircase of showbiz singing 'Sweet Life'. You are imprisoned in a role of your own devising." The blurb ends, obviously quite impressed with its own cleverness, with the kicker, "You're Barry Manilow and, what's worse, Adrian Deevoy is on your tail." Paranoid? Right.

Arguably the most puzzling compliment Barry has received came during a now-famous encounter between Manilow and rock icon Bob Dylan. Brought together at a party in one of those random acts of providence, Dylan reportedly embraced Manilow and said to him, "Don't stop doing what you're doing, man. We're all inspired by you." So shaken by this encounter was Manilow that he actually had to leave the party for a moment in order to pull himself together and begin parsing Dylan's statement for hidden meanings.

It's this seemingly odd pairing – Bob Dylan and Barry Manilow – that brings into focus the observations made by Fong-Torres and others that the business of entertainment is built in image and illusion[16]. In truth, there are as many similarities as differences between Manilow's career and Dylan's. For example, Dylan's trademark was his absolute lack of artifice, while Manilow has often been faulted for being almost entirely a creation of his own public relations machine. These are, of course, the images that have come to be hung on each of these performers. But Manilow's image has never been as false as assumed, nor has the complete honesty Dylan projects ever been based in reality. Bob Dylan was, after all, born Robert Zimmerman, and later went through a couple of name changes, from Elston Gunn (paying homage to both Elvis and popular TV character Peter Gunn) to Bob Dillon (after another television hero, Marshal Matt Dillon), finally settling on Bob Dylan, "because it looked better." When asked questions about his origins, Dylan would say whatever came into his head – he was an orphan, or he had joined a circus at 13 and

---

[16] Elton John tells a story that illustrates the point. One day one of his framed gold records fell off the wall, the glass in the frame shattering. Since the exposed record did have grooves, just like a normal LP, Elton decided to see what would happen if he tried to play the record. When he put the album on the turntable and lowered the needle, he discovered that his gold record was actually a gilded Barry Manilow album.

travelled with it around the Southwest, or he had played the piano on Elvis Presley's early recordings. "To put it frankly," said disc jockey Oscar Brand, who was host of WNYC's *Folksong Festival*, "he was a nervous wreck. "He came on my radio show, and he said nothing but lies about his life. Naturally, he was nervous all the time. He was living with these enormous lies. Here he was, a kid from Minnesota, and he came here to a climate where a number of people were already quite seasoned. He was afraid he couldn't compete and afraid he wasn't good enough, so he lied."

How, then, is Dylan's behaviour somehow more forgivable than, say, Barry Manilow's show of bravado when thrown in with Bruce Springsteen and Billy Joel? Why was it okay for Dylan to play down his relatively affluent upbringing (his father once gifted him with a pink Cadillac) to make himself appear among the downtrodden his songs championed, when Manilow, who could honestly report that he'd been raised in poverty, was sneered at as a melodramatist when he would speak honestly of his humble origins? How was Bob Dylan's bare feet and ragged clothing any less of an artifice than Barry Manilow's rhinestone spangled spandex?

"It's a matter of image," says Ed Sciaky. "The public just get sold images . . . every teenage kid in America wants the same stupid products for no reason at all. It's funny because Aerosmith can do the most disgusting Diane Warren ballad and get away with it, but Barry can't. I don't know what it is about him that riled the critics other than his songs were hum-able and what they considered to be overproduced."

Ben Fong-Torres would tend to agree, having noted, albeit from a distance, the change in Barry over the years. "The only time I ever saw him was when he was backing Bette Midler, and he was the arranger and pianist in her club act. This is at the Boarding House in San Francisco, a nightclub that held probably about 300 to 400 people on the main floor. And Bette Midler was the headlining act and Barry was onstage with her doing his role . . . I thought he did a great job anchoring that act. I was a fan of Bette's club act from the Boarding House all the way through to arena-sized lavish productions of hers. And he was very good in that job."

But of course a large part of Barry's job with Bette was providing a stabilising hand to keep her wildness in check. While Bette's frenzy was still hypnotic without Barry's disciplined counterpoint, without

Bette's unpredictability, Barry's discipline as a solo act could often come across as simply boring, particularly in comparison to his earlier association with Midler.

"Everybody has their own personal feelings about him," says Ben Fong-Torres. "And it is easy when someone is labelled a square or something like that. It's awfully hard to get that off, fair or unfair. I have never thought of him as a particularly great singer. That's a basic fact. I just don't identify with his voice and presentation. But you see him being lauded by fans, by adoring fans, Neil Diamond-like, for his entire stage presentation. And I think on the other level, speaking of Neil Diamond, there seems to be an adoration on the level of Neil that had to do with the entire package. Not only the singing and the songs, but also the whole show that he presented. And I don't know, I suppose that some people would say, this guy looks like a dweeb, and the fact that he's getting the kind of mob female adoration only puts me off more, whether it's male or female saying that, I don't know. But I think that's also part of the – the fact that he looked like a cartoon character, dressed in all white, not a particularly great looking guy, singing not particularly great songs, in a not great voice, and yet he's got this kind of outrageous response, does put people off. It solidifies for them the lack of taste on the part of many of their fellow Americans, and so then Manilow becomes the target for abuse about the declining values in pop culture. Fact is that they've been declining and haven't been at high levels in the very beginning anyway. So I think he's victimised by that. On the other hand, though, I find myself having a hard time defending him based on the quality of the music and his act and his show and his style and all of that. There's nothing there for me to latch onto."

But what of Bob Dylan's seemingly heartfelt tribute? Dylan is typically mute on the subject, refusing to either confirm the sincerity of his words or reveal his comments to be a cruel joke. Those who know Dylan can easily see it either way. "Well, Bob Dylan has a great sense of humour," says Fong-Torres, quick to give Dylan the benefit of the doubt. "Bob Dylan, for whatever else he is, is also in show business, and there's a certain etiquette. If you're a mature person, no matter what you think of a person – and it's the same thing in general social life – you by and large, unless you're a complete punk, you don't go around insulting people publicly without good reason. So you're kind, you're nice, you're part of the same fraternity overall – *we're entertainers, so I'm not going to abuse you and, in fact, I'm going to go out of my way to make you feel good.* Of course anyone who's seen D.A. Pennebaker's 1967 documentary *Don't Look Back* knows that Dylan has never had any trouble in the past behaving like, as Fong-Torres puts it, "a complete punk" when it comes to making sometimes bitingly cruel public statements about his fellow performers.

"There's a clown aspect of Dylan, for sure," says Fong-Torres. "And he may have felt like, oh, boy, he will get a kick out of it if I really go and overpraise him and make it so that he has a story to tell, and that's going to make it fun for me, too, because it's just a joke, but hey, if he wants to take it seriously, great, too. There's a [possibility] of that."

However Fong-Torres goes on to tell of a similar incident that occurred between Elvis Presley and Ricky Nelson. "When [Nelson] first broke out with his first recordings and began challenging Elvis Presley on the charts, he was at a party along with Elvis Presley. And when Elvis spotted Ricky, he brushed past a number of people and got to him, and greeted him, and bear hugged him, and lifted him off the floor, and praised Ricky's parents' show, *Ozzie and Harriet*, and his music, and just said, 'Hey, man, I'm really a big fan of the show, and I love . . .', and he starts recounting certain shows to Ricky. And he just made it very clear that he was supportive of him, and a big fan, and following his career. And just like that, and so generous, that Ricky was completely shocked and taken aback by it. And he would not have expected that of Elvis along with somebody who was perceived to be a rival of his for the number one position week after week there in the mid and late Fifties. So these things happen in the business."

"Don't play around with me . . ."

So Barry Manilow, it would seem, has been designated our national punchline. If he finds himself uncomfortable with his role as everyone's favourite celebrity fall-guy (with the possible exception of Joey Buttafuco, whose overall derision factor is cemented forever if not by his overall sleaziness, then certainly by virtue of having the most joke-worthy name since Fanny Hill) and tries to do something sincere and praiseworthy, there is a pack of pundits poised and ready, 'round the clock, to slap him back into place. A good example of this is Manilow's 1998 tribute to Ol' Blue Eyes, *Manilow Sings Sinatra*. Apparently unable to come to acceptable terms in order to forge a working alliance while Sinatra was alive, Manilow, after Sinatra's death, was finally able to pair up with the legendary singer, if only in spirit.

Of course the name Frank Sinatra carries with it the same kind of iconic imagery as does Bob Dylan. When it was announced that Manilow would be releasing a CD on which he would be covering a dozen Sinatra standards, there was, of course, no possible way that critics were going to let him get away with what they saw as an unbelievable display of chutzpah. "Had I thought about it a little more," Manilow told a reporter after the album's release, "I probably would have chickened out. I was dealing with my heart and not my head. Had I actually thought about it, I probably would have said, 'What's the matter with you?'" Luckily, there were no end of folks happy to pose the question for him.

An internet jokester quipped, "Barry Manilow announced that he's putting out an album of Frank Sinatra songs. Isn't that like LaToya Jackson putting out an album of Barbra Streisand songs?" Even campus newspapers couldn't resist a dig. In a faux "retraction" run in UCLA's *Daily Bruin*, student columnist Matthew D. Glaser wrote: "CORRECTION: Barry Manilow erroneously released a Frank Sinatra tribute album, thinking he was honouring Ol' Blue Eyes' memory and hoping to make a quick buck. Manilow regrets this error and his entire worthless career, except 'Copacabana'. I really like that song."

Manilow Sings Sinatra, released only a few months after Sinatra's death, did seem to some to be less a tribute and more a marketing ploy. "Awash in enough echo to swallow the band," writes Amazon reviewer Rickey Wright, "Barry Manilow does what he can to honour the memory of Frank in a (commercially) timely manner." Making unfavourable comparison's between Manilow's straight renditions of the Sinatra classics and Sinatra's own improvisational delivery of the songs, Wright concludes, "He's made poor homages to the past before this, but this one verges on the offensive."

Lloyd Sachs, writing in the *Chicago Sun-Times*, expressed similar dissatisfaction with Manilow's attempts to deliver Sinatra songs as anything but pale impersonations. "On ballads such as 'In The Wee

Small Hours Of The Morning',", wrote Sachs, "his imprint is mighty wee, indeed. When you have as many gaps to bridge as he does with this material and this legend, passiveness is the last thing you can afford."

In an ironic twist, for all the ire the album provoked among critics, it garnered Manilow his first Grammy nomination since 1978, when he took home the award for Best Male Vocal for 'Copacabana'. In 2000, the Sinatra tribute album was nominated for Grammys in two categories – Best Traditional Pop Vocal Performance, for Barry, and Best Instrumental Arrangement Accompanying Vocalist, for Johnny Mandel's arrangement of 'In The Wee Small Hours Of The Morning'. Though both awards would go to others – Tony Bennett and Alan Broadbent, respectively – it was a reassuring validation amid the hailstorm of criticism that the album's release had unleashed on Manilow.

Equally reassuring was the support of Sinatra's family. In a May, 1999 appearance on *Larry King Live* marking the one-year anniversary of Sinatra's death, Barry joined Frank's daughters, Nancy Sinatra and Tina Sinatra, who were announcing the establishment of the Frank Sinatra Foundation which, said Tina, "carries into the 21st century the works and visions of Frank Sinatra in education, medicine, the arts, and the individual in need." In the course of the show, Barry remarked that "even 'bootleg' Frank Sinatra is better than most other guys". In turn, Nancy Sinatra, referring to *Manilow Sings Sinatra*, said, "There's nothing wrong with your album either, kiddo. It's great!" In closing Barry noted, "I've got my stack of Sinatra albums out all the time," to which Nancy replied, "And we listen to you, Barry."

Later that year, Manilow spoke with a *Detroit Free Press* reporter who was obviously hoping to embarrass the singer. She failed. "Do you ever get tired of being a punchline?" she asked. "What do you think? How would you feel?" Barry replied. Not to be deterred, the reporter pressed the point. "No, how do you feel?" Manilow replied, "I've always been surprised that anybody would consider anybody a punchline. I'm surprised I would find myself at the end of a joke." Not willing to let it go at that, the reporter poked a little deeper into the wound. "Why do you think people make fun of you?" she asked. "That's what you get when you become terribly successful," answered Manilow. "I experienced it from the very first moment of my success. So have all of us – from Michael Bolton to Lionel Richie to Michael Jackson to Madonna." So, then, the reporter wondered, "Is there anybody out there you'd like to beat up?" Showing just how long his memory can be, Manilow harkened back to critic John Wasserman and his vicious review of Bette Midler's 1973 show. "When I was beginning and I really needed encouragement, there was a reviewer in San Francisco who tore me so apart and insulted everybody, including my family. I never quite forgot it. That guy was so horrible. But he died. So watch out. Don't play around with me."

"If you can't say something nice . . ."

For all the waxing and waning of his career in the past three decades, Barry Manilow, it would seem, leaves himself very little time to brood over anything others might have to say about him.

Seeming to be on perpetual tour, Manilow has managed to continue to sell out most of his concerts for the past twenty years, and into the 21st century. In fact, while Las Vegas' MGM Grand was, on December 31, still trying to sell tickets to Barbra Streisand's Millenium-eve concert (erroneously reported to have been sold out), Connecticut's Foxwoods Casino was adding shows to Barry Manilow's New Year's Eve/New Year's Day shows, all of which were sold out nearly as fast as additional performances were announced.

His concerts still rely heavily on old works, but in between 'Copacabana' and 'Mandy' and all the other favourites made popular in the Seventies, Manilow now inserts big band and jazz pieces, as well as selections from another new venture he's undertaken in the past decade, Broadway musicals.

Despite his usually heavy touring schedule, Manilow has been very gradually shifting his career away from the concert stage and towards the Broadway stage. Squeezing 'Copacabana' for the last dregs of marketability, Manilow adapted the song once again, this time into a stage play. Doing away with the unhappy ending that many felt had been a flaw in the song's television adaptation, *Barry Manilow's Copacabana* toured the world to mixed ticket sales and reviews. Unfortunately the mix was heavy on the negative side ("*Copacabana* is a Rotten Banana" read one headline), and the show folded in early 2001. Another stage show, *Harmony* was inspired by the true story of The Comedian Harmonists, a German singing group that was the toast of Europe from the late 1920s through the early war years. In addition, a tribute to Manilow's most memorable songs, either penned by the singer or simply made famous by him, is now being presented in the stage review *Could It Be Magic*, which opened in Chicago just before Manilow's 58th birthday. Though Manilow does not actually appear in the review, he seemed to be hovering over every detail of the production from his seat in the audience at every performance during the opening run in Chicago.

Of course with Manilow's ongoing success and diversification comes the continued taunts of critics. When Manilow sang the national anthem at the opening day of the Los Angeles Dodgers base-ball team, T.J. Simers of the *Los Angeles Times* wrote, "I liked the way the Dodgers invited Barry Manilow to sing the national anthem and then had a pair of F-16s fly over early to drown him out. I'm told the Fighter Wing wrote off the exercise as a smart bomb run." When it was announced that Manilow would perform at the Houston Rodeo in March 2001, one newspaper columnist couldn't help but quip, "Surely someone's going to be fired for this." But Michael D. Clark of the *Houston Chronicle* saw things differently. "Some may think it odd to see Barry Manilow at RodeoHouston," Clark wrote, "but why not? This showman of showmen has played nearly every-where else."

And it's true. Manilow's performance schedule is exhaustive and, one could only assume, exhausting. Manilow's charitable endeavours seem equally varied and numerous. Of the many charities Manilow lends his name to, he is most active in AIDS-related organisations, including the Pediatric AIDS Foundation, the Gay Men's Health Center, and the San Francisco Bay Area Destination Foundation. Edna Manilow was active in similar activities until her cancer-related death in September, 1994 at age 70. During the last ten years of her life, she volunteered at hospitals to help care for children with AIDS. "That was her passion," said Manilow's spokesperson, Susan Dubow, after Edna's death. "Rain, sleet, hail, snow, she would be there for these children."

"That's something celebrities do with their life," says *Playboy*'s Jim Peterson, of Manilow's charitable activities. "I don't have to go that far to admire him. This is part of a musician's lifestyle, to make himself available and to use the attention that centres on him to help other people. That's in the guidance counsellor's handbook on being a celebrity. And I'm sure he's done it more seriously than most."

It's the lack of fanfare for these endeavours that seems to mark Manilow's seriousness towards them. Unless his celebrity will help focus attention on a particular cause, most people would never know of Barry's hand in many of the organisations he supports. Certainly those who spend much of their time denigrating all Manilow does seem to turn a blind eye when it comes to his charitable endeavours. While reams can be written about Comic Relief, or Farm Aid, or Band Aid, or the 'We Are the World' venture (Barry wasn't invited to participate), when it comes to Manilow, the credo among journalists seems to be, as Dorothy Parker once said, "If you can't say something nice, come sit next to me."

"Everybody hates me . . ."

Herb Bernstein is in a unique position to judge Barry Manilow's work, having enjoyed the unusual privilege of first seeing Barry's talent as a high school student, when Bernstein was working as a gym teacher and coach at Brooklyn's Eastern District High School, and then later viewing Manilow's progress after both Bernstein and Manilow had left EDHS and each entered varying, but often overlapping, phases of the music business, each, at different times, working as performer, composer, arranger, producer and accompanist.

"I love his work," says Bernstein. "I think he's very, very musical. But unfortunately music changes. Everything that's so good a couple of years later is suddenly corny. But I love some of the stuff he's done. Very musical, very melodic. I guess by today's standards, with everything being so hip and rap, it's a little bit corny, but not to me. I love what he does."

Ed Sciaky says that his friends are astonished when he tells them the best concert he saw in 2000 was Barry Manilow's. But Manilow is, as *Rolling Stone* magazine dubbed him, "the showman of Our Generation", though which generation writer Bill Zehme was referring to is unclear. "I saw a concert at the Uris Theater quite a few years ago, and it was wonderful," says Herb Bernstein. "He started with just his little group out front, and then the curtain opened and suddenly exposed a 40-piece orchestra. He's a real showman, he's got all the shtick. And I love that. Like Elton John, Billy Joel – they're real showmen. And some of the others, they're recording acts and they don't have a clue onstage other than singing their hits and that's it. But every time I see Barry in person the place is mobbed. He's still a big draw, does great business wherever he works. He knows how to put a show together, he knows how to hit his audience. He knows how to pace a show. Almost like the old-time show business. I love what he does."

Bernstein discounts anything the critics might have to say against Manilow. "Everyone's a critic," he says. "If someone's successful, there's a reason for it. I see Barry's shows, I see the people reacting, I see him mobbed. I mean wherever he's appearing, they're sold out. So who are these guys knocking it? They're probably losers who never made it, critics who were singers before they became critics and couldn't make it, and they love to come with their clipboards and criticise. I really have very little patience for these kind of people. I've worked with acts where they got four standing ovations and I read the reviews and you would swear they'd bombed. I have very little regard for critics."

Manilow himself, after years of ducking the shots volleyed his way, and occasionally volleying a few back, seems to have made some kind of peace with the situation, choosing more often than not to join in the fun rather than fight it. On the popular, long-running (1988 to 1998) television comedy *Murphy Brown*, Barry became a running gag late in the show's run when the character Murphy Brown, played by actress Candice Bergen, gives birth to a son who can be soothed only by the sound of Barry Manilow songs. Though the butt of the joke on the show for a year, Manilow gamely appeared on the 1993 episode marking the child's first birthday, performing the Manilow-Panzer tune, 'I Am Your Child'. More recently Manilow made an appearance on the television show *Ally McBeal*, again gamely going along with his role as punchline. Does Manilow's willingness to participate in his own denigration denote a surrender to those who would reduce him to punchline status? Or does it merely mark Manilow's realisation that, after a career that is longer in years than the lives of many of his peers, he really has nothing to prove to anyone? As Ed Sciaky puts it, "What does Barry care? He's got fans all over the world who love him."

And when it comes right down to it, it's the audience that makes or breaks a performer's career, not the critics, and certainly not the cynics. Herb Bernstein likes to tell a story about the late comedian Totie Fields that illustrates the point.

"Totie Fields was working at a room here in New York – it's no longer in existence – called the Band Box in what was at the time the Americana Hotel. She performed there and the critics said she was dirty, she's not very funny, she's fat – every slander you could think of. And I remember she said to me, 'You know Herb, no one likes me except the audience.' "

When all is said and done, this may well prove to be a fitting epitaph for Barry Manilow: After a lifetime of singing to the world, no one liked him – except the millions who did.

Shadows Of A Book

Like an elaborate stage production, a book is merely the end result of months of preparation by many people who never set foot into the spotlight. It's my pleasure to take this opportunity to express my gratitude to a few of those who worked so hard to make this particular production happen.

First and foremost I'd like to thank my editor at Omnibus Press, Chris Charlesworth, who has been endlessly patient through numerous delays. His sensitivity to the demands on my time, and his tact when reminding me how I should prioritise those demands when I often muddled their order, made this process far more pleasant than it could have been had he responded otherwise.

That said, I would be remiss if I didn't also immediately acknowledge the equal patience, tact, and sensitivity of my favourite writer, Harold Gershowitz, as he, too, suffered seemingly endless delays in our work together due to my lack of coordination while trying to juggle far too many tasks. Hal's is a formidable talent, and I'm continually amazed that he finds anything I have to say worth his consideration. He also has very nice ears.

Another of the many men I answer to who deserves a special commendation for patience above and beyond the ordinary is John Ward. It's hard for me to believe that my contribution to his endeavors constitutes anything more than sheer frustration, yet still he always seems happy to see me. For that I'm grateful.

Of course this book would not have been possible without those who extended to me their time and trust in sharing their personal memories and mementos to aid my efforts. My sincerest thanks go to Herb Bernstein, Paul Brownstein, Dick Clark, Ron Dante, Robert Danz, Marshall Deixler, Susan Deixler, Ben Fong-Torres, Harry Grovier, Lee Gurst, Bro Herrod, Howard Honig, Maxine Horn, Jeanne Lucas, Steve and Lexy Mackler, Mary Moesel, Amanda

Mercer Neder, Pamela Pentony, Jim Petersen, Iris Richman, Ed Sciaky, Kyle Vincent, Jack Wilkins, Robert Windeler. A special note of gratitude to Mrs Anna Keliher, Harold Keliher's widow. Anna is a great Brooklyn broad, a sweet and lovely lady, a joyous human being, and a true pleasure to know.

Additional and equally heartfelt thanks go to Zev Gruman and the other intrepid folks at Paper Chase Research in New York City; Kalen Rogers at Music Sales Corporation, who did me the great favour of putting me in touch with Zev; Terry Mazeroski and Lester Eldridge of the former Eastern District High School, Brooklyn; friend and author Jerry Hopkins; the always accommodating Paul Lane of Photo Source, Evanston; Stroh's archivist Peter Blum, and Barry McGuire who put me in touch with Mr Blum; Michelangelo Signorile, who helped assuage my fears and put things in perspective; Paula Sweeney, at Selective Service Administration; Dr William Donnelly, a historian with the U.S. Army Center of Military History in Washington, DC; Mark Duran of Playboy Enterprises; attorney Renee Schwartz; Mark Foreit; Bill Lynch of the San Francisco Public Library; Mrs Denise Nielsen, fan and friend; the clever and helpful men and women of the Evanston Public Library as well as the Sulzer Library in Chicago, all of whom went out of their way to open new avenues of research to me, and make the old paths easier to navigate.

Of course they also serve who simply take my calls at all hours. I'm always thankful for good friends who are always so willing to listen to me read or rant or kvetch, who calm me down and cheer me up and generally make my life a more pleasant place to be. My special thanks to Michael Eldridge and Marianne Ahokas, my touchstones and too-frequent hosts, and Arcata, California, a gem of a place I wish I could put in my pocket and carry with me always. Thanks, too, to the Zimas – Bill, Debbie, Emma and – a new addition to the family since I acknowledged them in my last book – little Lucy. All are constant sources of comfort, creativity, and amusement. Even more thanks to my agent, Jonathan Dolger, the calm, quiet voice of reason; to Paul Desprez, the best husband I've had to date, and his sister Denise; to Tamsyn Griffith, who continues to lend generous moral and financial support; to Laurie Worrall, friend and fellow cheese hunter; to Cathy Weldy, the reassuring voice on the other end of the phone; to Dan Salomon, who is never impressed; to Kim Blacker and her beautiful and wise daughter Rachael Blacker; to October Crifasi, who got more – and less – than she bargained for when she raised her hand at that first book signing; to Beth Pearson, still my biggest fan; to Emil and Gertrude Francone, who still love me like their own.

And, finally, my sincere appreciation to all the Barry Manilow fans who wrote to express their support and add their personal thoughts and anecdotes. I'm sure their idol will shine no less brightly in their eyes for the revelation of a few new facets.

To anyone who I missed, please know that your omission is not an expression of any less gratitude on my part than I feel for those listed, but merely a reflection of my own poor organisation. While your name may not appear here, your assistance was truly appreciated.

Patricia Butler
Evanston, Illinois

Sources

"Through a Glass Darkly", Adrian Deevoy, Q, May 1990

"Can't Smile Without You", Giles Smith, *Sunday Telegraph Magazine*, January 9, 2000

The Selective Service System Headquarters, Arlington, VA

Social Security Administration, Washington, DC

"Barry Manilow Wants a Little Respect, and He'll Go Toe-to-Toe to Get It", Leonard Pitts Jr., Knight-Ridder/Tribune News Service, December 1, 1993

"Every Gay Blade's Fantasy", John L. Wasserman, *San Francisco Chronicle*, September 29, 1973

Liberace: An American Boy, Darden Asbury Pyron, The University of Chicago Press, 2000

Steppenwolf, Hermann Hesse, Holt, Rinehart and Winston, Inc., 1957

Anti-Rock: The Opposition to Rock 'n' Roll, Linda Martin and Kerry Segrave, Da Capo Press, 1988

"Looks Like Barry Manilow's Made It, To Say the Least, But Why Isn't He Happier", Robert Windeler, *People Weekly*, August 8, 1977

"Stuck in a Creative Corner, Barry Manilow Comes Out Swinging With Some New 'Old Standards'", David Van Biema, Todd Gold, *People Weekly*, October 22, 1984

"Still King of the Middle Road, Barry Manilow Ponders Some Careful Side Trips – Into Movies and Fatherhood", Carl Arrington, *People Weekly*, February 8, 1982

"Satirist Ray Stevens Turns Barry Manilow On His Musical Ear", Dolly Carlisle, *People Weekly*, May 28, 1979

"A Nice Mid-Life Crisis", Eric Levin, Jane Sims Podesta, *People Weekly*, November 9, 1987

"Human Tranquilizer", Kim Cunningham, *People Weekly*, May 10, 1993

"The English Dearly Love a Duke, But It Took Barry Manilow to Lure 40,000 to Blenheim Palace", *People Weekly*, September 12, 1983

"Manilow Can't Swing Like Sinatra", Lloyd Sachs, *Chicago Sun-Times*, December 13, 1998

"Classic Manilow", Glenn Gamboa, *Beacon Journal*, August 5, 1999

"On The Town", Penny Parker, *Denver Rocky Mountain News*, March 8, 2001

"An Unfunny Night at 'Copacabana' ", Joel Hirschhorn, *Variety*, February 25, 2001

"All Manilow Wants is a Little Retrospect", Karen D'Souza, Mercury News, January 7, 2001

"Psycho Nympho, Imaginary Manilow", Julie Hilden, *FindLaw Legal News*, February 12, 2001

"Everyone Has Been Lying To You . . . I Swear", Matthew D. Glaser, *Daily Trojan*, February 25, 1999

"Manilow Homogenizes Sinatra," David Wiegand, *San Francisco Chronicle*, December 6, 1998

"Can't Live Without You", Robert Drake, *Philadelphia Citypaper.net*, July 17–24, 1997

"1998: The Year In Review", Edna Gundersen, *USA Today*, December 29, 1998

"New Pop Music For Middle Age", Stephen Holden, *New York Times*, November 27, 1998

"The Burning Man Festival Sparkles", Joe Williams, *St. Louis Post*, September 13, 1998

"Smashed Hits, Here They Are", Jim Davis, *Daily Herald*, November 6, 1998

"Stranger-Than-Fiction Developments on Spring Rock Scene", *Albany Times Union*, April 27, 2000

"His Music and Passion Still in Fashion", Greg Morago, *Hartford Courant*, November 30, 2000

" 'Copacabana' is a Rotten Banana", Pamela Fisher, *San Francisco Examiner*, February 10, 2001

"Manilow's 'Copacabana' Comes Off as Very, Very Barry", Mark de la Vina, *San Jose Mercury News*, January 19, 2001

"Addicts Anonymous: Western Society Encourages Us To Be Dependent . . .", Helen Wilkinson, *Guardian* [Manchester], December 12, 1998

"Foreword: Zeitgeist", Tom Bussmann, *Guardian* [Manchester], December 19, 1998

CD Review Digest, 1983–1987

CD Review Digest Annual, 1989

"Fast Tracks", *Playboy*, May 1982

"Manilow Shows Audience What Makes Him So Great", Ed Masley, *Pittsburgh Post-Gazette*, July 15, 1993

"Barry Manilow: King of Schmaltz, With a Touch of Class", Henry Schipper, *Playgirl*, Mary 1983

"Barry Manilow", Alastair Sutherland, *Graffiti Magazine*, April 1988

"The Playboy Advisor", *Playboy*, December 1965

"20 Questions: Tom Waits", *Playboy*, [issue date unknown]

"The Playboy Interiew: Phil Collins", *Playboy*, 1986

20th Century Pop Culture, Dan Epstein, Carlton Books Limited, 1999

The Adoring Audience: Fan Culture and Popular Media, Edited by Lisa A. Lewis, Routledge, 1992

Barry Manilow: An Illustrated Biography, Richard Peters, Pop Universal/ Souvenir Press, 1982

Barry Manilow Special, Bev Gilligan, Grandreams Ltd., 1982

"Does Barry Manilow Deserve a Break Today?", Ed McCormack, *Oui*, November 1976

Barry Manilow, Tony Jasper, W.H. Allen & Co., Ltd., 1981

Barry Manilow: An Unauthorized Biography, Mark Bego, Tempo Books, 1977

Dennis Miller: The Off-White Album, Dennis Miller, Warner Bros. Records, Inc., 1988

Sweet Life: Adventures on the Way to Paradise, Barry Manilow, McGraw-Hill Book Company, 1987

Starlust: The Secret Life of Fans, Fred and Judy Vermorel, W.H. Allen & Co. Ltd., 1985

"Barry Manilow Music Catches Millions by the Ear", *Seventeen*, May 1976

Bob Dylan: Don't Look Back, Directed by D.A. Pennebaker, Produced by Albert Grossman, John Court, Pennebaker Films, 1967

"Fast Tracks", *Playboy*, February 1980

The Billboard Book of #1 Hits, 4th Edition, Fred Bronson, Billboard Books, 1997

Billboard Book of Top 40 Hits, Joel Whitburn, Billboard Books, 1996

"Give His Regards To Broadway", Jan Breslauer, *Los Angeles Times Calendar*, October 12, 1997

"Bound For Glory", *Vanity Fair*, May 2001. Excerpted from *Positively 4th Street*, by David Hajdu, Farrar, Straus and Giroux, 2001

"Barry Manilow", *Us Magazine*, June 26, 1989

"Barry Manilow: From Brooklyn to the World", Spencer Benedict, *Playing Keyboards,* December/January 1989

"Barry Manilow: Finding the Time for the 'Sweet Life' ", *Publishers Weekly*, October 16, 1987

"The Unseen Side of Barry Manilow", *Teen's Entertainment '80*

"Time to Spread the Love on Dodgers Opening Day", T.J. Simers, *Los Angeles Times*, April 3, 2001

Queer Noises: Male and Female Homosexuality in Twentieth- Century Music, John Gill, University of Minnesota Press, 1995

Queer in America: Sex, the Media, and the Closets of Power, Michelangelo Signorile, Random House, 1993

Fame in the 20th Century, Clive James, Random House, 1993

Passing Parade: A History of Popular Culture in the Twentieth Century, Richard Maltby, Oxford University Press, 1989

Red Lobster, White Trash, and the Blue Lagoon, Joe Queenan, Hyperion, 1998

A Massive Swelling: Celebrity Re-Examined as a Grotesque Crippling Disease, Cintra Wilson, Viking, 2000

"For Online Absurdity, Dave Barry's Your Guy", *USA Today*, December 2, 1999

"Barry", Stephen E. Rubin, *Ladies' Home Journal*, April 1979

"When Your Name is a Punchline, You Live in Hell. Barry Manilow Lives in Hell", Bill Zehme, *Rolling Stone*, November 1, 1990

CD Review Digest, Vol. 3, Janet Grimes, Editor, The Peri Press, 1989

CD Review Digest, Vol. 6, Janet Grimes, Editor, The Peri Press, 1992

CD Review Digest, Vol. 7, Janet Grimes, Editor, The Peri Press, 1994

"The Man Who Liked Paperwork", Michael Oliver

Mud Will Be Flung Tonight, Bette Midler, Atlantic Recording Corporation, 1985

"Out", Stephen Randall, *Playboy*, September 1990

"Fast Tracks", *Playboy*, December 1981

"Fast Tracks", *Playboy*, August 1981

"Fast Tracks", *Playboy*, June 1980

"The Answers: Barry Manilow", Imogen Edwards-Jones, *You* [*Mail on Sunday*], December 1999

"Barry Manilow", *Rona Barrett's Hollywood*, June 1979

"Barry Manilow, Producer-Arranger", *Planning Your Future* [*Teen Magazine*], 1980

"An Evening With Barry Manilow", *Preview*, December 1978

"What's Your Favorite Sport?", *16 Magazine*, October 1978

"Barry Manilow's True Blue Miracle: From Jingles to Hit Singles", *Bananas*, 1975

Will Pop Eat Itself? Pop Music in the Soundbite Era, Jeremy J. Beadle, Faber and Faber, 1983

Clive: Inside the Record Business, Clive Davis with James Willwerth, Ballantine Books, 1974

Follow The Music: The Life and High Times of Elektra Records in the Great Years of American Pop Culture, Jac Holzman and Gavan Daws, FirstMedia Books, 1998

Rockonomics: The Money Behind the Music, Marc Eliot, Franklin Watts, 1989

Man Enough: Fathers, Sons, and the Search for Masculinity, Frank Pittman, MD, Perigee, 1993

The Complete Directory to Prime Time Network and Cable TV Shows, 1946–Present, Tim Brooks and Earle Marsh, Ballantine Books, 1999

The Whole World Sings: The Fans Behind Barry Manilow, Mandy Strunk, Dowling Press, Inc., 1999

The Divine Bette Midler, James Spada, Macmillan Publishing, 1984

"Barry Manilow: The Musician Behind the Image", Bob Doerschuk, *Keyboard*, January 1983

"Barry Manilow: Writing the Songs to Get That Could-It-Be-Magic Feeling Again", Gerrit Henry, *After Dark*, June 1976

"Jingles and Singles", Jack Kroll with Peter S. Greenberg, *Newsweek*, March 31, 1975

"Barry Manilow: From a Hobby to a Habit", Paul Baratta, *Songwriter Magazine*, November 1975

"Barry Manilow: Photoplay's Star of the Month", *Photoplay*, August 1979

"The 1976 After Dark Ruby Award Party: Barry, Chita, and a Six-Year-Old Named Ruby", Patrick Pacheco, *After Dark*, July 1976

"Barry Manilow Redux: Maybe He's Not So Bad After All", Glenn Plaskin, *San Francisco Chronicle*, May 9, 1989

"Manilow Indulges His Jazz Man's Soul", Charles Passy, *Wall Street Journal*, April 4, 2000

"Housewives' Choice? Hey, the Guys Like Me, Too", Kevin Bourke, *Manchester Evening News*, January 21, 2000

" 'Copacabana': How I Wrote The Songs – and Learned to Act", Barry Manilow, *TV Guide*, November 30, 1985

"Barry Manilow: Master of Music", Joe Delaney, *Showbiz Weekly*

"He's a Survivor", Alan K. Stout, *Las Vegas Review-Journal*, December 15, 2000

"Swing Low, Sweet Manilow", Harry F. Waters with Mark D. Uehling, *Newsweek*, December 2, 1985

"Playboy Interview: Paul Simon", Tony Schwartz, *Playboy*, 1984

Gale Encyclopedia of Multicultural America, Volume 2, Gale Research, Inc.

The Jews in America 1621–1970, Compiled and edited by Irving J. Sloan, Oceana Publications, Inc., 1971

"Barry Manilow Refuses to See His Dying Dad", *Star*

"Music Preview: Could It Be Magic?", Lori D'Angelo, *Pittsburgh Post-Gazette*, August 6, 1999

"The Choice of Manilow", Mike Joyce, *Washington Post*, August 26, 1988

"The Democratic Party Planners", Lloyd Grove, *Washington Post*, June 25, 1988

"Personalities", Chuck Conconi, *Washington Post*, June 8, 1989

"Manilow Earns a Place Among Pop's Best Interpreters", Howard Reich, *Chicago Tribune*, February 8, 2000

"The Original Bathhouse Bette: My Interview With Steve Ostrow", *BetteWriter*, Stasey Tackett

"Stage: Miss M. Divine", Ian Dove, *New York Times*, December 4, 1973

"Divine Miss M. Is Set for a Tacky Gala", Paul Gardner, *New York Times*, December 29, 1972

"The Foreign Immigrant in New York City", Kate Holladay Claghor, Ph.D., *Reports of the Industrial Commission*, Volume XV, U.S. Government Printing Office, 1901

"Edna Manilow, Pop Singer's Mother", *Miami Herald*, September 10, 1994

"Edna Manilow, Singer's Mom", *Sun-Sentinal*, September 11, 1994

"The Playboy Interview: Billy Joel", *Playboy*, May 1982

"The Rocket Man's Rocky Flight", Jim Morekis, *Creative Loafing Online*, October 9, 1999

"The Rebirth of Elton John", Philip Norman, *Rolling Stone*, March 19, 1992

"Looks Like He Made It", Rafer Guzman, *Newtimes.com*, November 27, 1997

"Winter in the Sun: Palm Springs Loosens Up", Bernard Weinraub, *The New York Times*, January 14, 2001

"Sidney E. Woloshin, 72, Writer of Ad Jingles", Saul Hansell, *The New York Times*, November 10, 2000

"Barry Manilow Works to Please Himself", David Burke, *Lee News Service*, April 28, 2000

"Dubious Achievement Awards of 1992", *Esquire*, January 1993

"Point of View", Mark Evanier, *www.evanier.com*

"Just Like That Old Tie Rock 'n' Roll", Ann Norsworthy, *The Oracle*, October 18, 2000

"RodeoHouston: Some 'Splainin to Do", Tim Carman, *Houston Press*, January 25, 2001

"People, Places and Things in the News", *South Coast Today*, January 1, 1998

"Barry's Last Laugh", *San Angelo Standard-Times*, May 17, 1999

Behind the Music: Bette Midler, VH1

Behind the Music: 1975, VH1

Interviews with Anna Keliher

Interviews with Lee Gurst

Interviews with Ron Dante

Interview with Kyle Vincent

Interview with Jack Wilkins
Interview with Dick Clark
Interview with Robert Danz
Interviews with Pamela Pentony
Interview with Ben Fong-Torres
Interviews with Jeanne Lucas
Interview with Howard Honig
Interview with Mary Moesel
Interview with Lexy Mackler
Interview with Iris Pappalardo
Interview with Amanda Mercer
Interview with Jim Petersen
Interview with Maxine Horn
Interview with Paul Brownstein
Interview with Ed Sciaky
Interview with Herb Bernstein
Interview with Alastair Sutherland